Israel on the Couch

SUNY series

in

Israeli Studies

Russell Stone, editor

Israel on the Couch

The Psychology of the Peace Process

Ofer Grosbard

with a Foreword by Vamik D. Volkan

State University of New York Press

This work was translated from the Hebrew by Shosh Sappir.

Published by
State University of New York Press, Albany

Printed in the United States of America

For information, address State University of New York Press,
90 State Street, Suite 700, Albany, NY 12207

Production by Michael Haggett
Marketing by Fran Keneston

Library of Congress Cataloging-in-Publication Data

Grosbard, Ofer, 1954-
    Israel on the Couch: the psychology of the peace process / Ofer Grosbard; with a
foreword by Vamik D. Volcan.
    p. cm
    Includes bibliographical references and index.
    ISBN 0-7914-5605-6 (alk. paper) — ISBN 0-7914-5606-4 (pbk.: alk. paper)
    1. Arab-Israeli conflict—Psychological aspects. 2. Peace—Psychological aspects.
3. Political psychology. 4. National characteristics, Israeli. I. Title.
DS126.5 G694 2003
956.05'3—dc21   2002030975

10 9 8 7 6 5 4 3 2 1

In memory of my father
David Grosbard
A member of Etzel's chief command,
Tel Aviv District Commander,
Who taught me to experience our national life
As if it were my own.

Contents

Foreword

On the evening of May 10, 2000, during the fifty-second anniversary of the founding of the state of Israel, a ceremony took place in Jerusalem in the area surrounding Theodor Herzl's tomb. I was an Inaugural Rabin Fellow at the Yitzhak Rabin Center in Tel Aviv at the time, so I had the opportunity to attend this ceremony. The event was presided over by Avraham Burg, then Speaker of the Knesset. I had met Burg at the Knesset just a few days earlier, when both of us participated in a meeting that dealt with the themes of cultural diversity and coexistence. I remember thinking that he was an exciting speaker and I could see that most of the two thousand or so Israelis in attendance were stirred by his remarks. My Israeli friends who accompanied me to Mount Herzl translated Burg's remarks. He was urging his audience to live up to the vision of an idealized Israel where deep and troublesome societal divisions no longer exist.

The assassination of Rabin on November 4, 1995 by Yigal Amir, a Bar Ilan University law student, shocked Israeli society, and left them asking how it was possible for one Israeli to kill another. An Israeli psychoanalyst, Rena Moses-Hrushovski describes in her book *Grief and Grievance,* an Israeli "soul-searching" that took place after the assassination. Israeli intellectuals wondered how they could facilitate the coexistence of different political and religious groups and overcome the destructive splits among Israelis' multiple religious factions and ethnicities. In the long run, however, according to Moses-Hrushovski, this did not occur. At the time of the ceremony, the country still had deep divisions. Burg's address referred to this condition and cried out for a solution.

While I was a Rabin Fellow, my wife and I rented an apartment on the beach in Tel Aviv, a couple of blocks away from the American Embassy. At least four days a week I would take a bus to, and home from, the temporary location of the Rabin Center near Tel Aviv University. Each bus ride took about half an hour, and each time I observed a variety of Israelis who would, through integration and absorption, create a stable Israeli mosaic. Israel, in fact, has a minister of absorption, who is in charge of efforts to integrate various groups, especially the newcomers such as Russian Jews, into the society. My friend at the University of California, Los Angeles, Peter Loewenberg, an historian as well as a psychoanalyst, writes about "synthetic" nations, such as Brazil, Indonesia, and the United States: People from different cultures and with many variations of religious belief coming together to create a nation-state. Israel too is a "synthetic" nation.

When Burg's address was finished, twelve Israelis, representing different groups within the country, spoke briefly in front of lit torches and symbolically presented themselves as a unified Israel. A young woman, Oz (Sveta) Tokaev was a member of a group of one million recent "immigrants" from Russia. Zehava Baruch was the spokeswoman for Ethiopians. Boaz Kitain, whose son was killed in a helicopter crash, reminded everyone of grieving parents in a country where young people face real dangers. Two teenagers, one Jewish and one Druze, Ziv Shachar and Daniella Nadim Issa, spoke together, suggesting that Jews and non-Jews can coexist in the state of Israel. Others among the dozen speakers reminded the audience that there were citizens who were directly affected by the Holocaust and citizens who were representatives of women's rights groups; however, some Moslem Israeli Arabs and ultra-Orthodox movements were not represented. In the excitement of the evening, however, one could visualize an idealized and unified Israel.

As a Turkish-American living in Israel for only four months, it was obviously difficult for me to observe the divisions in Israeli society, especially those pertaining to religious differences—even though I made a specific effort to observe and understand them. During the first month of my stay in Israel, I met the author of *Israel on the Couch*, Ofer Grosbard, who has combined his enthusiasm for the intellectual understanding of the problems of Israeli society with his empathy for all. Whether we had lunch together in an Arab restaurant in Haifa or visited the kibbutz that his father-in-law, a pioneering Zionist, helped to establish decades ago, Grosbard explained to me what kind of societal problems, desires, and conflicts Israelis faced. During our meetings I observed his deep love for Israel, and its people who come from different cultural and religious backgrounds, as well as his concerns about the peace process. I found it very easy, rewarding, and thought-provoking to read Grosbard's book, and I believe that other readers will also find this book enlightening, even though Grosbard deals with extremely serious issues, painful events, and conflicts.

Grosbard, as a psychologist who has worked with youngsters as well as adults, has been especially interested in family dynamics. Parents can enhance or inhibit the development of their offspring. Grosbard applies his psychological insights about family dynamics to his explanation of political processes. He focuses on the divisions in Israeli society, between left and right, secular and Orthodox, and Israeli and Israeli-Arab. He also reminds us that it would be impossible to understand and deal with the divisions in Israel without taking into account how necessary and significant emotions are to human relationships.

At the one-year anniversary of my departure from Tel Aviv, a bomb exploded at a Tel Aviv beach and took many lives. As my wife and I watched the aftermath on television, I could recognize the trees that were in front of our Tel Aviv balcony and the promenade where we took frequent strolls. I was filled with sadness, and felt that saving the peace process would require a small miracle. It is not surprising that the news that we read here in the United States mostly deals with Israel's issues with the Palestine Authority and with its neighboring Arab countries. They also refer to the Israeli-Arab conflict within the general frame of international relations; examining the United States' role in the Middle East, and expressing concerns about the Bush administration's role in putting the peace process back on track. Thus, Grosbard's volume is most timely in reminding us that we also need to be aware of internal conditions in Israel. He gives us an insider's view of divisions within Israel and calls for resolutions, as Burg did at the anniversary of the founding of the state of Israel. In my opinion, what makes this book most enlightening is the fact that Grosbard has a wonderful style that combines the "innocence" and passion of a child with the wisdom and caution of a "wise man" in order to explore the emotional world of the people who call themselves "Israelis."

Vamık D. Volkan, M.D.

Preface

To understand the journey I took in order to write this book, I must share with the reader some milestones that tie my personal and national life together. I was born in Tel Aviv in 1954, as the youngest of three children. My father immigrated to Israel from Lithuania in 1932 with his family at the age of sixteen. My mother emigrated from Berlin in 1935 with her family when she was eleven. My father joined the anti-British Etzel underground, and eventually became a member of the top command and the commander of the Tel Aviv district. His emotional life to the day he died was indelibly tied to the Herut movement. My mother is a pediatrician and she too has right-wing views; both originally came from religious families. I was sent to the state-religious "Bilu" school, even though we weren't religious; we traveled on the Sabbath, and I only donned a yarmulke when I went to school. My parents thought a religious education was a good education, and that it was important for me to maintain a connection to tradition and religion. By the time I went to high school I was sent to a secular school. Around the dinner table we heard many stories from my father's years in the underground, and we took in the atmosphere of the right wing.

In those youthful days I felt like a rightist with all my heart. Today, looking back, I realize there always were cracks in my rightist views, and I expressed them in my rebellion against figures of authority (parents and teachers) and a difficulty to identify with what was offered to me. Since I was the youngest in the family, I may not have been expected to identify with my parents with the same strictness usually required from older siblings, which allowed me more freedom. I went into the army's Nachal paratroopers unit full of a spirit of volunteerism and a desire to serve in a combat unit.

In those days after the 1973 Yom Kippur War, in talks with comrades in arms while we were stationed in Egypt, my allegiance to the right was shattered. In the following years I found myself voting more and more toward the left (I voted for Moshe Dayan's Telem), until I was no longer ashamed to vote Labor. My parents, brother, and sister all voted for the right. My family treated me with patience, as the rebellious young child, thinking—well, he'll come to his senses.

My parents encouraged me from a young age to lean toward the natural sciences, which they respected more than the humanities. I always knew I wanted to be an engineer. At the end of my military service I was admitted to the Technion in Haifa and graduated with a degree in computer engineering. During my studies I became interested in psychology, and became more aware of myself and my emotions, to the point that I even dared go to therapy. A friend reminded me years later that I once said, "What, I should go to therapy? What am I, crazy?" I abandoned engineering and started studying psychology and went through the whole course of clinical psychology (B.A., M.A., and internship). I had a tremendous need to understand and know myself, to organize and make sense of myself from within, a need I could not compromise. I sought the emotion, the bond with people and not with machines such as engineering offered me. So the personal development that began with a change of my political views from right to left was later accompanied by a change of profession, from the natural sciences to the social and human sciences.

Indeed, I was less attached than the rest of my family to tradition, to the past, and especially to my parents. I rebelled and sought my way independently. At one point my rebellion was expressed by interrupting my studies and going on a trip around the world with a backpack. What I have noticed again and again with patients in the clinic is that in the course of psychotherapy they move more and more toward the left, and that happened to me as well too.

And then, wonder of wonders, just when I thought I had reached the last stop, I found myself again swinging toward the right to a certain extent. I feel I can understand the right and identify with it. Today I can take a more balanced look at the extremes between which I traveled, and recognize the importance of our religious and national past, like a child who rebelled against his parents with anger and rage, and now, after forming his separate, new and independent identity, is mature enough to go back to them reconciled, not angry, even loving and appreciating what he got from them. We know that from the clinic, too. A rebellious adolescent who prevails and finds his new identity can go back to his parents one day and reconcile with them. Today I have a greater appreciation for the importance of keeping traditions, the past and the roots of our Judaism, to maintain our historic continuity. Erasing the national past, just like erasing one's personal past, certainly causes emotional difficulties that are familiar from the clinic and that I will point out in this book.

Suddenly I understand for the first time the historic process in which my parents rebelled against their parents, abandoned religion, and no longer wanted to be Diaspora Jews; and what that meant (feelings of weakness, low self-image, and more). Their rebellion allowed the beginning of the journey from religion to state, and our generation continues that rebellion in its search for the kind of state we want to have. Like many adolescents, we are still confused and struggle to define who we are.

Election time is a hard time for me, because that is when I have to choose who is more right, whom I identify with, left or right. It is almost like choosing between one's father and mother. I am aware of the complexity of the continuum from left to right, with the right having a hard time parting with the past and with tradition and marching forward, while the left often severs itself from the sources of its past, and faces other national difficulties (guilt, repression of aggression to the point of being unable to recognize it, etc.).

When I examine myself, as we therapists are supposed to do in the course of our work in order to become aware of ourselves and our relations with our clients, I am aware that I sometimes lean more toward the left, but not to the extent I once did, and also understand that in the emotional development process of growth there is no right or wrong. Left and right are different aspects of a growth and development process that complement each other, and we as a nation must try to reach a balance between them. Therefore, if throughout this book I sound too much like a leftist, it might mean I have fallen into that deep rift that runs through our national body, and that I, just like the reader, should go back and reexamine myself, so as to get that much closer to the desired integration that I am trying to encourage in this book. Here the personal and the national become one, and some people can be expected to turn back to the values of the past and tradition, but this time in a more balanced and integrative way; after the rebellion succeeds, anger subsides, and it becomes possible to reconcile with the past, just as others will move toward Western, secular culture and identify with it. The deep rift in Israeli society is typical of the kind of rifts seen in adolescence, when everything is heated and stormy. Some of us rebel, some do not dare rebel, and some are tired of rebelling and want to go home and reconcile with our parents. Readers will judge for themselves where they are on this path, but we are all somewhere on that unending journey.

Before *Israel on the Couch*, I published *The Arab Within*, which I spent five years writing. That novel allowed me to delve deep into our national experience as only fiction can do, with no boundaries and obstacles, where everything is permissible (just as we ask therapy clients to say anything that comes to mind . . .). Only after the deep dissolution I experienced through literary writing could I go back and pick up the pieces integratively and use the therapeutic tool at my command to promote that holistic insight in this book, which actually brewed in my consciousness for many years. It would not be an overstatement to say, for my entire lifetime.

I greatly benefited from my close relationship with my daughters. The reader will find many examples in this book from parent-child relations. After all, childhood and politics are very similar. They are both so libidinous and primordial, so split and so entrenched in self-righteousness. Sometimes it seems as if politics is the only game adults have left over from their childhoods.

Another integration I underwent while writing this book is an integration between the world of clinical psychology, which I internalized over my years of study and work as a therapist, and my lifelong political allegiances. My father taught me to experience and live our national life, as I wrote in the dedication, as if it were my personal life. The link between politics and psychology was not obvious from the start. It demanded taking tools from the clinical arena and applying them to something that seemed distant and even its opposite—the political world. It is a fragmented area where each side is sure that only it is right, where one must not express deliberations and weaknesses. I believe strongly in applying clinical tools to politics and hope ardently that we can use those tools to advance our goals as a people. At a certain moment I sensed that "the coin dropped," and that two of my very deep allegiances, clinical psychology and politics, became condensed into one. I always breathed politics and surely breathed clinical psychology, so why not make them into one? It happened.

As a therapist, I belong to the intersubjective school, which is relatively new in clinical psychology and in psychoanalysis. It is an approach that maintains that both analyst and analysand are partners to the emotional process developing in the clinic, and the therapy cannot succeed unless the therapist is a true and equal partner. I find this approach to be all the more appropriate to conflicts between nations and conflicts between groups, because when you belong to a certain group you need to be aware of yourself and your emotions, and to try to understand how they effect the other group. Without examining what we really feel toward the other group we cannot examine our relationship with it, because we are full partners to the process. That is also the reason I wrote this introduction and told about myself. I have to be aware of myself and of my emotions throughout this process. I am not a neutral observer.

I wish to thank Dr. Rivka Yehoshua, a psychoanalyst and my psychotherapy supervisor. Our conversations over the years about current affairs from a psychological viewpoint stimulated me and deepened my insight into the emotional processes that fuel political processes.

I thank my good friend Dr. Meir Sa'adon, another clinical psychologist, for all those evenings in cafés on Haifa's Mt. Carmel, where he shared with me his sensibilities about discrimination, separateness, identity, and other areas, and helped me expand my horizons and open up to things I was unaware of.

A special thanks to Ika and Adi from Yedioth Ahronoth Books, whom I always found to be warm, calm, and down-to-earth; thanks to Dov, the director, who managed things from above and offered the security of a big Daddy who, even if he is not present at the moment, will be home any minute; thanks to Shirley, who had already given me some very smart words of advice; thanks to Ayelet, for her sensitive linguistic editing that avoided bruising my ego; thanks to Kuti, who gave me some good tips; and thanks to Zahava, who designed the cover and graphics.

Finally, thanks to my family, my wife Hagar, who allowed me to sit "with crossed legs" (that is what we humorously call my intense preoccupation with writing, which does not yield any income); thanks to Mor and Stav, my daughters, whose contribution I have already noted. And a final thanks to my mother, who although disagreeing with everything in this book and accusing me of being a flaming leftist, helped me economically and enabled me to attend to my writing. Without her, I doubt I could indulge in such a luxury.

Introduction

The goal of this book is to persuade the reader that the peace process is, fundamentally, an emotional process. Just as in the early days of psychology people needed to be persuaded that therapy helps, so today they need to be convinced that conflicts between nations can be resolved by understanding emotional processes. This book contains practical applications and clear and incisive recommendations that stem from that premise.

The argument that the Israeli-Arab conflict has psychological aspects is self-evident. Every conflict between two parties—a couple, parents and children, friends, and business associates—has emotional aspects, with each side bearing its own anxieties, defenses, and ambitions. This insight has been articulated by many leaders at different times. Issues of building trust, as well as feelings of hurt and insult on the national level, the desire to heal injuries, and the wish to triumph, are important not just existentially but also narcissistically. When we talk about relations between countries we are not talking about emotions and ideas invented specifically for international conflicts, but about human, everyday emotions, which generate the psychological processes in everyone. Therefore, these psychological processes can be addressed with the tools of clinical psychology. We know a lot about defense mechanisms, anxiety, impulses, desires, and so on. We do not need to invent a new psychology for these psychological processes, which have been studied in depth since Sigmund Freud. Therefore, throughout this book I will use tools known from clinical psychology, and bring examples from the clinic, from interpersonal conflicts, and from pathological and normal processes of growth and development, to analyze the peace process.

The first group into which we are born is the family. That is where our emotional world emerges and is shaped. That is where we learn how to live together, for better or for worse. The family is our first model of communal living. The family of nations is an extension of the family situation. There is no doubt that all of us, whether conscious of it or not, apply what we learned in our families, in the early years of life, to resolve difficulties throughout our lives. We approach the conflict between us and the Arabs from the same standpoint and with the same knowledge that we acquired to deal with problems and conflicts in our families. Just as conflicts within the family can be analyzed in a clinical psychotherapeutic setting, so can emotional problems between nations be analyzed in order to promote the best solutions. In the same vein, problems between groups in the Israeli public, such as religious and secular Jews, left and right, Arabs and Jews and others, can be viewed as emotional processes within the Israeli family.

The uniform character of emotions, which work in ever-growing circles, from the family to the Israeli family to the family of nations, can be understood by appreciating the primal bond between parent and child. That bond is deep and emotionally involved, because of the common fate that destines parent and child to live within each other's worlds so intimately and intensively. As Winnicott said, "There is no such thing as an infant . . . without maternal care." In other words, you cannot understand the development of an infant and what happens to him, without considering the mother. The mother-child relationship can serve as a model to understand other bilateral relationships between the groups and nations whose common fate destined them to live on this land together. There is no Arab without a Jew, and vice versa; there is no left without the right, and vice versa; there are no religious people without their secular counterparts, and vice versa, in this country. Those are inseparable pairs that are constantly reflected in each other's eyes, until you can no longer tell who is who or what is whose. This interconnectedness creates such a charged emotional system that you cannot understand either side without considering the feelings and emotions of the other. Therefore, I will use examples familiar to everyone from parent-child relationships to promote our understanding of complex and charged relationships between groups and nations.

As a nation, we had a traumatic childhood, laden with catastrophes and disasters. Working through this difficult past and understanding it would be enough to qualify us for therapy, so we do not carry our anxieties, defenses, and ambitions, which are sometimes unrealistic, into the present. And if our past were not enough, the difficult reality in which we live also calls for a deep, tough, and complex probing. Our troubles today are not only with the world outside but also, perhaps primarily, with our inner world. The grown child is gradually coming to understand that the war is not only between himself and the world, but that there are inner conflicts within him, and difficult emotional dilemmas, which require examination. Thus we are discovering, in a gradual process, how divided we are among ourselves. It is no longer clear what is more dangerous for us—the difficulties from within or from without. That is a condition for which individuals seek therapy. They are prepared, as a last resort, to admit that they have a problem they cannot solve by themselves. The problem is in the past; the problem is in the present; the problem is inside; the problem is outside; the problem is everywhere and with everyone. The growing process, characterized by working through emotional issues, is a prerequisite to ending our suffering, so that we can live a normal life in this country like other nations.

The emotional aspect of the peace process is revealed to us in its full force in simple people or children, who do not have the ability to suppress their emotions and to cover them with intellectual thinking. We may hear them say in political contexts, "If someone hits you, what do you do, hit them back or not?" The comparison between political and interpersonal relations comes up immediately, and the instinctive forces that inform their political positions become apparent.

A soldier at war does not need a psychologist. He does not need to lay bare his feelings, anxieties, and fears. On the contrary, he needs strong and solid defenses. He charges ahead and must not yield to his emotions. In the past it was clear that we were fighting for our survival, it was clear the enemy really did want to destroy us, and therefore we were cohesive and did not let our internal conflicts surface. Nor did we have a moral dilemma, because we were fighting for our lives. Only when the roar of battle subsided and the peace process began were we able to ask ourselves what we were feeling and how that effected our actions. Emotional awareness and clinical psychotherapy are the privileges of affluent, democratic societies that can relax a little from economic, military, or political existential dangers. It is no accident that there is no clinical therapy in Communist countries, or in dictatorships or theocracies. In order to observe our emotions we must be able to take a step back from them and not just be driven by them—in a climate of relaxation, which is not possible under existential threat.

Relations between nations or large groups of people usually reflect the most regressive and instinctive kind of interpersonal relations. In war, for instance, we are talking about murder. Would it be conceivable for either member of a couple to be sure that they and only they are right all the time? What would we think of such a partner? But that is a fixed assumption in politics—each side is convinced it is right. We expect members of a couple not to be too consumed with the question of who is right. We hope that each will show understanding and empathy toward his or her partner. As therapists, we are careful not to fall into the trap of arguing over "who is right." We know that life is not a court of law, and the question that is more likely to help the couple is "why are they suffering," and not "who is right." Such a dialogue cannot be taken for granted, and requires practice. The same is true among ourselves and with our neighbors. Empathetic listening is absolutely vital and requires practice. There is no other way to listen to one another.

Terms such as independence, setting clear boundaries, aggression, taking responsibility, recognizing the other, trust, security, and many more are part of both political and emotional jargon, in relation to the processes of growth and development that we strive to encourage in the clinic. The Palestinians want independence, while we hesitate whether to give it to them. We tell them: first fulfill your obligations; curb your aggression; then we will talk. Do we not function as authority figures in relation to them, dictating their lives in many areas? Do they not want to be like us in certain ways when they grow up? Are we not acting like parents who forgot what they were like as adolescents, and therefore have difficulty understanding the young adolescent who wants his independence? These emotional processes are not new, and they are quite familiar to us. Why shouldn't we use the vast knowledge we have accumulated to help the child and parent grow? After all, parenthood lasts for life, just as we can never separate from the Palestinians. Might that adolescent not remember for his whole life how his parents treated him in his youth, and whether they helped him grow or posed obstacles on his path? All of those questions are essentially therapeutic: How do you set limits on the child that are not too strict and not too lenient, limits that give both parent and child security, limits that help the child to grow?

To help the reader avoid resenting the analogy that compares us to parents and the Palestinians to children—an analogy that might be seen as patronizing and condescending—what I want to do here is refer to well-known human situations regarding relationships where one party is strong and the other weak, one big and the other small—parent and child, teacher and student, superior and subordinate, and more—and use the understanding of the emotional dynamics that take place in such relationships to shed light on a certain aspect of our relations with the Palestinians: the aspect that recognizes that our state is stronger and more developed than theirs. In other contexts the Palestinians are actually the older brother who was dispossessed of everything he had when his younger brother was born, while in yet other cases we can learn a lot about our relationship with the Palestinians from the emotional dynamics within couples. Not asking who is right, for example, but trying to understand.

I would like to state first of all that this book is written from a professional standpoint. It does not support a leftist or rightist position, Arab or Jewish, secular or religious, and so on. Moreover, I hope one of the things this book will clarify is how those twinned positions complement each other to the point that one cannot have a full emotional life while identifying with only one pole. That is because each side represses and denies the representations of its opposite that exist within it. Left and right, for instance, as I will show, are two sides of emotional life, and the ability to integrate them is the basis for a healthy process of growth and peace.

Still, some will ask even after reading the introduction whether I am a rightist or a leftist, religious or secular. The rift in the Israeli public is deep, and reminiscent of a person with a certain personality disorder who immediately asks you, "Are you for me or against me?" and cannot perceive that you can understand both him and the other. Such a personality demands that you identify with one side, and you, as a good parent or a good therapist, have to avoid falling into the stark, defined split between good guys and bad guys. In the early days of psychology therapists tried to adopt a neutral view on the issues raised by their patients. It took some time until it was understood that therapists have their own emotional stances and tendencies, and more importantly, conscious and unconscious sides in their personalities, and there is no human being who is neutral. Then it was understood that therapists have to be as aware as possible of their feelings so as not to be swayed without their being aware of it (e.g., therapists might have different moral stances than their patients', existential anxieties may motivate them, or they may have omnipotent wishes for the success of the therapy).

The same is true in the matter at hand. I have political preferences that stem from my emotional tendencies, and if I become aware of those tendencies I can be careful and make fewer mistakes. From knowing myself I know, for instance, that I have to be careful when it comes to compromising on security, or set red lines for myself that I mustn't cross, to counterbalance my inclination to get carried away by romantic fantasies and wishes for closeness and brotherhood with the Arabs. The reader may judge throughout the book whether I have succeeded in fulfilling this goal. Similarly, I would expect rightists who have a hard time believing in the possibility of change, and who find it difficult to be optimistic, to be aware of those tendencies, and to try to be honest with themselves and not erase from consciousness and repress evidence that contradicts their beliefs and shows that a serious change is in fact happening here. The process of self-examination has to be done honestly, and it is a very difficult process that takes a great deal of courage. How many of us have stopped at a given moment and said: "That information is incompatible with my beliefs and views"? It is so important, but happens so rarely. Therefore, there is no such thing as neutrality and objectivity. Everyone has personal tendencies, but self-awareness helps us get closer to those important values, and even more importantly, helps us build healthy relationships with others.

Besides self-awareness, we have to adopt another important tool from the parent and therapist—the ability to listen empathetically. After all, knowing the enemy, his emotions, and motives is a basic rule of war. We have a sore record of failure in that area and are surprised again and again (the Yom Kippur War in 1973, the Intifada uprising in the late 1980s, the belief that we could defeat terrorism, etc.). The best intelligence was, and still is, listening to the enemy like alert, small children, and not dismissing his feelings and negating his existence because it threatens us. There is a huge gap between the way in which we relate to statements by our own leaders and the way in which we relate to statements by enemy leaders. Anyone who is self-aware in the least will notice right away that when one of our leaders makes a statement we perceive it as the truth. When an enemy leader makes a statement we often see it as a manipulation or as a declaration that need not be taken seriously, and only seldom do we view it as a painful truth on which that leader cannot compromise. *The loss of our ability to listen is the greatest threat to our existence.*

Empathetic listening, expressed in the ability to identify with the enemy and understand him from within, is valuable not only in predicting war, but mostly in promoting peace. There is no alternative to empathetic listening, and its importance for the promotion of peace cannot be overstated. That is because that kind of listening locates the other party's pain, is able to identify with him and understand him, and to look at him with everything we know about emotional growth and development processes. Can the Palestinians possibly give up their desire for independence one day? Can they possibly give up their religious heart, the object of their desire, Jerusalem? Since we understand growth processes, we can say for certain that such a thing will not happen. The adolescent will give up neither his independence nor his belief. We know too that in the end he will achieve his goal. Therefore, the conflict between the Arabs and us cannot end in a worthy agreement unless both sides feel it satisfies them emotionally. An agreement signed by either side out of compulsion or temporary weakness will not lead to peace. The agreement has to be one that affords honor, independence, and the hope of continued growth to each side. As the Palestinians say, "Only just borders are safe borders." In other words, unjust borders will leave us frustrated and bitter, which will not allow for security.

Of course, we do not have to agree to everything they demand, but we must at least understand how they feel and what they are talking about. Then, even our "no" and our demands from them will be taken differently, like a parent posing boundaries for the child's benefit. Every parent knows that listening to the pain is half the solution. The very act of honest listening creates a dialogue of a different quality than the one that existed before the listening. But that is only a start, because throughout this book we will see that by listening empathetically we can help ourselves and help them in ways that were inaccessible to us heretofore.

A politician who thinks he is always right is denying himself the possibility of using those two tools. He is losing the possibility of listening both to himself and to the other. In therapy, the biggest breakthroughs sometimes happen when the therapist is wrong and can admit it. The same is true for parenting. I know several children (some of them grown up today) whose parents never admitted to them that they were wrong. I also know children to whom that happened just once in their lives, and they will never forget that one time. We are like children who yearn for an honest parent, who can be wrong and admit it, so that we too will be allowed to be wrong.

Our politicians are just the opposite. What a shame. There is no doubt that the most serious and dangerous ailment of Israeli politics is the rigid, paranoid, self-righteous stance, which doesn't allow open thinking. Its effect on educating the public and on the peace process is destructive, just as it is on the growth of a child whose father never admitted he was wrong. Without the freedom to deliberate, not to know, to make a mistake and regret it, and to recognize your limits and your emotions, emotional growth is impossible. In human and emotional processes, of which the peace process is one, when people can identify what their problem is and where they went wrong, their situation is much better. Call it "humility." When someone thinks he knows everything we have a real reason to worry. That is the omnipotent stance, which is compatible with Israeli arrogance. We also know that it serves to cover up the deepest anxieties and insecurities.

Exposing the emotional side of the peace process invites a more active role for women. At the risk of making a blatant generalization, I will say that women in our society have a better understanding of feelings and emotional processes. Politics are conducted largely by men, and in our country the military aspect comes into play. Introducing the female point of view to politics is of extreme importance, because if we are talking about growth and development processes, women are more open to these processes than men. The political world, which often lacks an understanding of emotional processes, which mothers know so well, and that clinical therapists deal with, is like a family that has a father but lacks a mother. It is not too hard to imagine what such a family would look like; after all, we all live in it. If we look at the family of nations as relationships and ties between patriarchal families, we can understand what a regressive world we are living in. One of the deep reasons for the regressiveness of many Eastern countries compared to the West is the lack of equal rights for women. In that sense we might be in for positive changes in the future. I hope the "Four Mothers" organization, which advocated the Israeli army's withdrawal from Lebanon, is the harbinger of a new female voice in the growth and development processes toward peace. The organization, which chose such an apt name that connected them with the power of the four matriarchs who gave birth to our nation, is not afraid to enter the military-inspired male world, and represent a different way of thinking, which is not motivated mainly by anxiety, and is closer to the emotional truth of a mother facing a child building castles in the air.

While writing this book I underwent a process of working through the material, internalizing and integrating it. Therefore, the latter chapters may be more integrative than the early ones, and also present more practical advice that stems from the insights gained in the process. I hope the reader will experience the gradual integration process in the course of reading the book. I had difficulty dividing the book into chapters, because in such a large orchestra, with all the instruments playing together, it is hard to separate them, and therefore there might be repetitions. But just as in therapy, where we sometimes feel as if each thing is connected to everything else, and everything together is one big package, we might want to make an artificial separation for a while, just to make it easier to understand and internalize—so I felt in the attempt to divide the book into chapters, and make order in the full, rich complexity of life as we experience it.

It is important that this book leads to a process of self-examination, because that is the most important process. This book offers a broad developmental, emotional model for the peace process, and exposes the emotional aspect of that process in our lives. We must be able to examine ourselves and ask ourselves where we have been wrong, in order to move ahead step-by-step. That is how a child grows up, and that is how we grow up as a nation. I am sure my perception of this book will change after it is published. It is not an ending; it is just one chapter in a long story, a first chapter in a lifelong growth process. I have no doubt that I will be rightfully accused of missing some aspects or misunderstanding others. But I am not offering a right answer, just a way of thinking, an approach, a way of life in which we try to understand ourselves, our anxieties, our mistakes, and what we really feel. *Self-awareness and empathy— the awareness directed at the self and at the empathy of the other, is the primary aim of this book.*

1

The Jewish People

The Patient

The patient, by the name of Israel, walks into the room and instantly bursts into a tirade of arguments conclusively proving his credentials, and says that he is better than everyone else. "Look," he says to the therapist, "Freud, Einstein, Marx, Jesus, and others, were all Jews. And it is an undisputed fact that, considering our small size, our people gave humanity more than a few geniuses, not to mention the Book of Books, the Bible, and our God, whom everyone else copied. No wonder everyone envies me and mistreats me," he says, adding, "it is simply jealousy and nothing else, because I did not do anything to them." Here the therapist begins shifting in his seat in confusion. For a moment it all sounded perfectly convincing. This patient really is incredibly talented and special. And he, the therapist, feels helpless in the face of the force of his arguments. Yet still, the experienced therapist recovers and realizes that it is not his credentials, the size of his nose, or other unchangeable things that this patient needs to change in order to get along with his environment. The therapist tells the patient that he appreciates and respects his special talents, which are indisputable, but that is not the problem. The problem is on another level, the emotional level.

The war between patient and therapist is on. Even an experienced therapist would find himself engaged in it, and ask himself how he ever got there, and what in the world it is that this patient does to him that neither of them understands. The patient keeps trying to prove to the therapist that he is wrong, that he, the patient, doesn't have any problem, and that everybody just hates him. And the therapist tries to show him that he does have a problem besides being terribly talented, and that he, the therapist, is right. This patient's arrogance and condescending attitude toward the therapist and toward everyone else bring out in the therapist complex feelings of envy, anger, and a desire to prove to the patient that he is neither the best nor the greatest in the world, and that the therapist also has something to say. Sometimes the therapist feels fear and uneasiness around this patient, Israel.

"What do you think is happening between us now?" the therapist will suddenly ask the patient. The patient will cut his vindication speech short, lean back in his seat, and wonder what the therapist is aiming for. "Look," the therapist will say, "What is happening between us now is what happens to you with the whole world. You surely didn't invent this behavior especially for me. You are trying to convince me you are right and I am trying to convince you I am right and we are stumbling into war. If we understand what is happening to you here, in this room with me, we can unravel this knot, and it can help you in your life outside of the clinic." At this point, the patient is prepared to admit there is a war going on in the room, just as there is a war going on wherever he goes, but he still doesn't understand why it keeps happening to him over and over again. The patient begins to feel there are things he has a hard time seeing.

The therapist will give the patient an example he knows from school. Everyone knows the type, the class genius who knows the answer to every question the teacher asks, but who doesn't have to jump up and answer before everyone else, doesn't have to prove his worth to others. He sits quietly, knows his own value, and knows that in the end, if nobody else knows the answer, the teacher will get to him. Another kind of class genius will jump ahead of everyone else and keep trying to prove he is the best.

Our patient, Israel, still doesn't really comprehend the analogy. But the therapist notes to himself that he understands from what is happening in the clinic why the patient quarrels with everyone. It is because the patient feels superior to everyone else, and invites everyone to prove to him that he is worthless. The therapy will be long and hard. "Like a stylus etching in stone," as someone once said, such is the progress of the paranoid patient, who feels everyone is against him. The patient will continue fighting tooth and nail to show he is the best. He won't easily give up his belief in his own grandiosity. The experienced therapist will begin to understand not only the anger this patient arouses in others, but how desperately this patient needs us to adore him, because he has a very hard time without it. Like every paranoid personality, he needs us to be very empathetic and attentive to him for a length of time, because he missed that experience in childhood, of someone really being with him, really understanding him. Only when he gets that experience that was missing from his past will he be able to calm down.

The therapist will also understand from the relationship growing in the clinic what this patient's relationships were with his parents, and that here, in this room, the patient is reconstructing and resurrecting his past relationships through the therapist. "Yes," the therapist will say, "in your childhood you really did feel persecuted, and those were your real feelings, as a child who had difficulty facing his threatening parents. But now you are grown up, and continue reliving your childhood experiences even where circumstances are different and you are not being persecuted." Slowly, the longer the empathetic line continues in therapy, and the more the patient feels the therapist understands him, he will start calming down. He will have a corrective experience: for the first time in his life he will have a different relationship, one that is not persecuting or threatening.

Then the patient will, for the first time, share his dreams and fears with us. He often feels he is not the best, but possibly almost the worst, and he hides this and tries to conceal it from himself and from others. And he really doesn't understand why he always creates a stir and raises a riot; he knows something is wrong with him, but can't say what. Slowly the patient will let on how hard it is for him to make space for others, and how he is absorbed mainly with himself because of deprivations from his past. And the therapist will rediscover with the patient how hard it is to recognize the other and give him space when you weren't given the space you needed in the past, and lived under constant threat and struggled to survive. Now the therapist and the patient are on their way. They still have a lot of work to do, but this patient is no longer thinking in terms of good and evil, that he himself is good and everybody else is evil, that he is right and they are wrong. This happened because he had a corrective experience in his relationship with the therapist, who accepted him and was empathetic toward him.

At this point we will end the analogy and go back to the Jewish people, not necessarily in chronological order. In therapy too the patient divulges his past in an associative order, sometimes beginning with what happened to him today and from there remembering events of the past. We as a people often look down on the Arabs from a position of superiority, and then are surprised by their reactions. One example is our attempt to develop the Arab countries through economic conferences, based on the correct assumption that we have the ability to contribute to them. But again, the emotional message that goes with the offer is the root of the problem, and the Arab countries immediately go on the defensive and don't want our help, fearing we will dominate them with our "helping." Wouldn't it be better to wait for them to ask us for help? Every parent knows how a child reacts to the parent's good intentions, when the child would prefer to do something by herself. A good parent will be there, will witness the child's experience and convey the message that the child can come to her for help when she wants to. The child will choose when to ask for help, and the request for help has to come from the child. Otherwise, the parent will be seen as dominating the child with her tremendous experience, and quashing the child's attempt to develop separateness and independence. That is how the United States treats us. It waits for us to ask for help, it helps us almost without our noticing, and surely does not flaunt its ability to help us; therefore we do not consider their help humiliating.

And who can forget the years of our contempt toward the Arabs, and the euphoria after the 1967 Six Day War, and the price we paid for it in the 1973 Yom Kippur War, and our dismissal and ignoring of the Palestinians until the 1987 Intifada uprising broke out unexpectedly, and the years-long belief that we could conquer terrorism with force, and the price we paid for that in Lebanon, and more? Indeed, with our personality disorder as a people, our patient receives blow after blow and doesn't know where it is coming from. That is because he has a very hard time seeing the other side, understanding what they are really going through, and therefore predicting their future actions. We know those patients who are beset by one disaster after another, and when we try to inquire whether they saw any warning signs, if they felt anything coming, they always insist that the blow came out of the clear blue sky. We understand that they were very self-centered and did not see the other. The Holocaust is, of course, another example of what happens to the paranoid-grandiose personality who is not alert to his emotional dialogue with his surroundings. Unconsciously, the person with that personality plays the role dictated by his inner worldview, and invites the other side to play the complementary role. In our case the roles are persecutor and persecuted. That is the dynamic of creating a self-fulfilling prophecy.

The Jewish people secluded themselves for years with their obvious difference and separateness from the surrounding nations. That isolation contained within itself feelings of persecution and superiority at the same time. If I am so great and so important, others must have a reason to persecute me, envy me, and hate me. In psychopathology we know that paranoia often goes with megalomania. We also know from clinical experience that the feeling of "I am the best" is usually connected with its opposite, the feeling that "maybe I am not as great as I think," and serve to cover it up, and there is a feeling of falling into an internal experience that says, "I am worthless." One could say that from such heights you can only fall. Thus, a personality pattern is created in the individual or the nation, swinging sharply between feelings of inferiority and grandiosity. One does not exist without the other, and there is no point in asking which came first, the chicken or the egg, because they were both formed simultaneously in the growth process, just as it is pointless to ask whether we are God's chosen people or can be wiped off the face of the earth. The Jewish people did preserve their singularity over the years, in a kind of package deal of balancing intertwined emotional mechanisms. In their dialogue with the Gentiles, the Jewish people felt and broadcast that they were superior, while the Gentiles reminded them of what they wanted to forget, that they also felt they were worthless, didn't even have a home of their own, and could be eradicated. There is a self-nourishing emotional system at play here. There is no doubt that the grandiose personality invites the envy and the hatred of others because of its arrogance, and that is how the person with that personality creates his own persecution and turns his emotional fantasy into a genuine, real experience. We, the Jews, find it very hard to think about and understand how we played any part in the age-old hatred toward us, and what feelings we aroused in others. That is the understanding the therapist tries to promote in therapy, so that the patient can become more aware of, and responsible to, what he brings out and invites from others. In the Holocaust the Jewish people connected with the peak of eradication and humiliation, so that from the arrogant experience of "I am the best" came the opposite inner experience of "I am worthless, and the evidence is, look what they did to us."

From that difficult starting point, a relatively small segment of the Jewish people decides to establish their own state, returning to their ancestral homeland. Those Jews attempt to return to their ancient country they had abandoned for two thousand years, thinking they could come back as if it had waited for them all that time empty and neglected. And here we already know these people are in for another surprise, because of that same old pathology, manifested in their difficulty to see the other and recognize him. And sure enough, the Arabs are going to revolt and refuse to accept them, and the Jewish state will seclude itself in its differentness in the Middle East. If You Will It, It Is No Legend, the motto by which we created the state, is a correct statement in a certain sense — that you must believe in your power in order to create new things — but it is also a problematic statement in the emotional sense. It is an omnipotent statement (often uttered by an adolescent) by a person who has only his own will in view, and feels that with it he can conquer the world. And here the old vicious circle is re-created again, because again they really want to destroy us. And I am trying hard not to be dragged into the question, "Who is right?" and say we deserve a place too. Because every therapist knows that question can sabotage therapy for a paranoid personality. The question is not who is right, the therapist will tell the patient, but why are you suffering so much, and how can that suffering be prevented (because life is more than a court of law)? How does one help that patient, who feels that everyone is against him — and this time the feelings are not just in his head, they are true in reality — stop that vicious circle and stop inviting everyone to be against him? How, in a state of threat and persecution, can you keep the balance that allows you to preserve your existence and your honor, along with the understanding that not everything is yours and that others deserve their share too? That is the dilemma of the paranoid personality who has already come to understand that something is wrong with him and wants to get out of the catch.

In the United Nations organization, in the group of nations, which is like any therapy group, we are the personality-disordered member. That is the member who sits in the group and everyone always picks on him, and everyone has to deal with him, and he thinks he is always right and innocent. That is, of course, a narcissistic disorder, where a person is absorbed in himself and in his own grandiosity, because he did not receive enough empathy in the past. We know that a child has to receive first, and only then can he give. What that patient really needs, as we said, is empathy from the world's nations. He needs to be treated with consideration, and needs his fears and anxieties to be understood, and rightly so, because others wanted and still want to destroy him, and that is why sometimes he gets aggressive, and has to hurt others and conquer territories.

This is where the different therapy styles of the European countries and the United States come in: The United States does not impose itself on us, and tries to give us security and a defense alliance. It understands that the peace process is a growth process that has to move at our own pace and come from within; that such processes cannot be imposed; and that direct negotiations are of immense importance, because this child has to grow up and be able to solve his problems himself, without others imposing solutions upon him and making him angry at them. That is the kind of parents every child needs in order to face the world. Parents that do not do things for him, but wait on the side and are ready to help when the child asks them. The personality-disturbed person also needs others to understand that he has to feel he is strong and standing on his own feet, in order not to be threatened and to be able to build trusting relations with the world. And what a therapeutic statement came from Secretary of State Warren Christopher when he said, "Only a strong Israel can make peace!" As every parent knows, only a child who feels safe can move forward in the growing process while recognizing the needs of others.

The European nations are, as therapists, less empathetic and less alert to our needs, and more inclined to try to impose their opinions on us. Therefore they are less effective in this therapeutic peace process and are less able to help the Arabs in the process. They approach this couples counseling like a therapist trying to impose her opinion, or at least who voices her opinion openly. They forget that their opinion is not that important and not so helpful, but on the contrary, blocks the eminently important ability of the partners to listen to each other. In that respect the right wing was right when it said for years that peace has to be made in direct negotiations between the parties, as equals, and not with the mediation of an outside arbitrator. During the governments of Rabin and Peres (1992–96) that personality-disordered being called "Israel" began to feel, definitely and possibly for the first time in its life, that the world loved it, a feeling that was ruined during the reign of Benjamin Netanyahu (1996–99).

Before we go back and try to understand how it all began, and how that personality disorder emerged and developed, let us say that the ultimate goal of growth in the lives of individuals and nations is the ability to integrate different parts of the personality. It is not only that I am the best, nor is it only that I am the worst, and it is not only that I am right, or that I am aggressive. The ability to see complexities grows during the growth process. In that respect, left and right as overt and covert parts of the personality represent different emotional attitudes that can change at different times, and are at work inside the nation's single soul. You can say the emotional structure of the right better represents the Jewish people's past, while the left is a relatively new and young offshoot. The therapist's task in treating this kind of personality disorder is to heal the rift and soften the fragmentation. That is the task of the growing process for a child who lives in the stormy world of monsters and fairies, and good guys and bad guys, and that is the overall task of the peace process.

So How Did It All Begin?

The Jewish people were born when God appeared to Abraham and said to him, "Get thee out of thy country, and from thy kindred, and from thy father's house, unto a land that I will shew thee. . . ." God chose Abraham, and, as we feel with certainty, chose us, to be his beloved children in this land. And that is how the Jewish people set out on their journey, a nation that began its course as different and special compared to other nations, because it was chosen by the omnipotent God. There is no doubt that Abraham had valid reasons to create for himself an authoritative, omnipotent father who loved only him. It surely took an active imagination to create such a new concept in those days, and Abraham used it creatively to resolve internal conflicts he must have had with his father, Terah. And so the group of people who had a strong emotional sense of singularity, including fear of their surroundings and arrogance, multiplied and grew. Let us consider for a moment that singular action in the human emotional experience, the invention of God, and try to understand it. Man created God out of his own needs; God did not create man. The goal of that human invention is to compensate for a very deep feeling of insecurity. That is because if there is a God, there is order and there is justice. Then you can predict the future, and events have meaning beyond cruel fate. Man's feelings of worthlessness and finality bred God as a great, omnipotent father, who watches over us, and whom we have to obey and appease.

But the Jewish people created a new model of God, an abstract one. Not a statue, not a mask, but the kind of God you cannot see, although it exists and is present in our consciousness, in our hearts, as an internalized image. That was of course a novelty in the environment of the Jewish people, because until that invention the nations surrounding the Jewish people were idol-worshipers (there are testimonies that the Jews were not necessarily the first people in the world to create an abstract God). That is an important developmental leap in the power of abstraction. We know that at a very young age (until the age of eight months) what a child does not see does not exist for her. If you hide her toy before she has acquired the ability to abstract, which is known as object permanence, she will not seek it because she does not see it. Indeed, the small infant has to see the object to believe it exists. At around the age of three another "object permanence" emerges, this time emotionally. The image of the parent is internalized by the child. The child can, for instance, go to kindergarten with assurance, and still feel the parent is there in her experience. That emotional object permanence is also a critically important developmental leap. If the parent dies before that internalized image of the parent congeals, the child experiences it as abandonment, and cannot mourn the parent she has not internalized. After the age of three, usually, there is an ability to mourn what was and no longer is. Before developing emotional object permanence, the child has to see the parent frequently in order to establish his existence in her consciousness, but after that stage, she does not have to see him as frequently. Only after the child has an internalized image of the parent can she actually separate from the parent. This is an opportunity to note how powerful internalized images are, and what complex relationships we can develop with those figures that exist only in our imaginations. Indeed, the Jewish people showed a strong power of abstraction and invented a God that is invisible, who cannot be touched, who is only an internalized image.

The concept of one God is another significant developmental leap toward abstraction and integration. We know from the child's development process how hard it is for her, and how much time she needs to understand that the same parent can be both good and bad, while remaining the same parent. That emotional integration of the image of a single parental figure, who is a human figure who has different personality traits, is an advanced developmental stage for the child, who is learning to view her parent as a complex personality. We know the fairy tales with the fairies and the witches and the dichotomy between good and evil. We also know from clinical psychology, from working with people with personality disorders, how they divide the world into good and evil, and how hard it is for them to understand that the same person can be both good and evil, and the split is in their own experiences but not in the person under consideration. The Jews created a God who is only good, but he can also be angry and cruelly vengeful when he is not obeyed. And again, relating to one single deity requires the integration of different feelings in the same figure without the possibility of a split.

Indeed, it has been hard for the Jews all these years to keep their God abstract and unique, and not to turn him into a statue, and not to give him children, such as Jesus, for instance, or the offspring and the multitude of Gods with different characteristics created by the Greeks. The concrete need to touch the object as well as fragment it, and not to stay with the abstract, is a very strong regressive need. The Jewish people did give humanity the abstract and single God, and other nations adopted that model in later times.

Let us go back now and examine the relationship between the Jews and the

God they created. We must remember, of course, that this beautiful fantasy existed nowhere else but in the minds of the Jewish people, who, since that moment in the life of Abraham, the patriarch, have lived by the story they told themselves. God chose the Jewish people, and God rewards them and punishes them time and again but he, God, is always right, and he must always be heeded and obeyed. That authoritative father figure is omnipotent, always right, and punishes severely and cruelly, especially when he is abandoned. In the Ten Commandments, the first commandment is, "I am the Lord thy God which have brought thee out of the Land of Egypt." The second is, "Thou shalt have no other gods before me." And the fourth is, "Thou shalt not take the name of the Lord thy God in vain." Thus the Jewish people created an infinitely narcissistic figure, which the first three commandments place in the center of the individual's world, and who requires absolute loyalty. The reward was, undoubtedly, the experience of differentness from all the nations of the region. The feeling of superiority and specialness runs like a thread through all of Jewish history, and is symbolized by the God who is only ours, the one and genuine.

The relationship between the Jewish people and their God has, among other things, a deep sadomasochistic element. God is always right and man is always wrong. And if something terrible happens to us, such as the Holocaust, we simply do not understand why we deserve that punishment, but we do deserve it, and God knows what he is doing. He is never wrong. In other words, the dialogue between man and God always ends with man saying, "I am guilty; I sinned," and so on, taking all the blame and the responsibility, and God always remains the good, strong, and right one. Surely it is not easy to grow up with such a parent, who, when he hits us, we have to say he is right. It really is not humane, but that is how the child, at least at certain moments, experiences the authoritative parent. The child, at those moments, identifies with the aggressor. It can be assumed that most of humanity grew up under such strong hierarchies most of the time, and therefore that is their projected image of God. But the Jewish people had a compensation for all the blows inflicted on them by God. They experienced them as blows of love, a sign of God's caring and desire to discipline them. That is how battered wives and children often feel about their batterers. Those women and children justify the beatings they get, see them as a sign of love, often invite the beatings, then run to the batterer asking forgiveness and comfort. That is the sadomasochistic relationship at its best. Yes, said the Jews, God is angrier at us and punishes us more, but that is because he loves us more and keeps us by his side, and that is where we derive our compensation and singularity. That child, named Israel, thinks his father loves him best, and transmits that feeling to his siblings. He is sure they are jealous of his closeness to God, the parent.

It is no wonder that such an inner experience is a self-fulfilling prophecy. All the other nations have to do is assume the role the Jewish people assigned them over the years, to try and harm them, and thereby the Jews will continue feeling they are right and everyone is mistreating them because they are God's beloved children (this is not intended to justify the offending nations, only to understand the Jewish people's responsibility for the suffering they underwent). But let us not forget that everything we are talking about is happening in only one place, in the mind of the Jewish people, who invented God and the whole story. They did not invent it by accident. The Jewish people are projecting their inner experience outwardly and telling us about the quality of their initial relationships as a people. Now all that remains is for them to live by the story they invented, and thereby reconstruct and relive their inner historic experience as a nation again and again (those are emotional processes that can be seen clearly in the clinic).

The Jewish people preserved their uniqueness and their religion for years, and tried to establish a state during the periods of the First and Second biblical temples. The current attempt ("The Third Temple") by the Jewish people to establish their own state is different from the previous ones, because the world around us has changed. We no longer have a monopoly on God. Moreover, a more universal and less religious Western culture of thinking has evolved; a new stream with a more romantic and less dramatic emotional capacity has emerged; the developed world has undergone a change that reduces the role of religion in our lives and places the secular state above it; and emotional, impulsive, and totalitarian thinking are being replaced by democratic thinking, which is more relative and less absolute, and gives space to different voices, in the outside world as well as within the soul. It is both an emotional and intellectual maturation. The original need to create authoritative parents for ourselves has lessened, and our intellectual capacity for more abstract and less concrete thinking, as expressed in science, has increased.

2

The Dynamic
of the Peace Process

The Peace Process: A Business Negotiation
or an Emotional Bond?

In business negotiations we apply various manipulations and tactics to get a better price. We might insist on every detail and demand a clear and binding contract. Emotional relationships, such as those between partners or friends or with children, put emotions at the center and give them the stage. The questions we ask about emotional relationship are whether they include partnership, trust, mutual appreciation, and so on.

A person with paranoid personality traits will argue with us and use every small detail to prove she is right. It is hard not to be drawn into a discussion of the details and lose sight of the forest for the trees. The forest in this case is the emotional bond. A person with paranoid tendencies thinks she is right, but my role as a therapist is to tell her I am more interested in her suffering than in her vindication. The therapeutic question in this case is, of course, why the person feels so threatened that she has to cling to the minute details to show she is right and to use various manipulations and tactics to protect herself. What is she so afraid of that she cannot think in terms of the relationship? It is also true that you cannot build a good relationship if you are over-preoccupied with details. On the contrary, such a preoccupation invites more and more wars. The therapist will try to be empathetic with the patient's emotional suffering and to give her the stage in order to create a corrective experience. Only then can the patient relax and put aside the details and tactics.

Prime Minister Benjamin Netanyahu got overly involved in the minute details and led us to a dead end. He was not aware of the fact that his concern with the details projected a basic insecurity, which had to be dealt with. The perception of the peace negotiations as a business negotiation, where you start at one point and end at another, and therefore have to raise the price in advance, and so on, needs to be examined. It is a distorted perception of the peace process. It is a superficial approach. It is true that during the process we made more and more concessions, and moved further and further away from our opening positions, but if you look at it that way you lose sight of the fact that at the same time a genuine emotional process was underway; we went deeper and deeper in asking ourselves what is really important to us and what we could and could not give up.

Had we approached the negotiations this way from the start, recognizing the Other's needs as well as our own red lines, that would have aroused more trust and not created the illusion that we can be bargained with. True, as in therapy, like in any growth process, there are no shortcuts, and the emotional process has to take place (we learned we could give up the Sinai, that we could agree to the establishment of a Palestinian state, etc.). But not revealing our truth, our cards (in general, any association between negotiations and a card game is not an invitation to peace but to war)—our opening positions, as the right always maintained—before we sit down at the negotiating table, and artificially raising the "ante," is an emotional position that invites mistrust and war. We know that the truly big deals are often made without contracts but only on a handshake. We, for instance, can by no means compromise with terrorism, and if we bring honesty to every area, that demand to fight terrorism will not be seen as another manipulation that can be bargained over.

Therefore I think saying, as Ehud Barak did, that within a year we can solve the Lebanon problem, is not revealing our cards nor is it a commitment to our public that the Syrians can later use against us. It is the truth, that we want to get out of there as soon as possible and there is nothing to hide here. On the contrary, that statement is a trust-building measure because we come without manipulation and from an emotional stance that allows contact and trust.

Besides, for years the right had a negative view of the repeated statements by the left that it wanted peace. It claimed that that pursuit of peace projected weakness. OK, you want peace, it maintained, but you have to hide it. Today it is hard to remember that, because we are in another place emotionally. Today statements about peace are appreciated and not seen as weakness. Now these quarreling children have learned that asking to make up does not make you a wimp. Indeed, the era of the manipulations and tactics has undergone a far-reaching change, which I will expand upon in chapter 3. Former Secretary of

State Warren Christopher understood that in a sense when he said, "only a strong Israel can make peace," and the Americans, in the help they give us, understand that too, at least intuitively. A growing child who feels secure will not need so many defenses, and will understand the other better and be less suspicious.

The question arises: Are the Arabs cunning and manipulative, or are they suffering because they feel threatened by us? Those are very different emotional stances, which call for very different responses and require clarification. For years there were many among us who said that the Arabs could not be trusted, that their word was worth nothing, and that they would not keep their agreements. There is no doubt that if we felt more secure, we would need fewer manipulations and would attribute less cunning and manipulation to the Arabs. We could be more empathetic to their feelings. We know this well from treating partners or parents and children or people in general. Only when someone is secure can he understand the other. When Yitzhak Rabin said, concerning the negotiations with Palestinians, that he will not have a Middle Eastern bazaar, he did not understand that even if they were manipulative, they were doing it because they felt weak and were fighting for their home and independence, and could not compromise on that. It was not that they were such sophisticated negotiators that they got the impossible even from Netanyahu. It is simply because they are fighting for their independence and their lives, and not for one percent more or less, like us. We of all people should be able to understand that because of our past, because we too fought for our home and eventually built a state. Today we are arguing as much as they are over each percentage point, even though we are not fighting for our survival and they are. Perhaps we are projecting our manipulations on them.

I want to stress again that in a relationship such as ours with the Arabs, where we have no chance of separating, as in a Catholic marriage, with both peoples living together in this land and being reflected in each other's eyes, the best comparison is with the emotional bond between partners because our intensive cohabitation brings up very deep emotional contents that cannot be ignored. We know to what extent relationships between partners are effected by the baggage each partner brings from his or her parents' home. It is natural for us to expect that in the most meaningful relationship of our adult life, the marital relationship, we would experience the same feelings, doubts, and conflicts that characterized our early lives. Our relationship with the Arabs is also influenced by our past as a people, by our anxieties and the traumas we have suffered, from aspects of our personality as a people that were formulated during our history. The question I want to raise here is whether we are attentive to the emotional parameters of the peace process, or whether we are too preoccupied with the details, which are important in their own right, but that must not come at the expense of the emotional aspect of the process. We should ask ourselves, for instance, what statements by us can bring about a change in the process, empathetic statements that recognize the Palestinians' suffering.

Jordan's King Hussein made a big impression when he came to Israel to offer condolences to the seven families whose daughters were murdered by a Jordanian soldier. We saw how an emotional gesture can change the whole picture. He did not give up anything, he just expressed feelings of partnership and empathy, and aroused in us feelings of warmth and caring. Not to get carried away, but when Syria announced that it was glad Barak replaced Netanyahu, and said that it felt it could do business with Barak, how that moved us and changed the way we felt about the Syrians! And it was only a statement. Sometimes it seems as if the Arabs understand the emotional aspect of the peace process better than we do. Arafat avoids details and refuses even to remember them. When you watch him you realize how much he is influenced by emotions. In general, great leaders are motivated and guided by emotion: Ben-Gurion, Begin, Sadat, Churchill, Lenin, and others. Sadat, for instance, asked Begin to withdraw from Al-Arish before the designated time as a gesture for his daughter's wedding, but was refused, because of our entrenchment in our fears and the suspicion, voiced quietly at the time, that the Arabs always want *bakshish* (money that is given under the table) and do not know how to keep agreements.

Indeed, it is hard for us to be generous, because to be generous you have to feel more secure, and we are still far from that emotional stance. The goal I wish to suggest is the ability to treat the peace process as a growth process for both sides, which should be done out of love and not threats. *The reversal from threat to love is the fundamental change we are seeking*. The Gestalt phrase, "the whole is larger than the sum of its parts," fits this understanding, where the peace process should be seen in terms of its emotional quality, beyond the collection of concrete details. In a process where the parameters are qualitative rather than quantitative, our thoughts should not be directed at how to give them less and keep more for ourselves, as in commerce, but should be comparable to the growth process; it is important for us to care about them; we must ask what this Palestinian child needs in order to grow. We must recognize his difficulties and sometimes think for him, whether he can accept one agreement or another, even if he wants it. We must not, for instance, accept an agreement that does not respect them. That is of course very different from a commercial negotiation. Our ultimate goal, which I will discuss at length in the chapter about Jerusalem, is for them to have a capital in east Jerusalem with honor and pride, and even if they are willing to forego it, we should not agree, because we can guess how giving up your own interests will end. Nobody can give up himself, and attempts to do that end in anger and war. A child does not always know what he needs, and a good parent can give him what he needs without his asking, just as he can impose limits even when the child resists them. Developing them in all areas (airport, seaport, safe passage and so on), for instance, is in our interest as much as theirs, and they should be encouraged in those directions even if they sometimes resist. The question is what emotional stance we choose. Are we defensive and avoidant, or are we taking responsibility, initiating and warm? A good parent understands the child's inner world and what he really needs. If the parent is always threatened, he cannot experience the "together" feelings and the common interest, and will stress what he is against and will perpetuate the commercial style of negotiation.

The Third Way Party, which carried the banner of finding the middle road, did not understand that there is hardly any argument between right and left anymore about what to give back and what to keep. The difference, which the Center Party understands, is in the different emotional positions, and different emotional messages, because the peace process is primarily an emotional process. The integration for which the public is so hungry is on the emotional level rather than on the operative level of how much to give back. The more time that goes by, the more we understand that the question here is not territory but the relationship, like a child arguing with his father over how much allowance he will get. More allowance will give him the feeling that he is bigger, but the father knows the question is not more or less allowance; the question is emotional, whether the child will grow, stand on his own, make a living, and be responsible for his actions. The father has a limited amount of money, and can give a little more or a little less. The child and the parent might argue over the marginal details and forget the main point, whether the child is responsible or not. The adolescent wants more and more, but the parent's role is to see beyond the adolescent's legitimate wishes and assess whether his growth process is correct.

The Peace Process as a Process of Emotional Growth

When we try to reconstruct how we felt as children, it is not easy to revive the sensations, the smells, and the experiences of childhood as we experienced them at the time. That is how a patient feels when he is undergoing a process of change. He is in a new place, and often has a hard time reconstructing just what went on in his past, when he thought differently and saw things differently. Such is our situation in relation to our positions and feelings regarding the Arabs in the course of the peace process. We have already forgotten how things looked back then. But it is important to take another look at the emotional process we underwent in order to understand the direction it has gone, and learn something for the future.

The Role of Despair in the Growth Process

Israel was born in massive denial and repression of feelings of anxiety and helplessness. Without such defense mechanisms it is hard for a child to grow. The desire to establish a Jewish homeland in the Land of Israel was motivated mostly by emotional rather than by rational forces. Such powerful processes are not driven mainly by logic. It would have been more logical to go to the United States or to other countries, as most of the Jews did, rather than come to a country that needed to be built and that was populated by Arabs. Herzl's statement, "If you will it, it is not a dream," is fundamentally an omnipotent statement that says that we can actually do anything we wish. Of course this statement contains the denial of impotent feelings of weakness, anxiety, and helplessness, feelings the Jewish people experienced for all the years of their exile, in the same way a child may grow up with defense mechanisms such as repression and denial. Indeed, every child goes through the omnipotence stage, with magical thinking and fantasies of his unlimited ability. The opposite emotions will often emerge in dreams, where a monster may pursue him. The more omnipotent, the greater the underlying anxieties and fears. Thus our state was founded with a lot of joy and fanfare, with euphoria in the victory of the War of Independence, and a lot of trepidation inside. It is no accident that our developmental process as a nation reborn in its land is identical to the development of a child from infancy to maturity. *During his growth, the child gradually gives up his omnipotence, through stages of despair and depression, and increasingly recognizes the Other.* We too increasingly recognize the Palestinians as well as our own ethnic and national complexity, that we cannot vanquish terrorism and have to give up territory. We are learning this just like a child, with a lot of pain and disappointment. How many more disappointments does this child need in order to grow up and realize his true ability, to give up his magnanimous fantasies, and still recognize the existence of the Other? The baby, we have already said, does not recognize his mother or see her as a separate entity. For him she is a part of his body that needs to fulfill his needs. And how painful for him to learn that she has her own life; she is not just his and for him alone. And that is just the beginning of the long journey of life, where he will suffer one disappointment after another when he discovers that he is not the center of the world and has to give up his egocentricity and narcissism by repeated injuries. And how much suffering did we endure before we recognized the Palestinians and their right to independence, whereas we have yet to recognize, emotionally and morally, the suffering of the Palestinian refugees, which we caused.

Now we have done some growing up and we are around fifty. Slowly the beat of the drums of victory is dying out, and new voices are emerging, more mature and ripe. Some of the cries of joy were actually a reversal of our emotions in the wake of the Holocaust, and stemmed from our need to overcome some of our traumatic experiences as a nation in our two-thousand-year exile. Adolescence is another omnipotent stage, after infancy, when the adolescent feels that the whole world is open to him, and that he can do everything his parents could not. Disappointment and despair come later, when the adolescent gradually comes to recognize his limits. If it weren't for the Yom Kippur

War, for instance, it is doubtful that we would have made peace with Egypt. That is because the war taught Egypt that it could not destroy and decimate us. We too began internalizing the fact that not every victory is as swift as in the Six Day War, and that it's painful to live by the sword, with all the casualties, over the years, not to speak of the constant existential danger. In that general respect there is no real difference between left and right. Both camps lived over the years of our growth as a nation with feelings of euphoria that denied the feelings and existence of the Other, and both have undergone a long phase of depression. In this depression or despondency we experience reality hitting us cruelly in the face again and again—the Intifada, for instance. We are still struggling, mainly with ourselves, to recognize the Palestinians' right to their own state. I mean a real recognition, from the heart, with a desire to help them. The recognition of the Palestinians as a people takes time and seeps into our consciousness more and more, and each time requires another process of grief. The same is true in the life of the individual: giving up narcissism and recognizing the other is a prolonged mourning process. We might accept a Palestinian state on paper, logically, but not yet emotionally. For that we need another period of depression. We have not suffered enough to give up our grand ambitions as yet. We understand that peace has to come through difficult feelings before we are able to really welcome it. Therefore, it is no wonder that many of us are experiencing despair. There are many years of despair ahead of us because we are still far from full recognition of the existence of the Other.

How often do we see this in the lives of married couples? How hard is mutual recognition of each other's shortcomings, giving up the attempt to change the other and impose your worldview upon him? It is hard to endure the hurt and insult over the fact that things are not the way you wish they were, and that what seems so vital to your existence, at least in your experience, is not happening. In the despair stage you give up the pleasant fantasy that at the end you are going to win. That is what we always said about the Arabs, that they would not make peace with us as long as they had not given up their attempts to destroy us. They too have undergone and are undergoing a mourning process in their recognition of our existence. The same is true for us. So long as we do not give up the attempt to erase the existence of Palestinian refugees, and do not recognize the Arabs' legitimate desires, we will not have peace. As long as we do not understand that as far as they are concerned we landed on them from another world, settled in their land, expelled them from their homes, and ignored their existence, there will not be reconciliation. Recognizing the other is almost the essence of the individual's growth, and giving up the belief that "the world revolves around me" is very painful for a child. It comes from a series of blows and disappointments from the environment and signals the end of the era of omnipotence. Sometimes, out of despair can suddenly come love for the enemy. With recognition, the anger starts to dissipate, and we recognize the limits of our partner. We are no longer angry at him and blame him for our common fate anymore than we blame ourselves, and understand that he is just like us; he is not omnipotent; in the same way a child might feel guilty for what he did to his mother, and tries to make it up to her.

Let us look at the relationship between these partners, us and the Arabs, who are changing together. First of all, it is worth noting that when you give up your omnipotence, you also rid yourself of the powerful anxieties that reside alongside the omnipotent fantasies. In emotional life, those two opposites feed each other and are inseparable. The dejection that goes with recognizing the other relieves deep anxieties of a paranoid kind, as well as raises our awareness of our red lines, the things we can absolutely not give up. Just as when a child grows up, first he learns the boundaries of his body, then the boundaries of his abilities, and becomes aware of their implications.

I think most Israelis today, unlike in the past, feel that we can give up the Golan Heights. Yes, it is very painful, and we feel as if a part of the Land of Israel, a part of our body, is being ripped away. We must go through a mourning period as we did when we gave up the Sinai, but today we can give up the Golan in terms of our inner feelings, in exchange for peace. On the other hand, if you look at the Syrians and at their feelings, it is clear that they experience the Golan as an inseparable part of Syria they cannot give up. Due to the process they have gone through they now recognize our existence and agree to peace, and like us they are examining what they can give up in the painful process, where they can compromise, and where they cannot.

I think many of us still mourn the loss of the Sinai, surely those of us who loved the sand dunes of Nuweiba, Sharm A-Sheikh, and St. Catherine. We became very attached to those regions, not to mention other aspects of our national mourning, such as the feeling of becoming smaller, giving up the income from oil and tourism, and to top it off, the stinging insult of losing Taba too in the international court. The mourning process has not ended, and the need for passports to go to Sinai still makes some of us bitter. But this mourning is so important because we forget that once we were in an earlier developmental stage, a paranoid stage when we feared the Egyptians would not keep the agreement and would attack us. Today we are in a depressive stage, sorry for what is gone. That is tremendous progress. The Egyptians, on the other hand, felt the Sinai was their home, and could not make any compromises. Today there is no one who would say that peace with Egypt was not worth it, or, conversely, that it could have been achieved without fully giving up the Sinai. But then, recognizing the red lines of the other and understanding that there are things upon which the Egyptians could not compromise — and the Sinai was such an asset for them, just as we have our own red lines — was not so obvious. Our feeling was paranoid and manipulative, that it was just another negotiating trick rather than an inner truth they were shouting. They could compromise over recognizing our existence and everything that implied through a mourning process they have not finished (there are also other voices in Egypt), and indeed they made a cold peace with us. Emotional processes take a long time. And these were not things they could take for granted, just as we could not in the past.

We no longer perceive Arafat as another terrorist the left and right refuse to speak with, and we no longer necessarily view a Palestinian state as an existential danger to us. Today left and right are negotiating with him, and a Palestinian state looks more and more possible, maybe even desirable. The Palestinians, on their part, cannot give up their independence, but in a slow and gradual process that has only just begun they are realizing that they have to take responsibility for the aggression that comes from them, and stop terrorism. True, they are just at the beginning of a real war against terrorism, and have not yet disarmed Hamas. Recognizing our existence is a deeper process than voting at the Palestinian National Council, and takes time. Their declarations that they recognize our existence are just the tip of the iceberg of conscious and unconscious fantasies that require processing. We know the process well and know how hard it is for some of us to give up the dream of the Greater Israel and how hard it is for most of us to give up the Golan Heights, the West Bank, and Sinai, not to speak of recognizing the refugees, and so on. Therefore, the Likud was right when it insisted that the Palestinians at least make a clear and unequivocal statement that they recognize us, as an opening to a deeper emotional process of actually recognizing us. The Palestinians made another concession, at least declaratively, in not demanding the massive return of refugees to Israel proper, and that is the beginning of a deeper process.

We have to understand how processes of change work. Even when we accept a certain reality that is imposed upon us, we still have various conscious and unconscious fantasies that require deeper processes of acceptance and processing. Partners can maintain their marriages but still really want their partner to change in certain areas, and have fantasies about it. Children may take years to come to terms with their parents' shortcomings and hope they will change. Even in adulthood the children do not always reach an integration that recognizes the parents' weaknesses along with everything they gave them. Mourning processes over what we want but cannot have take time, and there is always tension between reality and fantasy and our wishes. Comes the extreme right and says the Arabs have never given up their desire to destroy us. How true is that? I think they are talking about a fantasy harbored by some Arabs, just as some of us have not given up our wish for the Greater Israel. In our public too you will find those who say they are waiting for the opportunity to realize the vision of the Greater Israel. We as a nation sign agreements whereby we give the Palestinians parts of the West Bank and Gaza, but we also have desires and fantasies of holding onto those lands. Among the Arabs too you can find the whole spectrum, from thinking peace will be good, through mourning and acceptance of our existence and all the way to fantasies of our destruction. Therefore, when our Right claims that we all think as they do but are afraid to say it—that the Arabs want to destroy us—it is actually referring to regressive parts of our personality as a nation and as individuals. True, sometimes, especially after a terrorist attack, those feelings come up with greater force, feelings of anger and insult and the desire to break down negotiations with them, but those are just certain parts of our personality. Those parts require and will continue to require further processing both by us and by the Arabs, but just as in the individual the ego forces that are responsible for contact with reality usually succeed in containing our most primal and impulsive fantasies, so that we don't fall apart (psychosis), so do the peace accords contain within them worlds of fantasies of each side, which require long processing so that the peace agreement can survive. Therefore the negotiations between us and the Palestinians about the PNC decisions regarding Israel's destruction demonstrate what is known from clinical therapy, that changes of this sort have deep levels that require long and slow processing.

In therapy we can, at best, help the patient change. However, we cannot change his environment. Therefore we have to educate ourselves toward a more complex view of the peace process in this national therapy, built from all the details, and the details of the details. We have to become more sensitive to our statements and how they are received by the other side, and develop ties with the Arabs on the basis of smaller joint goals, like Shimon Peres's vision of regional economic development. Just as in therapy, where emotional listening and working on the details of feelings are as essential to the process as general sweeping statements, in the form of one agreement or another. Putting an emphasis on the publication of nonhostile textbooks in the Palestinian Authority and Arab countries, for instance, is of critical importance to this process. The soldiers should be polite to the Palestinians at the roadblocks and minimal social benefits should be provided to the laborers. We know that emotional development comes from the smallest personal examples. Whether in the case of babies, or in therapy, generalizations come from the details. I do not want to belittle the importance of agreements, but if we do not put an emphasis on the emotional details that comprise them, the agreements will stay empty. It will be a cold peace. The more peace agreements are signed with the Arabs, the more real work we will have, in processing our deepest fantasies about the essence of our relationship with the Arabs. During that processing, our fantasies have to constantly be checked against the details of reality on both sides. These are emotional materials that will emerge into our consciousness, and need to be processed and checked against reality again. Just as a person grows, so does a nation.

And Now, A Look at the Future

We are not yet ready to know which of our settlements across the Green Line should be dismantled and which should not. We are in the process of clarifying our permanent borders and modes of coexistence with the Palestinians, and this takes time. I think and hope that the further the peace process moves between us and the Palestinians, we will not just look at the question of which settlements to dismantle and which not, but also how. In other words, if we do not dismantle a settlement, how can we use its presence to promote good relations? And if we do dismantle it, it is very important to ask for what purpose, and what will become of it. Perhaps it can be used, for instance, to house refugees. And if we do not dismantle a settlement, maybe it can be used as a base for economic cooperation with the Palestinians. We are apparently not ripe yet to internalize that emotional position. And the Palestinians may not be ripe for it either, because it requires a sincere belief in peace. But it is important to point to the right direction, because that is the meaning of real peace, and that is where we should be heading. The question is not only what belongs to whom, but how it is done. Because the how represents feelings, and it is the most important thing. In simple words, the settlements may and may not be dismantled, but that alone will not promote peace. There might be peace with or without the settlements. Because what matters is not what we do, but the emotional component.

The same goes for the insight, which I mentioned before, that Israeli Arabs have a very important role in promoting peace. Even if they do not serve in the army for obvious reasons, they can serve in the "peace corps" and help their Palestinian brothers in various ways. This is a different way of thinking, which does not exclude the Israeli Arabs out of our fear and feeling of being threatened, but recognizes their importance and uses them constructively as promoters of peace. Therefore there is no reason not to let them join the coalition. On the contrary, they should be included in the peace process out of recognition for the tremendous contribution they can make.

Another example is the settlements on the Golan Heights. In this case we should not agree to the destruction of settlements as in the case of Yamit, because that contradicts the spirit of peace. We have to think with the Syrians how to use those homes for some peace-promoting purpose: housing refugees, for instance, tourism, or even simply as a gift to the Syrians, but by no means should we demolish them. Rather, we should use them to develop the region, because that is the emotional meaning of peace. And that is another example of *listening to the emotional logic of the process.*

Neither can we put up with any terrorism. The Palestinians are going to have to learn how to live with that demand. In the long run it is the emotional truth that wins out, not manipulation. On terrorism we will never compromise, just as the Palestinians can never give up their demand for independence and a capital in east Jerusalem. The mutual recognition of each other's "red lines" and inner truths is the key to peace, because that is where arguments stop, and nobody will accept a threat to his survival. But both sides will need some time to find our inner truths out of the tangle of emotions that flood us. Our inner truth is, for now, that we will not give in on the matter of terrorism, but if they prove themselves, we will give them independence. In every growth process, closing gaps between inner and outer worlds, and reconciling with reality, lead to closing gaps in one's inner world and mending rifts and splits. Today there is no significant gap between the positions of the left and the right regarding what to concede and what not to, and time will continue closing that gap and leading to the point I am talking about, our emotional truth as a nation. That split in our personality as a people, between left and right, is slowly closing, and that is a sign of the positive mental process we are undergoing as a people, which is also evident in our foreign relations (this is another illustration of the principle of separation).

There remains a problem regarding Jerusalem. Our emotional truth on that matter is severely repressed, and we need more time for the emotional processing of that issue. Yes, there is room for both them and us in Jerusalem. Extremist religious declarations that in Jerusalem there is only room for us, and that it can only be our capital, come from a narcissist place of hurt, and require us to go through a deep emotional process so that, like growing children, we can make space for the other and believe there is room for both. If we listened to the Palestinians we would hear that they cannot give up Jerusalem. They repeat it again and again. Emotionally they cannot and we cannot do anything about that, just as we cannot give up Jerusalem. And they, the Palestinians, know what we, for the time being, only know in our unconscious, that there really is room for both. We always said we won wars because we knew what we were fighting for. When we fought for our survival we were right about that. But today it is true for the Palestinians, who are fighting for their independence and for their state.

If we look back, we will realize that we have undergone a process that took us through the muddle of our anxieties toward an emotional truth that became clear. It is not a question of arguments about 1 percent more or less of land. Indeed, we and the Arabs are each going through an emotional process, with each side slowly coming to understand what its red lines are and what it can give up, and there is less room left for manipulations. We cannot get real long-standing gains through various tricks, because the truth will prevail. That is the nature of intimate emotional bonds in general, and our bond with the Arabs in particular, which is coming into sharper focus all the time.

True, it is not always easy to see in advance, at the beginning of the emotional process, what our red lines are. Because when someone is threatened they have difficulty seeing what their truth is and what they can give up. It is even harder when you are afraid to enter the shoes of the other whom you view as an aggressor, and to understand him. But we really are in the midst of a couple's therapy with the Arabs, and are going through such dramatic changes that we can hardly remember opposing the withdrawal from Sinai, refusing to speak to Arafat, and so on. In the future, when we feel more secure, we surely will not understand how we couldn't see that there was room for both us and them in Jerusalem, moreover, how we adopted a threatened and combative emotional stance toward the Palestinians, and did not help them when they needed our help.

Emotional Resistance to the Peace Process

People resist change and progress in any natural growth process, including a peace process. Even though the child understands that he should grow and that it is for his own good, there are still powerful forces at play, many of them unconscious, which try to keep him in his current state. The difficulty is in giving up familiar habits and securities for something that is unknown. Getting weaned from the pleasure of breastfeeding—giving up the breast for the bottle—is not easy for a baby; nor is not being able to excrete whenever he feels like it, but holding it in for the convenience of others. The child feels as if he is letting someone else take control of his own muscles. In the oedipal stage, the child gives up erotic wishes toward the opposite-sex parent. The tension between the individual and society, between one's egocentricity and the common good, between the child who thinks he is at the center of the world and the adult who has to assert himself in balance with the needs of the environment, is a peace process that never ends.

In adolescence, for example, you have to sever yourself from your original family, give it up and create your own family, a process that is not easy emotionally. That too is a kind of peace process between the growing person and his environment. The person has to give up old securities for new balances, and the question of whether people can live together and whether there is room for everyone keeps coming up in different ways throughout life. In therapy we try to clarify those resistances to growth and bring them into consciousness. The patient refuses to give up old defenses for a new mental balance. Why should he give up his aggressive actions, which release impulses, for the sake of recognizing the other? He might understand that it is in his interest, but it is still hard to give up. It is hard to give up obsessive rituals that quell anxiety. Why should he give up his depression, which is so cozy and comforting, and leaves him supposedly free of malicious intentions and aggression? Why should he give up his paranoid stance, which leaves him as pure and innocent as a newborn baby, and the other person evil and monstrous? Why should he give up his omnipotent thoughts, that he is the best, and feel its repressed opposite, that sometimes he feels like a zero, as if he is worthless? Why should he give up the clearly divided world between good and evil, for a more complex view, including painful things that are difficult to recognize? Those are all emotional prices we pay on the way to growing up, painful prices people are not always eager to pay.

The peace process is a growth process of knowing ourselves and knowing the other, while the pathological state of war has many derivative *benefits*. The first obvious benefit is that beyond the border there is a monster whom we can blame for everything. If there were no monster there everything would be fine. In other words, the feeling is that I am the poor victim of difficult circumstances. I project all of my troubles on the war that was imposed on me, and attribute all my difficulties to it. It allows me to say, "What can I do? If there weren't a war, the economic situation in the country would be better, and so would mine. I wouldn't have to go into the army; I could do things I can't do today. People, including me, would be less edgy." When there is peace there will be no one to blame. Then the entire responsibility will fall upon the individual, and it is no small matter not to have anyone to blame and to have to take responsibility. Another even more common projection is that in a state of war and lack of prosperity we can blame the leaders and place all our problems on them. "It is all because of this damn country," is a statement we hear again and again, and implies that if we had better leadership I would be in great shape.

War as a defense mechanism unites the whole nation, so that we don't have to see ourselves as the conflicted human mosaic we are, Arabs and Jews, religious and secular, Ashkenazi and Sephardi, left and right, men and women, and so on. The army is surely a melting pot for some of the population, and in a state of peace those gaps will surface in even starker relief. In family therapy we sometimes see one member unconsciously taking a symptom upon himself, or the family assigns him that role in order to rally the whole family around the emergency. "The child wets his bed," for example, or "the child has problems at school." Then the whole family rallies, and stops talking about other problems, which are usually deeper and more severe. What may emerge in family therapy is that the parents do not get along with each other, and the child wets himself so that the parents can rally around his problem instead of constantly fighting with each other. Indeed, the common external enemy unites us. And with the peace process moving forward, we can see the rifts between religious and secular and Jews and Israeli Arabs coming to a head.

Another example (which I mentioned in "The Rabin Assassination") is of the personality-disordered individual who seeks a war outside to justify his inner turmoil. In the absence of war, the noise from inside gets louder. Then the person with the disorder realizes that those voices are only his own and are not generated by an external reality. He will do anything to create and initiate confrontations with others. Indeed, there are people who function better in times of stress and war. It is a deep unconscious statement about the connection between our internal rift and the peace process, and how hard it is for us to give up the fight and war against the external enemy and reveal our inner conflicts. There have been more than a few countries that went to war because of internal conflicts. In that way, war can serve emotional defenses.

Another defense mechanism or pathological benefit from war is the fact that sometimes it is nice to find comfort in the sea of pain and national bereavement. Memorial Day for Fallen Soldiers, for instance, is a day when people feel relief from all their personal troubles, not necessarily ones that are related to the pains of bereavement. The sadness and collective mourning are comforting, and you can take a personal ride on them. If others are suffering, my relative position improves. We each have individual processes of mourning on different issues, and the conformity between our inner and outer realities is a real comfort.

But giving up our emotional defenses for the sake of peace is even more painful. What does it mean to us to give up our absolute righteousness? To deeply recognize the great suffering we caused so many refugees who were banished from their homes and remained destitute? It is hard for us to recognize our own aggression, after we worked so hard to erase it from our national consciousness. In therapy it takes years to melt and crumble such defenses.

And what about our concept of ourselves as a chosen people, "a light unto the nations?" We will have to give up that grandiosity too, because it is hard to make peace from a position of superiority. Paranoid and grandiose stances go hand in hand, and reinforce the split that says that everything about me is good and that all the evil resides with the other. I am not persecuted for nothing, but because I am so special. We have nurtured our specialness and arrogant singularity to repress our existential anxieties, which were tremendous for years. We were a people without a home, who lived in the homes of others. What did we have left, just the fears? It is hard to give up defenses. *It is hard to realize that we are not that special, and that everybody is not against us, because both of those feelings operate within us as one solid unit.* So we will have to understand the other, recognize him from a more equal position, and give up our joy of victory for a quieter, sadder music. We know what a developmental leap it is for a child to go from the egocentric stage to the stage where he is not the center of the world and can see the other and recognize him.

But beyond that, we must remember that real peace is initially a *sad* event and not happy for many of us, because it requires recognition of the other. As far as developmental stages go, it is a difficult transition that cannot be taken for granted. A baby does not easily recognize his mother as a separate entity that has its own difficulties and problems. For him she always has to be there for him, and fully available to serve his needs. It takes him many years to understand that she is a separate person. Sometimes, he cannot understand it all the way through adulthood and until the end of life. Recognition of the other, separation from the other, is an impressive developmental achievement that many couples do not reach. It requires seeing the other through their eyes, not just as a means to fulfill my needs. Such a mature stance requires giving up narcissism, egocentricity, and my basic needs, for the other.

Can there be peace between us and the Palestinians with such a great lack of symmetry? When they are filled with hatred toward us, feel we have everything, and they, whom we expelled, have nothing? It is so hard for us to recognize their experience, that we expelled them from their homes and now live in them happily, while they are watching from the side how we plant and possess their land! To illustrate their associations, it is worth mentioning that the land is often perceived in the deep levels of our consciousness as a woman whom we plow and sow and that bears fruit. Our emotional defenses, which come from repressing guilt, prevent us from recognizing the depth of their ongoing suffering that was caused by us. Our emotional resistance to the peace process comes from the tremendous difficulty in opening that painful wound and recognizing what is happening here. *It is not easy to look the Palestinians straight in the eye, because that requires first recognizing them and their pain,* recognizing the tremendous gap between what we have and what they have, and agreeing to give up part of what we have for them. These are all both emotional and material concessions that it is hard to make. We prefer not recognizing their suffering and remaining in a state of confrontation.

Can there be peace when there is no water in Hebron, when the Palestinian laborers feel exploited and devoid of basic rights, and so on? Are we able to give up something of ours for the well-being of the other? We are scared to death that it will have no end. Therefore, out of fear, we erase their existence from our consciousness. As they sometimes say in the right, "OK, so give them Ramat Aviv" (Ramat Aviv is a rich neighborhood in the suburbs of Tel Aviv). That is what happens when you repress something: you are terrified of the thing you repressed; otherwise, of course, you wouldn't have repressed it. Then you stay swinging between two extremes: erase their existence or give them everything. You have no ability to think about what you can give up and what you cannot, or even what suffering you can recognize and what you cannot. You can choose. We can, for instance, take part in their suffering and show understanding of their pain without feeling guilty (later I will discuss this distinction) or without thinking that we owe them material compensation. We can help them in some areas that are less burdensome for us. But when you repress, and are unable to bring painful contents to your consciousness and look at them openly, you do not have such flexibility, as partners sometimes say to each other, or parents to children, "If I give one finger you want the whole hand." The fear is that suddenly all boundaries will be violated; I will give myself up and be drawn into an endless process of giving (Ramat Aviv for peace). And then, of course, out of defensiveness, we give nothing, and pay the price in war. *Those are the rules of emotional life.* There is a price to be paid for the inability to look the Palestinian in the eye, to repressing what we feel. And there are advantages to looking straightforwardly and being able to face repressed feelings. What are you so afraid of, the therapist will ask the patient. And he will wait for the answer for many years. The therapist knows how hard it is to really recognize the other. And he also knows it is inevitable.

There is another price we pay for not taking an honest look at ourselves. The price is the unconscious guilt feelings we carry within ourselves. We do not even know that truly, we are right too. In a peace process, when the other side stops being a monster and turns into a person, we can no longer dehumanize and eliminate him. Then we have to see him, relate to him, and sometimes help him, especially if we are making him suffer. Are we ready to pay this price of peace, or will we continue to choose to defend ourselves emotionally with war?

I will not expand on the Syrian question for the moment, as I only want to refer to the emotional resistance to giving up parts of yourself, parts of the homeland; perceived as body parts; staying small and shrunken with a "narrow waistline" and a "soft belly"; severing Jerusalem, the heart. It is very hard to give up the grandiosity of a big country, which wants to view itself as a superpower, and stay a small country. Accepting the depressive stance that recognizes our true size, our limitations, is not easy, especially for a people who considers itself a "light unto the nations," and for those of us who want to create a "new kingdom of Israel." Not to speak of the very idea of making concessions to the Syrians, which we experience as an insult and capitulation. On the Syrian issue, too, we have more of an emotional obstacle than any rational resistance to the peace process.

The Whole World Is Against Us

This is the well-known paranoid stance. The question of whether everyone really is against us cannot be resolved rationally, only emotionally. A person with a paranoid personality assumes that he is good and that everyone else is bad and that they are against him. That assumption has to do with his past. Once it was true and he experienced his parents as persecuting him, and the relationship must have had some kind of threatening quality; otherwise he wouldn't have that problem. But today, in his adult life, he is not as dependent and helpless as in his childhood, and not everyone is out to get him. The paranoid person wants the therapist to give him the warmth, love, and acceptance he did not get before. If their relationship is good, it can be a new and unusual experience for the patient, which can be a starting point for changing his attitude toward the world.

The Jewish people have plenty of reasons from their past to feel persecuted. Worse, the present reality is very threatening. So maybe we are not paranoid, but realistic? Our therapeutic job is very hard: to sort it all out and discern what is reality and what is fantasy. Some of us say, this is our fate, it cannot be changed, and there is nothing to understand here; they simply hate us. *A good therapist will recognize the truth of the argument that there is anti-Semitism in the world, but will try to turn it into an understandable experience.* First of all, there might be people in the world who feel differently toward the patient, that is, us, some who may even like or love him. In addition, perhaps we can help the patient to understand why those who hate him feel that way and what he brings out in them, and perhaps he can change those feelings. The therapist will also try to help the paranoid patient see that he is not that special in being hated, and that there are other people and minorities in the world who are hated. And finally, the therapist might try to help the patient clarify his feelings toward others, and help him understand why other people might view him as somebody who does not particularly like or appreciate them. In other words, the therapist will present the patient with a much more complex scheme of emotional attitudes, and try with the patient to give meaning to the difficult experience of persecution.

Throughout our history we have always maintained that "We are better than you, we are more just than you, we are special, and our god is the true god." We kept ourselves separate and different for years with those arrogant statements. True, Islam and Christianity copied from us, and they concede our copyright to the concept of the one and only god, but they have felt very hurt by us and remain very angry with us. Yes, something about our grandiose stance has been very infuriating, and was experienced as humiliating and aroused fierce reactions from a lot of people in the world. If we add to that our weakness in the Diaspora, that is a sure recipe for attacks and pogroms. Everybody knows there are two kinds of good students in a classroom: one, whom everybody likes, and the other, whom everybody hates. The difference is not in the competence of the two students, which in both cases is high, but in the way in which competence is conveyed to others, and whether it insults and hurts others or connects with them and helps them. We were perceived by other nations as insulting and hurting, which is surely connected to our deep inner experience as a people who always had to defend itself. We know from clinical therapy how much insecurity and worthlessness there can be behind arrogance. For years, we defended ourselves as a nation without a land, who maintained its cohesiveness and singularity, by saying and feeling that we were the best. Clearly it is possible to be the best without gloating. That is a clear difference between our objective qualities as a nation and the arrogance we project onto others in a hurtful and insulting manner. Even the best student in the class does not have to be a show-off. It is true that not everyone hated us, there were some who loved or appreciated us. It depends a lot on the other party's self-confidence and the degree to which they were hurt by the arrogance. The more self-assured the other is, the less hurt he will be by someone's grandiosity and megalomania. But we, as a paranoid personality, experienced our persecution as another proof of our singularity, our importance. Otherwise, why would they persecute us? We felt, as the sages have said, that we were destined to suffer because we were the purest of all, and our righteousness would ultimately prevail. It is clear from clinical therapy that paranoia and megalomania go hand in hand. I am persecuted because I am so great, important, and special. Thereby the paranoid personality arouses and invites from others just the thing he is so afraid of—persecution.

We have to understand that not everyone hates the Jews, and that sometimes there is a great deal of sympathy toward us in the world. The hatred toward us, as we have seen, is no accident. It has reasons, some of which we can control. To put it simply, we are not that special, and the world did not invent for our benefit emotions that do not exist toward other nations in the world. The more the peace process advances, the less special we feel, and therefore less persecuted and more similar to other nations. I am condemning our feeling of singularity, the feeling that we have special abilities, which trips us up again and again and draws persecution. We know how much we enjoy hearing that the Jews are the smartest and the best and the most just, and what disasters we have suffered as a consequence of that emotional stance. We know where our dismissal of the Arabs led us in the Yom Kippur War, and how our dismissal of the Palestinians led to the Intifada that caught us off guard, as did the Rabin assassination. Our arrogance and failure to recognize the other misled us into thinking that such things could not happen to us.

The dissipation of a child's paranoid-grandiose feelings comes from two opposing directions: first, the blows dealt to the child by reality, and second, the parents' empathy toward him. The blows we receive from the Arabs bring us back to ourselves and force us to look inward and to examine ourselves in a painful but necessary developmental process. That is how, in the last years of the peace process, we have arrived at insights we might not have had if we had merely vanquished the Arabs. I am talking about recognition of the other. In a child's world, conflicts are perceived as primarily taking place between him and the world, and he is not ripe yet to look inward. Only when he meets reality, which he experiences as a wall he cannot break despite all his efforts, can he go back to examine himself in the spirit of inner dialogue, rather than in a conflict with the outside world. The patient's ability to see conflict as existing inside himself and not just between him and the outside world is a very important developmental stage, which allows the patient to benefit from therapy. Otherwise, the whole story would be that he is right and everybody else is wrong.

The second way to soften the paranoid stance is with empathy, which touches the roots of grandiosity and melts them. Warm and love toward the paranoid personality speak to his insecurity in a way that allows him to relax. The international community can help us with that. The United States succeeds in helping us in peace negotiations more than the European community because it is more empathetic toward us. It gives us security and understands how badly we need it so as not to become entrenched in our positions and act arrogantly out of our anxieties. Therefore, the U.S. is also better for the Arabs in promoting peace. What does that mean? It means that the way to our hearts is through empathy rather than through coercion. Indeed, the paranoid personality—we as a nation, or the growing child—needs a combination of reality hitting us in the face and an empathetic parent, to help us move out of that tough position.

Most of the world finds it easier to connect with Palestinian dejectedness and with the homeless refugees, and support them, rather than us. We are seen as powerful, and it is harder to understand what we are so afraid of. Both we and others have a hard time seeing through our arrogance to our fears and our threats, which we have to explain first to ourselves and then to the world. Our Shin Bet, our Mossad, our air force, are all among the world's best. Our brains, our developments, and our military innovations are all renowned. As a grandiose personality, first we show the world how able and how strong we are, and then we don't understand why unreasonable demands are made upon us in the peace process, and why they do not understand our weaknesses and fears.

For years we talked about our existential anxieties and explained to the whole world why, for example, we needed strategic depth. But at the same time, in various ways, we told the world that we are the best and the strongest, and in fact, are a world power. Those arrogant qualities came across to the world stronger than our attempts at apologetics, that did not fall in line with the image of the new Israeli that we created. The Palestinians, on the other hand, show the world their weakness rather than their strength, as a people who want independence and do not have it. They are connected to their weakness and feel it as we once did ours, and therefore they gain a lot of sympathy, just as we did at the time the United Nations recognized our state. We repress and hide our weakness from ourselves, and therefore are unable to present that truth to the world. That was and still is the trap of Israeli propaganda, which has not been effective for years.

People who view us as strong still cannot understand why we are afraid to give the Golan Heights back to the Syrians, or why we are afraid to give the Palestinians independence. It took years, for example, until the world understood that Palestinian terrorism is an obstacle that has to be surmounted before there can be peace. The rest of the world also underwent a long process of internalization until it recognized Palestinian aggression and stopped seeing them only as victims—a process that culminated in the 1996 Sharm A-Sheikh conference against terrorism. It also took us years to understand that because we were captive to our omnipotent ability to defeat terrorism. We tried it in the Lebanon War and elsewhere, and told our own public and others that we would defeat terrorism. We did not present terrorism as stronger than we are; we did not tell the truth, that we cannot defeat it, and that we need the Palestinians to restrain themselves. Our repression of our helplessness in the face of terrorism was so strong that we had no answer when the Palestinians said to us, "What do you want from us; you failed to defeat terrorism too." They too attributed omnipotent power to us, and we could not tell them simply that it is their job, not ours, to control their aggressive impulses and drives. Today, after a painful internalization process that took years, we realize that we cannot defeat terrorism, and are willing to expose our vulnerability and helplessness against it. That new position of ours, which is developing with the peace process, surely increases the world's empathy toward us.

That process of giving up our grandiosity comes with terrible disappointment every time terror strikes again, every time there is a failure of the Shin Bet, the Mossad, or the army, every time we need others and cannot do something by ourselves: produce the Lavi fighter plane, fight Iraq, receive economic aid, and expose corruption—then another crumb from the huge rock of grandiosity we built comes tumbling down. We convinced the world of Israeli heroism and could not tell ourselves and others the truth, that we are a small country with many problems within and without, and that we live in constant fear that we will not survive. A reported decline in motivation to serve in the army, whether true or not, reflects a process of our turning from heroes to human beings. Heroic myths surrounding the establishment of the state, that represent adolescence, have softened over the years and made room for concern for the individual and the ability to recognize our weaknesses. We are like a paranoid person who slowly starts talking about his fears and anxieties and recognizing them, thereby helping himself not to be so paranoid and helping the world understand him and connect with his feelings. In clinical therapy it is evident that it is hard for people to see the weakness behind aggression and arrogance. It is hard to be empathetic toward a husband who beats his wife (to cite an extreme example) and to understand that he suffered as a child and feels threatened. And if he does not share his past and his feelings, will we have any way of connecting with him and understanding him? An older child picks on a younger child. As parents, it is hard for us to identify with the aggressor, understand that he is having a hard time, and that his aggression, like any aggression, stems from an injury. Indeed, how hard it is for the world to recognize our chilling inner experience, which is hidden deep behind our inflated confidence and arrogance! As a people we are undergoing what amounts to a process of therapy, are connecting with our anxieties, letting go of our inflated singularity and grandiosity, and therefore are growing closer to other nations and are less isolated from them. That is how the paranoid person breaks out of his cherished loneliness for the sake of human relations with the environment. Only after he connects with himself and understands how anxious he is, and is not afraid to reveal that anxiety to others, only after he becomes softer on himself, recognizes his own suffering and stops thinking himself omnipotent, can he arouse in others empathy and identification.

The Deterrence Factor

For years we thought inflating our military was a deterrent factor. Again and again we anxiously asked ourselves whether the army's power of deterrence was harmed by one event or another. We quickly answered ourselves that it was not. And we failed to notice that we are the only ones living in our house of dreams. The children of the Palestinian Intifada uprising were not afraid of us when they wanted independence. Syria and Egypt were not afraid to declare the Yom Kippur War after our startling victory in 1967, even though they knew we had nuclear power. Neither did our power of deterrence do us any good when Iraq fired missiles at us in the Gulf War. The Arab countries are not attacking us, not because they are afraid of our tremendous power of deterrence, but simply because they do not want to. Is the truth so intolerable, that we have to create a fantastic deterrence force in our imaginations, which does not exist in reality?

Do we really think that if we and others know our true strength that will be our end? True, there are animals that grow a lot of hair on their heads to appear bigger than they really are. "Come on, let's see you!" a teen will say, thinking he is terrifying us. But are we monkeys or that kind of kids? Are the Arab countries so ignorant that the only thing that is keeping them from attacking us is our bluff? It is no wonder that we live in incredible anxiety, because we do not believe our power is enough to defend ourselves, and we are waiting for the balloon to burst. Then everyone will see how helpless we really are. This is mainly a dialogue we are having with ourselves. A bluff we tell ourselves, and then really believe it. The bluff is that we are so strong, and that is why every time something happens that shows our weakness we wake up in horror. So we swing between desperate weakness and the magical powers we attribute to ourselves, and we have no idea of our real power. Could we defeat all the Arab countries if they attacked us together? We have asked ourselves that question again and again, and relaxed when we answered that we could. The Arab countries, when they decide to attack us, are less concerned with how strong we are than with what price they are prepared to pay for what they want to achieve. They understand better than we do that war does not necessarily mean victory or defeat, destruction or survival. They understand that we neither want war nor to pay its price.

In the Yom Kippur War, Egypt and Syria thought war would bring them toward their goals faster than any other method, and they were apparently right. In that case, the deterrent force of the Six Day War worked negatively—it encouraged war, just like a thug who pumps up his muscles and asks, "Who wants to fight me?" and invites everyone to prove he is not so strong. That is because it was important for the Arabs to restore their lost honor. But we are captives to the inflated world we built for ourselves, misled by the lies we tell ourselves about how intimidating we are, and then we are afraid of our own shadow. One day we are alarmed when we hear of a decline in motivation to serve in the army, in another case we try to conceal the dimensions of emigration from Israel, or we try to hide from the Arabs our mishaps and corruption, and so on. Is our real force not enough, so that we have to lie to the world, and of course, pay the price I am talking about? The price is that we, the strong, the side with the deterrence, are viewed by the world as aggressors. The Arabs know our true power is not unlimited; yet they do not want to launch war for various reasons. In the short term and at certain moments, during combat, for instance, there is value in deterrence. A company of soldiers would hesitate to storm a position that seems to be more powerful than they are. But in the long run, with a global strategic view, only the truth can win. A bluff that is exposed leaves us weaker than we really are. And how great is your desire to attack when you discover the party you were afraid of is not as strong as you imagined? Indeed, bluffs such as the ones we tell ourselves and others cannot survive for very long. Rather, they survive in our consciousness, but not in the enemy's.

Again and again we discover what all enlightened countries already know, what people learn throughout their lives, what we try to convey in therapy: that being open and exposing problems inwardly and outwardly is what makes you really strong. Democracy, which allows open and critical debate, protects human rights, rejects torture, and does not present an inflated and unfounded "posture," is more powerful than any other system, and is also the only system that survives over time. We learned that the death penalty for terrorists is not a deterrent, and that open discussion and criticism of the army, the Shin Bet, and the Mossad help promote their interests more than any omnipotent deception. We need look no further than to the collapse of the Soviet Union to understand that deceit and false deterrence cannot endure. The United States may have paid a price for its openness, its public discussion, and its democracy, but it has prospered. Indeed, our false deterrence turns the world against us, besides all the other needless prices we pay for it.

The world is not against us personally, in the sense that we are not important enough for it to have an interest in being against us personally. We often invite the world to be against us, or at least do not help them understand our fears, by denying the biological, chemical, and nuclear threats from Iraq and Iran, for instance. It is hard for us to admit even to ourselves that we feel threatened! We raise the subject cautiously, careful not to set off a panic, not to look afraid. The Gulf War scared the daylights out of us, but we have already repressed it, and do not dare think it can happen again. Just as repression in the life of the individual has implications for that person's relationships, so is our repression as a nation reflected in our foreign policy and in the way we explain our positions to the world. This important subject, which could draw a lot of sympathy for our cause, takes a secondary place in our propaganda policy. Again we see the price of repressing our fears and putting on an omnipotent face, which makes it hard for others to understand us. That is not how the Americans behaved during the Cold War. They discussed the nuclear threat openly in their media, as difficult as that was. We are like paranoid personalities whose progress in therapy is slow and arduous. We are still in the midst of an emotional process of connecting with our real weakness, our fears, which are legitimate and can be understood by the world only if we recognize them first.

In this long therapeutic peace process we will find that the world is less and less against us.

One of the explanations we maintained for years was that the world was against us because of its interests: Arab oil that everybody needed, the Arab boycott of companies that traded with Israel, the advantage of trading with the populous Arab nations, and so on. That view of the world as a place guided mainly by cold and alienated interests, without emotions or morals, is a paranoid view. All we have to do now is explain why most of the world's nations voted for recognizing Israel at the United Nations and what transpired between that time and the UN resolution equating Zionism with racism. And if, since peace negotiations took off, we have more support again, then why? Lately it is harder than before to say that the world is amoral, when the United States sends peacekeeping forces to Iraq and Bosnia. There are, of course, considerations of self-interest in the world, but what we have a harder time seeing, and is no less important, is our emotional stance, which invites anger. The paranoid personality always complains that it has to explain itself and is misunderstood. And we, in therapy, try to help that person understand himself first.

But if the world is *not* against us personally, and if it is not motivated purely by egocentric interests, perhaps we can listen to how it views the peace process, and really use its input, just as a patient uses the therapist's objective view of the patient. That happens only after the patient realizes that the therapist is on his side rather than against him, a difficult process in its own right. For years we grew accustomed to ignoring the world. Ben-Gurion said that it doesn't matter what the world says; it matters what Israel does. The paranoid personality feels that it doesn't matter what others say; he will do what he thinks, because everybody is against him anyway and he does not have to listen to them. As of today, we are not in an emotional position to really consult other countries; we are still defensive and view them as opponents. It is true, of course, that most countries in the world support the Arabs, but what we are unaware of is how we contributed to that situation.

That is why Americans are correct when they walk one step behind us instead of one step ahead of us. They let us lead the process and stay away from any hint of coercion. The paranoid personality is so sensitive to any trace of coercion, and so desperately needs to feel he is being allowed to lead at his own pace, and that that is the only way for him to slowly drop his defenses. A feeling of coercion will only make us take the opposite action—entrenching ourselves in our righteousness. To this day we stress our desire for the peace talks between us and the Arabs to be direct, without European or even American mediation, while the Palestinians would prefer such an involvement. Clearly, the peace process succeeded over the years only when there was no external coercion.

The same is true for a therapist working with a couple. It is clear to him that the partners have to understand each other and get along, and no imposed arrangement can promote peace. Therefore, the Americans have succeeded more than the Europeans over the years in promoting the peace process. The Americans, as opposed to the Europeans, were like therapists who were sensitive to the process itself, rather than jumping ahead of the patient and telling him what solution he should eventually reach. A good therapist, like a good teacher, understands that you cannot shorten the process and skip over processes of understanding and internalization. True, the Europeans spoke years ago of a Palestinian state that would serve Israel's interests too, but we were not ready to listen. In the therapeutic process, the therapist can say the truest and most correct thing in the world, but it will be worthless if it does not promote the process it is meant to serve, if it is said at the wrong time, or in the wrong tone of voice. In other words, in our growth process as individuals or as a nation, being right is just part of the picture. Parents know this, and we all need parents who let us develop in our own good time.

The European countries need to ask themselves, as we ask, how they fell into the trap of leaning toward the Arabs, and even tried at various times to impose a settlement, or at least took public positions that were perceived by the Arabs as supporting them, and by us as opposing us. We know where they went wrong: while we were flaunting our power and our might, the Arabs were flaunting their weakness and dejectedness. Until lately, their terrorism was not viewed as a serious matter, but as a weak protest in the face of ongoing occupation and discrimination. The Arabs were the little child who kept running to his parents to tell on his big bad brother. It took time—more for the Europeans and less for the Americans—to understand they should not intervene, that the parent is being manipulated by the little one's crying and by the big one's arrogance. The parent started to understand that in this situation there really is not one side that is right and one that is wrong. He can ask the kids to get along with each other, he can advise them, give love to both of them, but not say who is right. Those kids have to live with each other, so they had better start talking to each other and understanding each other. The Palestinians have started to understand that the fact that the parent thinks they are right does not do them much good. Their salvation will not come from other countries, only from talking to us directly.

In that sense our peace process is not only with the Arabs, but with the whole world. We are like the paranoid personality who only remembers the latest blow, which at the time seems like the worst. Right now we are focused on our conflict with the Arabs, but throughout our history we suffered confrontations, pogroms, and a Holocaust imposed on us from members of other religions and nations. We are still unable to learn lessons from our past. That is how psychotherapy works and that is how the peace process works. You learn to know yourself, your feelings, and your shortcomings, and at the same time your relations with others improve.

Denial of Aggression and Fear, and Its Price

Denial of Aggression

With denial of aggression we fall into the same trap Arafat falls into in relation to Hamas. Unconsciously, both we and Arafat do not want to totally renounce our aggression toward the other side. We make declarations of peace, but do not restrain our dangerous and threatening extreme right. The Rabin assassination, which came as a surprise, clearly exposed what was there all the time but that we did not want to see: the huge aggression of the extreme right toward the Arabs, which was surprisingly directed toward us, and should have been snuffed out before Rabin was assassinated. The extreme right is directing its aggression inwardly when it calls President Ezer Weizman a spy, accuses Netanyahu of hugging Arafat when he knows the next murder is being planned, and so on. Both right and left are responsible for the failure to repress the extreme right. The deep reason is our identification with their aggression toward the Arabs, and an unconscious desire for that work to be done by others. When Minister of Justice Tzahi Hanegbi said in a news interview with Channel One television on August 28, 1998, that Baruch Marzel and his friends produce news items but don't have any real significance beyond that, he is failing to understand that they have significance in the depth of our unconscious as the ones who do the dirty work of aggression for us, and why should we stop them. We know the mechanism well in children: the child says, "it was the bad boy that lives inside me, not me," thereby splitting his own personality, so as not to recognize the aggression he possesses. Another child may simply be unaware of his own aggression. Likewise, it is easy to understand why it is hard for Arafat to fight Hamas and terrorism. He too is not free of feelings of aggression toward us, *even if some of them are unconscious.* Even if he wants peace, there are still unconscious desires at work full force in Arafat's personal unconscious, as well as in the collective unconscious of the Palestinians, which need to be worked through. We need to understand that the impact of the right-wing Jewish minority that enters Palestinian villages and throws rocks at windows, overturns vegetable stands, and takes the law into its hands, cannot be measured by their numbers. It has to be measured by the drives they represent, which have to be restrained and put under control. *Those impulses exist in each one of us,* and a tough government position would convey a message of curbing aggressive impulses and imposing order. That will help, first of all, to restrain each of us.

Those impulses of ours, as I will show in this chapter, not only hurt the Arabs and the peace process, but are a boomerang that comes back and hurts us and terrifies us. We know how scared an aggressive child can be who lashes out in every direction and cannot calm down. We keep telling parents that order and clear boundaries in the right place are very calming to children. We need a parent or prime minister who takes responsibility for the child and places borders, not a parent who says, "I did not hear or see what was happening" and secretly cooperates with the aggression. It is hard to overstate the importance of placing boundaries on our extreme right in a peace process that demands integration, restraint of drives, and recognition of the other. If we speak about educating ourselves about peace, this is what we are talking about.

This aggression toward the Palestinians exists both in the left and in the right in different versions. The right, which has less of a tendency to repress drives, and to its credit, is less wont to deny the Arabs' aggression toward us, collaborates with the extreme right more openly. The left collaborates with its aggression more subtly. The epithet Bleeding Hearts that the right attaches to the left comes from the feeling that the left is fake. The fakeness in question is the left's defenses against its own impulses. Therefore, the left denies the Arabs' aggression toward us, and, as people who ignore aggression, also represses our aggression toward them.

I am sure that our demand that Arafat fight terrorism would be received differently if we showed a firmer determination to fight *our own aggressive impulses*. In this light we can understand statements by people such as Benny Begin, who claimed that Arafat does not really want to fight Hamas and terrorism. Out of the full picture of Arafat and the Palestinian leadership, which has various sides, such speakers have chosen the side they want to see, their aggression. But they forget that we are in exactly the same situation of unconscious conflict, and the other side accuses us of not reining in the settlers and our extreme right. The absence of a clear decision to impose the law on the extreme right, even after the Rabin assassination, shows again that there is an unconscious factor at play here that is very hard to deal with. Otherwise, our difficulty in asserting authority would not be so great. Like the rest of us, our attorney general has an unconscious too, and should have seen before the assassination, rather than speaking afterward, that he could not hide behind statements in support of the freedom of speech and democracy, because it is simply a matter of aggression with which we are unconsciously cooperating. We can use therapeutic tools to examine whether letting the extreme right call the president a "traitor," or letting the grave of Baruch Goldstein, who massacred Palestinians in Hebron, become a place of pilgrimage, stem from a humanistic position that allows others to express themselves, or from our identification with the aggressor and fear of confronting him, which is why we secretly cooperate with him. The answer can only be found by soul-searching and really listening to ourselves. Are we not like the parent who secretly smiles when he sees his child directing aggression at another, either in support of him or out of fear of confronting him? That parent who does not set boundaries has to start listening to himself and asking how he puts up with such a thing in his own house. But for that, the parent needs to really start listening to himself.

If a person is really honest with himself, he might sometimes detect that forgiving smile that quickly slips back into the unconscious, the smile that is really so human, that says, "the Arabs deserve it," "they need to be taught a lesson," or is just happy that yet another Palestinian was hurt. Those are aggressive drives that exist in all of us and automatically react to our continuously being hurt. Therefore, our secret collaboration with the aggression of the extreme right, and our difficulty in curbing it, are understandable.

Hamas, like our extreme right, poses a real danger to the peace process and Arafat, like us, has not quite accepted that. What he has not internalized is that each side has repressed aggression toward the other, and the extremists on each side are merely its representatives who express it overtly. Curbing the extremists means curbing the extreme emotional elements in each person's soul. Therefore, neither side understands the extent of the commitment to fight aggression and terrorism. When Minister of Justice Tzahi Hanegbi says that the extreme right is a marginal minority, which exists more in the media than in reality, he is ignoring *the extremist emotional element that resides within each one of us in this difficult peace process*—the element of *aggression,* which is mostly *unconscious.*

The tremendous aggression of the extreme right toward the Arabs was finally directed inwardly, at us. The assassination of Rabin should put an end to any doubts anyone has as to *the close link between our treatment of the Palestinians and our domestic violence.* The extreme right's aggression toward the Arabs was displaced and directed inwardly. Clinical psychology maintains that aggression that can harm someone else can be directed at oneself and turn into suicidal harm. The same violence is directed in different directions at different times. Now we have an opportunity to explore the rise in the dimensions of violence in Israel. The denial of our aggression toward others is coming back at us. When children come to school with knives and everyone ignores it, that is the denial I am talking about.

The occupation itself and the control of another people are not what corrupt us and effect the level of violence in this country. The elements of the occupation that come out of self-defense, from our need for security, do not corrupt at all. Those are very important elements, which seek to prevent violence. We know that a position of victimhood can invite aggression while a strong stand against aggression can prevent it. But the emotional elements of the occupation that hurt and dismiss the Palestinians, which deny their humanity, are the parts that come back to hurt us. Denying and not accepting the other's existence are not things that stay within certain borders, and such aggression has no limit. We are in an emotional developmental stage where it is not at all easy for us to ask ourselves honestly *where our self-defense ends and our aggression begins.*

We are like the difficult child in the family of nations, who grew up with considerable emotional problems, who is having a hard time, and who needs long-term therapy to achieve internal order. This is also an opportunity to say the other siblings in the family have some responsibility for what is happening here. The whole world shares the emotional and moral responsibility of helping both us and the Palestinians. But getting back to our own case, it may make us uncomfortable to note that one of the definitions of the psychopathological personality is that it is unable to identify with the other and to feel his pain. I think in relation to our attitude toward the Palestinians we meet that definition, and over the years we have done everything, as a society, so as not to recognize their existence and their suffering. As a nation we have yet to master the distinction between an act of self-defense and an act of aggression—something we demand from a child in the growth process. Surely, the world has yet to discover how to raise an adolescent who doesn't manifest severe expressions of aggression. The adolescent's ability to express himself fiercely after the long years of childhood when he was in his parents' custody expresses an important developmental process, which is necessary for the adolescent's ability to achieve independence and self-confidence. But at a later age the adolescent is expected to be able to integrate his different needs and emotions and to control his aggression. We as a nation banished the Palestinian refugees. It is hard to imagine what we would look like without that aggressive act. It gave us independence in a state with a Jewish majority, and we had no choice. Many countries experienced violence on their way to consolidation and independence. But what is permissible for an adolescent, or at least inevitable in the growth process, is not so for an adult or for a nation that has already achieved independence.

If we deny the aggression of the extreme right and fail to curb it, we thereby convey an unconscious message to our children about ignoring aggression, and it surely affects our society. The voice that says, "in my case it is allowed," or "in certain places it is allowed," is undoubtedly transferred to our domestic problems and sure enough, violence is on the rise. Just like a therapy patient does not invent a particular behavior for the clinic that he does not express elsewhere. And we know that when a patient exhibits aggressive behavior, we should see where else he demonstrates the same behavior or problematic attitude. Another illustration would be the parent who lets her child run wild at school or outside the home, thinking it will stay outside the home. Our aggression, which at a later stage is directed inward, is expressed in beating Arabs, humiliating them at roadblocks, and treating them dismissively, even unconsciously—letting them stand in line for hours, ignoring their basic needs like water and electricity, and imposing long curfews, as well as the attitude of "so what if they don't have schools" (those of us who are more honest will recognize harboring such secret thoughts).

The term "morals of warfare," upon which we were raised, touches upon a deep understanding that it is not force itself that corrupts, but our impulses, which are locked up for all our lives, and that can break loose when they have the chance. When unbridled aggression is released it is not clear what direction it will take. Violating rights and human dignity in the territories, treating some people as less human or less valuable and ignoring their pain, are aggressions that will come back to haunt us. If a soldier receives tacit approval from his commanders, by their disregard, and checks the Palestinians roughly and contemptuously, he will carry his unbridled aggression into his personal life. Our treatment of Israeli Arabs since the establishment of Israel has been undoubtedly aggressive. To the Jewish public, they are nonentities and less than human. There is a direct link between that attitude toward Arabs and violence in our daily life. Therefore, the people in our country who fight for human rights are doing a great service for the prevention of violence. The decision by the High Court to forbid torture is an indirect and partly unconscious message to the public about the need to control our impulses even in situations where it is very hard. The absence of a death penalty is also a positive message, which is also partly unconscious, and that teaches restraint and the prevention of violence. The lack of sufficient rights for homosexuals, the disabled, the retarded, prisoners, and so on, all those expressions of internal violence, can never be entirely unrelated to the violence we direct outward, and reflect it like a mirror image. It is true in the life of the individual and in the life of the nation. Depression, the cruelty of the individual toward himself, and the aggression directed at others, are twins that interact so that at times you see one and at times the other. A parent who lets her child treat the other parent, a sibling, or a playmate rudely, cannot expect that behavior to stop there. It will come back to her one day. That is the price a parent pays for ignoring her child's aggression and smiling to herself. Therefore, the "morals of warfare" are as important domestically as they are outwardly.

Denial of Fear and Its Price

But we deny our fear too, the fear of the aggression that now is directed not only outwardly but also inwardly. It is like a child who protects his classmates but beats up the kids in the other class. His classmates are already afraid of him, because everybody can see that the aggression that is now directed at others, supposedly in their defense, will sooner or later be turned against them. Therefore, a good parent or teacher will realize early on that the aggression has to be stopped, not only out of concern for others, but out of concern for themselves. But we know how hard it is for students to ask for help, to admit their fear, and how their silence serves to perpetuate terror and violence in our schools. The class in this analogy is of course the country, and the child is the general public. The message is that it is important for the public to admit its fear. We fear the settler who says if anyone tries to evacuate him, it will be a disaster. We fear that another Israeli prime minister will be assassinated. Indeed, most of us are afraid, some more and some less consciously.

What is the deep meaning of violence in the political system? Some claim there is no violence; others say there is but it does not effect public opinion or people's personal choices. That is because ultimately you vote behind an opaque screen, and nobody sees who you voted for. Therefore, there is nothing to be afraid of. Yet, fear does play a decisive role for many of us in formulating our political views and deciding how to vote. When Barak was a prime ministerial candidate, he smiled through the Popolitica program, mediated by Ya'acov Ahimeir, unperturbed by the heckling of a rightist audience that did not let him finish a sentence. We know there is a large leftist public that is afraid of confronting crowds of rightist protestors, and avoids taking to the streets. These people are not just indifferent; they are afraid. It is not easy for them to protest opposite extreme rightist protestors, to overcome their noise, and to put forward their own message. There is no doubt that the crowd that shouts and takes us to impulsive and regressive places knows what it is doing, consciously or not. By shouting, it actually drives some of us to support its views. That is what the extreme right did in Rabin's time. The education of a child is fundamentally based on fear of punishment. That is the strongest motive to obey parents. That is how the parent controls the child even when he is not with him, and that is how some of us can be controlled while we are behind the voting screen. Fear often makes people think in the direction that is most desirable to the threatening force.

Yes, fear can arouse hidden resistance, as when a parent forces the child to do things he does not want to do. But not everyone can rebel against a strong authority, and identifying with the aggressor is a powerful developmental mechanism in all of us. As children, we often identified with the intimidating angry parent and justified him. As the Israelites said at Mount Sinai to the greatest authority figure of all, "We shall do and listen." First do, and then listen and understand what we did. That is how fear effects us. The truth is that shouting can convince some people to act in certain ways, and it is not true to say shouting does not convince. Shouting scares, and fear surely drives some people to prefer to be on the delivering end rather than on the receiving end. We often hear politicians say, "do not scare us." When somebody says again and again that he is not scared and will not be intimidated, we know that he or the public he represents has some trouble with that. When Netanyahu stood on a stage and chanted with the crowd, "they are scared; they are scared!" it was clear that crowd had a need to at least believe that the left was scared, even though it was partly their own projected fear; otherwise they would not have needed to repeat it. But again, fear plays a central role in forming their views. In this respect there is a difference between right and left. The right lives its drives and fears more openly, and uses, as I explained, a dramatic language. The left represses its drives and fears, but fear can surely influence and direct its views. In most cases such an influence is unconscious.

Many people, especially adults, are ashamed to admit fear. People fear admitting fear not only because it is immature or unrespectable to be afraid. The reason is deeper, and it is that we know deep in our hearts that fear does influence and convince us. Fear makes us think differently, as happens to children in the education process. The evidence is apparent in totalitarian regimes whose citizens identify with them, and repress any other feelings or thoughts until they become unconscious. In such regimes, people vote from the fear they don't admit, even behind the screen. The denial of fear proves how strong a motivator it is.

Rabin was assassinated at a demonstration titled, "Yes to Peace, No to Violence." That is another example why *in our nation's collective unconscious it is very dangerous to insist on your opinions,* because the end will be bitter. Indeed, just a few years later, what is left of the assassination? There is less of a focus on the killer and his prey, less of an aggressor and a victim, and more acceptance of what was seemingly inevitable, a decree of fate, in other words, a repression of the violence that took place there, so as not to confront the threat and fear that exist within us. Suddenly people started saying, "Rabin died" instead of "Rabin was murdered." Because if Rabin just died, we can supposedly be less fearful. From this act of repressing the aggression it is not too far a leap to identify with the aggressor and feel that the victim asked for what he got. That is how many people view women who are victims of rape, and secretly think they asked for it; some women go along with that because they feel guilty; that is how battered children justify their parents who abuse them; that is how as children we all identified with our punishing parents. From that point, there is not too great a distance to saying that Rabin asked for it.

People who have weak ego forces tend to join the strong and the winners rather than the weak and the losers. A child who disrupts class often takes many others with him. When Netanyahu used the slogan "A Strong Leader for a Strong People" in the 1999 elections, he was addressing the emotional elements in the public who identify with power. He was playing on the well-known emotional mechanisms of repressing fear and identifying with the aggressor as a way of escaping the threat. It is no accident that players on the ballfield are cheered with loud shouting. The power and spirit invigorate us, although many, especially on the left, are ashamed to admit the effectiveness of those means of persuasion, at least on them, who have such solid views. The bureaucrat who is nicer than usual to prevent his client from having a fit knows that force does help, and people who are afraid that if they put a Peace Now sticker on their cars, they will be vandalized, know that fear.

The triumph of the right in the 1996 elections, following the assassination, can partly be interpreted as an unconscious identification of the public with the aggressor rather than with the victim. In any case there was no sweeping identification with the left, the victim, as the left hoped. When the left said, "Have you killed and also taken possession?" or, "The messenger was murdered and now so was the message," it expressed its deep feeling of getting a double punishment. The double punishment was the identification of the majority of the public with the aggressor, like a raped woman who is later found guilty. The wounded left came out the loser, while the assailant right won. In this situation it is hard to admit fear and to stand up to aggression.

There is no doubt the extreme right sounds and looks bigger than it really is. The extreme right drags us into the world within which it lives, a world of fear and existential threat. We would rather stay in our more depressive world, and it takes us backward, than resort to screaming and threatening. It is hard for a person with a depressive stance to say, "I am afraid" and feel his well-repressed existential anxiety. After all, he tends to direct his aggression at himself. He has already taken responsibility and forgets that once he was threatened, and took upon himself too much responsibility. In other words, a leftist is supposedly immune to threat and fear, because he has already been crueler to himself than anyone else is going to be. As I said, this is just defensiveness against fear.

A leader who tells the public that he is not afraid of violence would be better off saying he is afraid. He should not be ashamed to be afraid. That way the discussion of the fear and terror of the extreme right can be put on the table. Just as in therapy the first stage in dealing with a problem is talking about it. Looking at the feelings that direct us without our being aware. Just as in therapy, when we are willing to own up to certain feelings, they have less power over us. Saying, "I am afraid" is the first step in facing fear without surrendering to it. *Denying the existence of fear, which is so typical of the emotional stance of the left, promotes surrender,* because some people can unconsciously be driven by repressed fear. As a rule, a feeling we become aware of has less power to drive us in directions we do not want to go. Therefore, it is so important for the public and the leaders to admit the fear we do feel. The first thing a child abused at home or at school, a battered woman, or a blackmail victim needs to do to break out of her difficult predicament, is to say to herself and others, "I am afraid and therefore I obey." Admitting fear is half the solution.

If the nation has an open discussion of its fear of what the Golan residents or extreme settlers might do if their settlements are dismantled, and how threatening that is, we will all be able to look that fear in the eye and calculate our moves in a way that is not dictated by fear. In our situation today, when our leader says that he understands the settlers' fear and is empathetic to the Golan residents, it is not clear whether he is truly empathetic, which is an important emotional act, and how afraid he is, which is an entirely different motive, which gives them greater weight than their true weight in society.

By being afraid to say it is afraid, the public is tacitly collaborating with the repression of the extreme right's aggression. Fear and aggression are mirror images of each other, and we ignore both. The tacit consensus is that this is a matter each person has to deal with privately and we do not talk about it. There is an absence of a collective admission that since the Rabin assassination the public is much more afraid. It is very possible that the extremist settlers are given exceeding consideration because of the fear and threats they generate. It is no accident that the law has not been imposed on them to this day. Is not their broad exposure in the media a defensive act we call "reversal," where we give them power out of the repressed fear we feel? It is no accident that they get more attention than society's poor and take up more space in our consciousness. A good parent or sensitive teacher can identify unspoken fear and the desire to ignore existing aggression and will not give too much attention to the disruptive, noisy child. He will understand that he may be having trouble, but will know how to stop him and will not let him drag everyone with him. That parent or teacher is the prime minister. Like everyone, the prime minister has an unconscious. And he is unquestionably motivated by such repressed feelings, surely after another prime minister was assassinated. It would be good for the prime minister to admit his fear and thereby serve as an example of a person who is not afraid to be afraid.

Is Our Sense of Reality Valid?

When a patient tells us that he is surprised again and again and doesn't understand why things happen to him, when he tells us about misfortunes he feels befell him out of the blue, with no early warning, we try to help him understand how that happens and what it is that he refused to see. Our goal in this section is to examine *whether we have a thinking disorder, which distorts our sense of reality, and if we do, what is the emotional reason for that disorder?*

The Yom Kippur War came after the tremendous victory of the Six Day War. Much has been said about the power-intoxication we experienced, the euphoria over the military victory and the feeling that we could do anything and were unbeatable. Perhaps the songs of those days speak of our hubris better than anything else. Various inquiries such as the Agranat Commission are surely important, but I think it is no less important to understand the emotional background of such disasters. The euphoria that was shattered was nothing but a massive defense against the opposing feelings that were powerfully repressed. I mean the feelings of threat to our security and to our very existence. In six days we went from real existential anxiety to extreme feelings of euphoria. The end was predictable. We were like an insecure child who puffs up and gloats until somebody takes his air out and takes him back to the place he was trying so hard to escape. That hurtful and insulting arrogance invites the other side to war, because it humiliates the opponent and leaves him no choice but to engage in confrontation.

Yes, our story is tragic. A group of refugees from many countries gathered here to create their own state. Then they turned many Palestinians who lived here into refugees. It is hard for a refugee who is fighting for his life and existence to recognize the suffering he caused his enemy by turning him into a refugee. Again, without discussing who is right and who is wrong, I am talking about recognizing the suffering we caused others and our duty to take responsibility and to try to help as best we can. I repeat, recognizing the suffering of another is an emotional stance, and does not imply particular action. This is a point that needs clarification. Operative action has to stem from understanding an emotional stance, but it also has to be grounded in reality. Recognizing the pain of the refugee and our part in causing it does not necessarily lead to the conclusion that we have to let them back into Israel's green line borders and commit suicide. We are still free to take different decisions that show our recognition of their suffering and our common fate. Even words of understanding have value if they replace alienation and infuriating statements to the effect that they are to blame for their suffering. Reparations are also an option we are not yet emotionally ready to consider.

Personally, it took me many years to recognize and understand the refugee problem. I grew up in Tel Aviv in the 1950s and I don't remember any deep discussion in school, in the media, or at home that helped me understand the depth of the problem and the harsh feelings it involved. For years, Palestinian terrorism was nothing but more proof that they wanted to destroy us, which is still partly true, but now as in the past, we find it hard to connect it in our consciousness to the Palestinians' feelings of frustration and rage over becoming refugees. We denied and repressed the refugee problem for years because we could not deal with it emotionally. *Emotional repression leads to a distorted sense of reality.* That is because we are ignoring important information. We felt threatened, persecuted, and just, so how could we feel the pain of others from that emotional position? That is the tragedy of the paranoid personality, who grew up in a threatening environment, and who now has trouble adjusting to a less persecuting reality. The repeated blows whose source he does not understand are the price he pays for his distorted sense of reality, that thinking disorder that prevents him from seeing the other as he is and leads him to repress and ignore emotional information that is so important to seeing the whole picture.

Indeed, in the years until 1967 one could say with certainty that the Arabs had not given up on the option of eliminating us by force. We were not paranoid, we were very realistic, we knew only our force would guarantee our existence, and we were right. Our perception of reality was right, and the moral question regarding our relations with the Arabs was irrelevant. Right and left were in agreement that we were fighting for our home and for our existence. Surely, you cannot ask someone whose existence is being threatened to be empathetic to the party that wants to destroy him, although, in our case, that could have spared us from the Yom Kippur War. That six-day transition from acute anxiety to feelings of omnipotence is fundamentally pathological, in the sense that those repressions distort reality and lead one to believe that all his troubles are over. The Six Day War was the peak of repression of feelings of existential threat and the peak of failure to see the whole picture and not to distort reality. Later Sadat interpreted the Yom Kippur War as a great victory for the Arabs, and said it made peace possible. He had to restore his honor after the 1967 defeat before he was prepared to make peace. He needed to make peace from a position of strength and not from humiliation and defeat. But who among us could think about the enemy's emotional needs (which is a correct perception of reality), in the "high" we were in after the Six Day War? The Yom Kippur War, as Golda Meir said, made our lives sadder. We understood on a deep level that there are two sides here; we were not alone and were not omnipotent. But as happens to paranoid personalities, who massively repress the recognition of others, one single blow may not be enough, as harsh as it may be, to allow the repressed emotions to emerge and to arrive at an integration of different parts of the personality.

So *what* are we repressing so strongly? We are repressing the feeling that our whole existence is a *bluff*, that we are living on borrowed time, that the dream is about to vanish with us, that our true weakness will be revealed, and that will be the end. We will give the Syrians the Golan Heights; we will let a Palestinian state be established; there are one million Arabs within Israel's borders; we are splintered and divided; so what is left? I admit, *this way of thinking makes me shudder*. But first, we have to admit to shuddering so that we can examine whether it is true. Some say Israel lives on the assumption that "everything stays the same." That is an inductive proof that says that if we existed yesterday and the day before, we will probably exist tomorrow. In other words, a feeling that our whole existence is a miracle or magic, and that the only proof of our future existence is that it happened before. *That shuddering is a signal of the things we repress and do not want to see.* Our fears demand recognition and containment, as in therapy, so they do not turn into undesirable actions. In therapy we call it "acting out"—acts of aggression manifested toward others that stem from anxiety and distress that the individual cannot contain. That is our story in a nutshell, and the reason why we distort reality and why we cannot see the other.

The second national repression that surprised us was the Intifada. Again our distorted perception of reality was exposed and we paid the price. We thought we could occupy another nation and they would not rebel. We thought we could oppress them and they would not rise up against us. Another surprise. The reason for that repression is that at the time it was very hard for us to think we could allow a Palestinian state to exist and that it would not necessarily endanger us. We had erased the existence and feelings of the Palestinians. This was another mistake that stemmed from egocentric thinking, directed by the threat we perceived, and prevented us from looking up and seeing the other. This is exactly the vicious circle from which the paranoid personality cannot break free. He is afraid of being hurt, then unconsciously invites it out of defensiveness, and incessantly relives his past anxieties. A soldier in combat has to repress his fears and anxieties in order to fight and survive. But even for a soldier in combat it is dangerous to go from those repressions that are necessary for his existence, to euphoric feelings and to an inability to correctly read the enemy.

In a peace process there is not the same need to repress anxieties. Now we are free to let the anxieties rise to the consciousness, so we can feel them, deal with them, and let them slowly dissipate. That is the power of the therapeutic process that cannot take place during war, during the threat, because then all defenses need to be mobilized. Every soldier knows you do not ask an attacking soldier how he feels. Because that is exactly what he is repressing (in the many television interviews with soldiers, they generally do not admit fear or fully acknowledge it. They may sometimes speak about concerns, but not much more than that). This is the change I am talking about: we are no longer soldiers in combat, as we could have called ourselves in the past, but need to discuss our feelings openly, without defensiveness, to correct our thought distortions, and to spare ourselves from having more surprises.

In therapy too we encourage the patient to face his "shuddering" and feel it, look at it and get to know it in a safe environment, so that it will stop controlling and motivating him all the time. Rabin ordered the army to break the arms and legs of the uprising Palestinians, and thought that way he would put down the uprising. Again he was power-struck. Meir said earlier that there is no such thing as a Palestinian people. She denied the existence of the other because she felt it contradicted our own existence, and therefore was too threatening. It touches on the shuddering I mentioned, the collection of associations that ends with annihilation, which prevented us from thinking differently, that perhaps there is space for two. The "shuddering" is what is responsible for turning those difficult feelings into a victory march. That is how emotional mechanisms work. We know those reversal mechanisms. What stands behind boasting? No doubt our anxieties guided our thoughts and led to our erroneous conclusions in not foreseeing the Yom Kippur War, the Intifada, and other examples I will cite in the next section.

And wonder of wonders, both right and left moved toward the left. Today the existence of a Palestinian state seems much more plausible than in the past, and Arafat is no longer a terrorist we must not negotiate with, as both right and left maintained in the past. Undoubtedly reality has forced us to gradually lower our defenses, recognize the other, and give him space. Just as we gradually adjusted to the withdrawal from Sinai, and it no longer makes us shudder as it did before. The Arabs have undoubtedly also changed, from their desire to destroy us, which peaked in the Wars of Independence and in the Six Day War, to a quiet and sad acceptance of our existence. They too needed time to adjust to the Zionist infiltrator, who arrived without their permission to take over the country. They are not driven by love of us, but by a recognition of the grim reality they face, along with the understanding that peace will have advantages. Without comparing, our conciliation with the German people did not come from love of the Germans, but from the desire to receive reparations, to promote our economic needs, to get closer to Europe, and to put the pains of the past behind us. That is how the Arabs see us. That is the meaning of the cold peace we have with Egypt and with other Arab countries. It seems that both we and the Arabs moved from a paranoid stance to a more depressive stance, which is so necessary for peace. Therefore our trepidation slowly melts away, but it still has tremendous power over us, like a giant iceberg that is only peeking out of the water. Again, that unprocessed fear and the defenses we mobilized against it are the reasons for all the unpleasant surprises that befell us both during the era of war (until the peace with Egypt) and after the peace and reconciliation process began.

We needed to use force in the first twenty years of Israel's existence (until the Six Day War). In the second half of its existence we needed brains, or better yet, emotions, even more. Understanding the emotional logic of the peace process should lead us in the future. Force was very important. Without it we would not have survived, and everybody agrees on that. Now we are at a stage where force and deterrence are still important, but our emotional stance toward the process of peace and conciliation is even more important, and that is the next stage. Since the Yom Kippur War, for twenty-seven years, more than half of the years of the state's history, we have not experienced a war that threatened our existence, and nobody has tried to annihilate us. Before the Yom Kippur War we had frequent wars: the War of Independence in 1948, the Sinai Campaign in 1956, the Six Day War in 1967, and the Yom Kippur War in 1973. These are facts that have to be reexamined in light of our "shuddering." On the other hand, at the same time, we made peace with Egypt and Jordan, and began serious negotiations with the Syrians and the Palestinians, as well as building ties with more distant Arab countries. Those are not insignificant changes, but a slow and sad recognition of Israel on part of the Arab world. Indeed, it is because of that shuddering that in this era of peace we still think war, because we have not adjusted to a different way of thinking. We distort reality like paranoid personalities who see everything through a prism of threat, even though the threat has been considerably reduced. It is a way of thinking that stresses the negative, which sees our interest as opposing theirs rather than being identical to it. It is a way of thinking that has lost the ability to approve, to show warmth, not to speak of love. Loving the Palestinians and really thinking about how we can help them grow are dirty words these days. Possibly we will pay heavy prices in the future for our emotional difficulty to break free from feeling threatened and for allowing ourselves to be directed by that feeling.

I am talking about a way of thinking that is rooted in war rather than in peace; for instance, saying Jerusalem is only ours, and that they can "go to hell," instead of thinking that they have feelings too, and that we can accommodate the capitals of two states in Jerusalem; or the spacious Jewish settlements in the heart of crowded Arab settlements, which are poor in land and resources. But mainly I am talking about our emotional stance, which is not really trying to help the Palestinians and support them, not just out of moral responsibility, but from a deep emotional understanding of the essence of the peace process. So that we come out both bad and stupid, instead of being good and smart. Because we know where such unempathetic thoughts can lead, to something we don't want. What happens to paranoid personalities can happen to us. Yet we do not have the nerve to think differently and to change our way of thinking. It is all because of that "shuddering."

The third national repression or evidence of our defective concept of reality was the Rabin assassination. For a Jew to kill our own prime minister? People thought maybe an Arab would, but a Jew? Inconceivable. In other words, the refusal to see reality was not only directed outward—we failed to see that the Egyptians and the Syrians were very hurt, and would want to restore their honor, and that the Palestinians were oppressed and would revolt one day—but also inwardly—that the rift and the hatred within our people were great enough to lead to the murder of the prime minister. The national repressions do not necessarily distinguish between left and right. We all share them.

When a therapist gets to know a patient he can say with pretty much certitude that this person invites trouble, and that by the way he leads his life he predicts that there are more problems ahead. The therapist knows the patient's pathology, and knows that with such a pathology, there is no other way but to clash with reality, sooner or later. In the clinic we try to help him clarify the unconscious emotions that motivate him and cause him damage. To understand, for instance, that his aggression comes from anxiety that is not always realistic. We understand that once, when he was very young, the anxieties he feels were realistic. Then he was small and weak, and the environment was probably not warm and supportive enough. But now that he is big, he still carries that trauma with him, and it motivates him even in places where there is no threat such as the one he feels. Yes, this patient often distorts reality. If we return from the analogy to ourselves, our thinking still is, mainly, defensive. Who today would offer Iran and the movements it represents a historic conciliation between Judaism and Islam around our agreement to divide Jerusalem between us and the Palestinians, and turning it into a symbol of peace instead of a focus of war and tension? As of today, our shuddering and our thinking disorder do not allow us to think that way. We have to understand we are talking about an emotional position that is conveyed to the other side. Even if we get a negative response, just making the offer changes everything.

What can we learn about Israel's pathology? That there is a certain deeply repressed feeling, that although we discuss it often, is still far from being worked through and understood to the point that it stops motivating us in undesirable ways. I call that feeling the "shudder," and it is the existential threat we are under. The "shudder" is not just based on the Arabs' wish to destroy us, a wish that still partly exists, but also on our past: pogroms, Holocaust, and so on. That shudder makes it hard for us to discern where there really is an existential danger, and where, on the other hand, we distort reality and refuse to see things in a different light than our difficult past dictates.

The deepest Israeli problem, the shudder, is the difficulty to believe that it is really possible, more or less within the 1967 borders, to live a normal life. We have a deep feeling that we can only live through struggles and the use of force. We are really afraid of becoming small again. This is a deep psychological problem of a country that feels small and weak whenever it is not fighting. Confrontation and muscle-flexing play a well-known role in allaying the deepest anxieties—a negative role, of course. When we struggle and fight we are less able to feel the shudder and the fear. The real and most chilling question we are hard-pressed to answer is whether we can survive in the 1967 borders with about one million Arabs inside the country, and with such deep rifts between religious and secular Jews, left and right, Sephardic and Ashkenazi, and more. Time shows that it is more of a mental and psychological question than a military one, as we always assumed. Therefore, the "shudder" has to be dealt with with the tools of psychotherapy not less than as a security issue. But we are still busy wondering whether we are perceived as strong or not. We put tremendous energies into building a deterring and frightening image to the point where we have forgotten who we really are, what we really think, and what is good for us, just like a person who is always busy wondering what people think of him instead of what he thinks about himself. That is our thinking disorder, our distorted sense of reality, which stems from our "shudder."

If the Arabs were willing to launch the Yom Kippur War shortly after the Six Day War, when we were at the peak of our strength and deterrence (and had nuclear weapons), and it was partly due to our failure in the Yom Kippur War that promoted the subsequent peace with Egypt, does that not show something about our defective thinking, or about our disordered sense of reality? True, it was not the recognition of our weakness that brought peace; there is no question that we have to be strong, but we do not have to be full of self-importance and vainglory and contemptuous of our adversaries as we were after the Six Day War. Being seen by the Arabs as human beings who can and will defend ourselves, but are also able and willing to see the other side and be considerate, is what will bring peace. In that context, it is important to stress the fact that the Arabs launched the Yom Kippur War even though they knew we had nuclear arms. That shows the strength of the power of humiliation and insult, as well as the tremendous desire to restore one's honor. They could not stand the humiliation, but after the Yom Kippur War they were even ready to make peace with us. It appears that the deterrence factor, when it threatens and humiliates the other, actually invites war, and maybe we sometimes forget that.

There is no doubt that we are too defense-oriented, obsessed with our strength and with declarations of what we will not give up. We will not give up on a united Jerusalem, we will not return to the borders of 1967 in the West Bank and Golan Heights, we will not dismantle settlements, and so on. As if those are the most essential and important questions. We are like a child shouting that nobody will take away his toy, who really seems to be making that statement to convince himself not to give it up. At least based on past experience, that was the fate of our declarations that we would never speak to Arafat, we would never allow the establishment of a Palestinian state, and we would never give up the Golan. We are less concerned with thoughts about how to create peaceful relations, to build them, and to nurture them. Our obsession with our strength invites war, just like the child who will not let go of the toy, just like the thug who flexes his muscles and invites everyone around him to a confrontation. Our excessive concern with our deterrence, without making space for the more emotional-human aspect of recognizing the Arabs' feelings, invites an attempt to test our strength by confrontation. Again, the question that arises is how we live with the shudder and how we contain it in order to seriously examine whether returning the Golan Heights, for example, is an existential threat or actually promotes peace and security. And whether Barak is right in being stubborn with the Syrians about whether we should go back to the exact borders of 1967 or not, or should he be fighting over the meaning of peace in a broader sense, without losing the important emotional aspect, through deep and creative thinking, about the fate of the Israeli settlements on the Heights, for instance, which can promote peace. Indeed, the shudder makes our thinking more concrete and limited. That is what happens when you are afraid.

One of the implications of that shuddering, that existential threat, is the difficulty in seeing and understanding the feelings and needs of the party that is viewed as threatening. That is where the distorted sense of reality comes from. A person who feels he is being attacked can hardly understand the emotions and motives of the attacking party, or consider the fact that the person he sees as an aggressor is actually hurt. We see in the clinic how hard that is. It is so hard for us to respect the Palestinians. Out of our vulnerability, it is hard for us to see that what is good for them is good for us too, and that a happy and prosperous Palestinian state nearby us is the only guarantee of peace. Even the left does not understand the extent of the emotional commitment that means. *As long as there is no corrective experience that shows the Palestinians that we really care about them, there will not be peace.* They need a corrective experience from us, just like a child who needs his parents to apologize for any injustice done to him. Even if it is too little too late, it is better than nothing. The child will be able to understand that the parent had a hard childhood too, and forgive him a little bit someday, only after the parent is able to touch the child's pain, and appease him, even if just somewhat. Of course it does not mean that we do not have to place limits upon them and make demands on them, but the guiding principle should be helping them grow and develop. That can only be done by someone who has worked through his shuddering experience. Treating them as enemies because of our emotional problems is what feeds the cycle of hostility and that sums up our distorted sense of reality. When you want to help a child grow, you may place clear limits, but it comes from a loving emotional stance that wants to help, and understands that sometimes a parent has to be firm, rather than from a position of dismissal and contempt. That is the difference in a nutshell. Our repressing of the Palestinians' suffering is what will not let us live in peace. And we will not be available to see the Palestinians' pain, recognize it, and deal with it, as long as we have not worked through our own "shuddering," our existential fear, through a mental process.

The real emotional process that has to kick in is dealing with the "shudder" and repeatedly checking our sense of reality. Our national repressions and the failures that followed them came from that shuddering fear that we cannot exist as a small country. It is time for us to ask ourselves what we are really afraid of. Is our fear so realistic? Are we not inviting the very disasters that fulfill our fears, by our concept of power? In our national therapy we have to recognize the shudder, contain it, and not let it motivate us in the direction of incorrect action, just in order to erase that difficult feeling. A therapist works hard to help the patient feel his insult and humiliation, so that he does not turn those feelings into vainglory or aggression, which supposedly restore his confidence and good feeling. Our national need today is to contain our intolerable feelings and to try to examine them slowly and carefully, without running into major wars and damaging actions. Can we exist without a war to unite us, in small borders, and divided from within? That is the question that scares us the most. Only after we can answer it will we be able to relax.

More evidence of our defective sense of reality (besides the three I cited of the Yom Kippur War, the Intifada, and the Rabin assassination) is terrorism. We are surprised anew by each act of terrorism. After each one, we repress it until the next one happens. We refuse to look at the force that generates terrorism. Why are there people who are prepared to die only to hurt us? We continue looking at the phenomenon and not at the cause; we look at the symptom rather than at the disease; we refuse to recognize that this problem is caused by emotional forces. What we teach our children, that "force does not solve anything," is true for us too. For years we believed that we could defeat terrorism with force, and said that they understand only force. The Lebanon War, one of whose goals was to put an end to terrorism, is further evidence of our distorted sense of reality that I am talking about. We could not accept the fact that we could not defeat terrorism, yet our leaders promised the public for years, every day afresh, that we will not put up with terrorism and would finally defeat it. Only lately do we hear braver leaders say that the solution in Lebanon has to go through a peace agreement with Syria. At issue is a chronic thinking disorder, which comes from the shuddering and existential fear aroused by terrorism, which makes us become defensive and closed, and as a result, unable to understand that terrorism is fed by the hard feelings of homeless Palestinian refugees. It is true that terrorism is also fed by religious incitement, but without the frustration and the bitter feelings, the religious incitement would not take hold. In our consciousness, Palestinian terrorism is severed from its roots, the Palestinian suffering that feeds it. We thought the Palestinian bitterness, frustration, and rage could be solved by force. The only way to fight their tremendous emotional pain is with warm feelings of love and caring, a real desire to help them and *taking moral responsibility* for them. Only a real emotional process between us can appease the Palestinians' deep feelings of insult and hurt. But when we are wrapped up in our shuddering, how can we give them the love they need so badly? They need a warm relationship, support, and help in every area and every sense, and we are sunk in our shuddering over our heads.

We have a basic ongoing problem in our sense of reality, beyond one example or another. We distort reality because of our massive emotional repression of our "shudder." We can expect unpleasant surprises in the future too, perhaps an atomic, biological, or chemical war, possibilities that we have already repressed since the Gulf War. These too will take us by utter surprise. I will address that latest national repression in a separate discussion.

We are just like a patient who has to work hard in therapy to extract himself from the intolerable situation of being surprised again and again, and never knowing where it is coming from. As a nation, we have a paranoid personality, which cannot create normal human relations with others or see them, because of tremendous anxieties and defenses, and therefore is constantly surprised. Such a personality is preoccupied with itself all the time, narcissistically and egocentrically, because that is its war of survival, and in such a war it is not free to see the other and give it a place in its consciousness. We know it well from therapy, and we know that when the patient relaxes he will start to see the world differently. To this day, *security* is a magic word. Like Rabin, Prime Minister Barak took over the defense portfolio, thereby signaling that it is top priority. That is what the paranoid personality says: "There is one thing above all else, and that is my security, and I cannot compromise on that." Try arguing with such a patient, and what can you say? That there are other important things? That he is not seeing the whole picture? That with his behavior he is reducing his own security and bringing a disaster upon himself? That he is insulting others and inviting them to a confrontation? Whatever you say, he will say the same thing: security, security, security. That paranoid personality's "shudder," and ours as a people, motivates all of our actions unconsciously and powerfully, without our understanding that it is the reason for our actions. A paranoid personality will never feel secure. He will arouse and invite quite the opposite from his environment.

That is the painful paradox of human existence. Of all children, the one who is most afraid is the one who will invite others to attack him, and to increase his fears. The child is actually continuing to revive and reconstruct his past and to prove to himself that what he feels is true, that everyone is against him. There is no other way but being aware of the shudder and of its tremendous power over us, and the way in which it activates and motivates our actions. Only that awareness can change the story of our lives and make it different: the story of a peace-loving nation that can live in peace with its neighbors. But if there is one thing that is difficult for the paranoid personality, it is being empathetic to the other side. How can he be empathetic to a party he sees as threatening his life? That is a real paradox. If he could, all his relationships with the world would reverse and change completely. The question is, Are we really unable to do that?

3

The Story We Tell Ourselves,
and the World, about Ourselves

The National Anthem

From the start of the anthem, with the words "As long as the Jewish heart yearns," it is clear that it is focused on Jewish feelings. It raises the question of how a non-Jewish Israeli feels about his national anthem. Israeli Arabs wish we had a more universal anthem, which would reflect the yearnings of the Arabs who live in Israel. Giving Israeli Arabs full recognition is very hard, because it requires us to change from a Jewish state to an Israeli state. That change touches our deepest strata as a people, our right to exist, our drive to prevail and survive, and so on. That change is a very hard developmental crisis for us, which I discussed in the chapter "from religion to state." If we liken the nation to an individual, the anthem is one of the deepest recesses of the national unconscious, which is hard to change, because it is essentially primal, instinctive, and egocentric, and can only endure very slow changes. Indeed, the egocentricity of our anthem, which reflects our developmental stage and our mental state as a nation, does not let us, as of today, see the possibility of any other anthem. In that way we say, unconsciously, that there is no space for two peoples here. We cannot conceive of creating an anthem with which Israeli Arabs would feel comfortable. We could do that by adding one line about members of other nations, for instance. But it is hard to argue with instincts. We will only reconsider when reality slaps us in the face. And it will.

The anthem begins with anxieties and fears: As long as the Jewish heart *yearns*. Indeed, the music also begins quietly. The Jewish heart is aroused and yearning. Then: "Toward the East, the eye beholds Zion." This is about the streaming of Jews to Israel from all corners of the earth. To the sounds of a magical tune, everyone is drawn, after years of exile, to Zion, which is Jerusalem. Then comes the most important part of the anthem: *We have not lost our hope of two thousand years / To be a free people in our land, the land of Zion, Jerusalem.* The main feeling conveyed in the anthem is that we are wretched, weak, and hurt, but we have not lost hope of being a free people in our land. Are we not free today? That is what children ask at the Passover seder, when everyone sings: "This year we are slaves; next year we will be free." We have not been slaves for so many years, but we still feel like slaves, poor persecuted victims, and that someone else controls us.

Our anthem is the anthem of a paranoid nation. The paranoid personality feels that it is the poor victim of an evil and cruel world. There is a clear accusation of some abstract entity that is causing our suffering, which is preventing the realization of our two-thousand-year-old dream. That undefined other can be anybody, and actually means the whole world. What is missing here is the emotional position that realizes that we are not alone in the world, and that we make others suffer too, an emotional position that recognizes that we are not the most despondent in the world, and must consider the feelings of others as well. According to our anthem, nobody is as righteous as we are, and no nation suffers more than we do. Of course there is not the slightest mention of all the help we received from other nations.

It's as if nothing happened since the anthem was composed more than one hundred years ago, and as if we did not grow from the stage when we did not have a state and independence. The truth is, the anthem should be changed. We need a new anthem that contains a more open vision than the vision of an adolescent who is victimized and deserves everything. A vision that includes the foreign minorities that live with us, a vision that recognizes that there is room for everyone, and that we can live together as good neighbors. In other words, an anthem upon which we can raise generations of children with a more complex and correct view of reality, not an anthem that shouts, "I am a victim" and nothing more. The truth is that we are an emotionally undeveloped nation, because of our religious and egocentric elements. Yet we have to sustain emotional burdens that more developed and mature nations would have a hard time sustaining, to bridge over deep emotional rifts within us and between ourselves and our environment.

Hatikva is an anachronistic anthem of a state that feels adolescent because it does not recognize that it is already fully grown, and continues its rebellion against those who supposedly do not give it what it wants. It still feels that it is fighting against the establishment, even though now it is the establishment. It is a state which, according to its anthem, still lives in its heroic past, when it had nothing, and feels itself entirely despondent, and refuses to acknowledge that now it is a relatively stable country, and that others around it have nothing. But our hearts still yearn. And we still look toward Zion as if it weren't ours. And we still talk about not losing hope while our hope has already been realized. Now our problem is giving that anthem that was ours to others. Today it is the hearts of the Palestinians that are yearning, and they are dreaming about their capital in Jerusalem, and they too are saying these days, "We have not lost our hope of being a free people in our country." They sing that song, because they don't have a state.

We know that an anthem reflects the spirit of the nation. We all grew up with it and it is hard for us to change it. That is because what's at stake is changing our emotional position as a nation. What happens to a parent who continues to behave like a child, who continues rebelling against anyone above him, against any authority figure, as if it were the parents who oppressed him? Now he cannot see that he is the parent who oppresses others. He is the battered child who becomes the battering parent, and feels he is the world's most righteous victim. That blindness is well-known in clinical psychology, the blindness that comes from the reconstruction and revival of difficult past experiences. Once the small child really was weak in relation to his abusive environment, but is no longer so today. Yet he relives his past and sees others as if they were his abusive parents. Today we have to help others realize their dream; we have to be good parents to others. But we cannot grow and replace the emotional stance of adolescents with that of adults; we cannot go from feelings of victims to the recognition of our power and aggression, from someone who had things done to him because he was small and powerless, to someone who can see what he is doing to others. We are fighting with all our might to stay the most wretched in the world and the most righteous in the world and not to recognize our aggression. We are like any adult who swears he would never do to others what they did to him.

Every nation chooses an anthem that reflects its feelings. The British ask God to save the queen; the American anthem speaks of courage and freedom; the French is about fighting tyranny; the Egyptian is about the need to defend the country; the Brazilian anthem is about the beauty of nature; the Chinese anthem stresses the importance of uniform thought among millions of hearts; the German anthem (which once was "Germany above all, in the whole world") today speaks of freedom, justice, and unity; the Indian anthem stresses victory and prayer; the Pakistani anthem is about its sacred soil; the New Zealand anthem asks God to protect the country; the Turkish anthem is essentially belligerent; the Canadian anthem stresses the importance of vigilance; the Finnish anthem is calm and quiet; and the Tanzanian anthem asks God to bless all of Africa.

Indeed, most anthems ask God for protection, talk about the need to be strong, describe the beauty of the country, and mention its highest values such as freedom, justice, and unity. The Israeli anthem stands out. First of all, the strong suffering and pain it expresses set it apart from the other anthems. Hatikva, as its name means, is about hope for something that has not come to be yet. Other anthems talk about preserving what is, while ours is about what has not come into being yet. Judging by our national anthem, you would think that we do not yet have an independent state. The melody that started relatively quietly reaches a high pitch toward the end. The drama we created and live in reaches a climax. Only then does the crowd, who stood at attention, disperse, calmer. It has told itself that pipe dream again, that we have not lost hope. Now it has filled up its batteries until the anthem is sung again.

A different anthem could actually turn our weakness into strength. We could have an anthem about the fragile and difficult coexistence in our region and the duty upon us all, members of all religions, races, nations, and ethnicities, to unite and live in peace in Israel and in its capital Jerusalem. An anthem of rising above conflicts and emotions, and marching toward peace, but an anthem that reminds us and does not forget that we must always be strong. Such an anthem would suit our region and our future, and it is with that kind of an anthem that we can raise our children, not as suffering saints.

A suggestion:

As long as the Israeli heart yearns within
And the eye beholds Jerusalem and Zion in the East
We have not lost our hope of many years
To be a free nation in our land
A land of Jews and Arabs.

And maybe we could add another dramatic verse to the anthem regarding our greatest problem these days, the domestic problem, an anthem that encourages religious and secular people, Jews, Arabs, and rightists and leftists, to live together. And another verse about the need to be strong. Everything is possible except continuing to play the tune of the "righteous victim."

4

Foreign Affairs

Syria

The negotiations with Syria offer us an opportunity to take a close look at the paranoid experience, the feeling that we are the poor victims of aggression directed at us from without. Syria's demand during peace negotiations with Prime Minister Yitzhak Rabin, to receive early warning stations on the Golan Heights so that we do not attack them, seemed to many of us bizarre or manipulative. For them to think we would attack them! We really could not conceive of that, as people who feel so victimized and hurt by the other side. Paranoid patients take years and years of therapy to recognize their own aggression and difficulty in giving up the posture of the tortured saint or the righteous victim. A person's ability to recognize his own aggression is a significant developmental achievement, which leads to the more advanced feelings of guilt and a desire to make amends. At that point the person gets out of the egocentric stage where he is at the center of the world and the only one who is important. That is when he can recognize the other and his suffering. I want us to develop our ability to listen to ourselves. The strange sound of the Syrian demand does not fit our understanding and our perception, and needs clarification. It is what will enable us to gradually change our perception of reality. They think we might attack them? Strange . . . whatever made them think such a thought? That needs clarification. When somebody tells us they see us as aggressive, the question that arises is not whether they are right, because we all know that feelings are neither right nor wrong. That is how the person feels

67

about us, and the question is whether we can relate to that. In simple words, it is important to understand why they feel that way, and what we did or said that made them feel that way. Our ability to understand what someone else is telling us can expand and enrich our world. Our emotional defenses lead to our surprised expression, which does not understand how the Syrians reached that feeling. So what are the Syrians really talking about?

They are of course talking about our war-riddled history with them, in which we prevailed and conquered: the War of Independence, the Six Day War, the Yom Kippur War, and the Lebanon War. They are also talking about the fact that we banished Palestinians and some of them live in Syria today. What did the Jewish people feel throughout their history toward all the nations who conquered their country and lived in it? As we saw in a beautiful film by a Syrian journalist about the Golan Heights, which was aired on Israeli television, the Syrians miss the Golan Heights very much. They talk about it with yearning and longing, just as we spoke about Zion.

To understand the depth of the emotional gap between us and the Syrians, we must listen with therapeutic ears to Syrian Foreign Minister Farouq A-Shara, who says the Israeli government has to educate the Israeli public toward real peace, where we do not occupy other lands. Educate us? Isn't that a little insulting? Do we not know what real peace is? It is the Syrian insult speaking from his mouth. It is also an honest statement that expresses deep pain. But we really do not relate to the emotional meaning the Syrians attach to the fact that the Golan Heights is under our control. For them it is blatant injustice. For us it is a morale-boosting achievement. We also have often said that Arab leaders have to educate their people toward peace wholeheartedly. In saying that, we were actually saying it was the Arabs who were uneducated and did not understand the meaning of peace. We too treated them in a condescending and insulting manner, as if our feelings were more correct and justified than theirs. The Syrians feel very hurt by us. They wanted to destroy us for years, but they have no problem with that, because to them we were a cruel conqueror. Their willingness to recognize us is inherently connected to a feeling of humiliation and failure. They changed because they had to. We are changing too—a few years ago, who thought we could give the Golan Heights back to the Syrians?—but we are still far from understanding the Syrians' feelings and emotions. Therefore A-Shara is not so wrong when he wants the Israeli government to educate the citizens to better understand what the Syrians want, to recognize their feelings and understand how they arrived at them, and to realize that they did not invent them.

For the Syrians it would be humiliating to establish more extensive peace relations to get more land. Rabin's formula, "the more peace, the more withdrawal," is very humiliating to the Syrians. They heard Rabin say, "in exchange for more warmth you will get more land." Therefore they did not send a condolence message or participate in Rabin's funeral. Similarly, they did not participate in the Sharm A-Sheikh conference against terrorism. They feel terrorism is legitimate, because it is resistance to occupation. They often say that they refuse to go through the humiliation Israel puts Arafat through. They feel as if they are being forced to make peace, and their feelings are being bought in exchange for the return of parts of their homeland. They want to make peace, but from a position of freedom. One can understand their feeling that they do not want to be forced to make peace, because you cannot force a person to love someone. Therefore, we cannot expect a warm peace in the coming years (with Egypt or Jordan either).

Unfortunately, we learn only by force, in this case as in others, that we have to be considerate of others. If we withdraw from the Golan Heights it will only be because we have realized that our might no longer does us good. The withdrawal will not come from a real recognition and understanding of the Syrian position, of how they perceive us, what the Golan means to them, and how they experience it as an inseparable part of their country. It is a shame, because if we make a concession, we should at least understand where it comes from as well as the real needs and feelings of the other side. We will need those emotional insights throughout the entire peace process. Those are typical mistakes of military thinking, because what army can think of emotions?

We need to listen to the Syrians differently, empathetically. Being able to understand them through their eyes is the crux of the matter. Only if there is a part of us that can bring itself to understand the Syrians will we be able to live together. Without that element, called "empathy," there will not be peace. Only when you are empathetic to the other side can you know if its intentions are honest and really understand it. That is how parents relate to their children; that is how couples relate to each other. Therefore, for the benefit of people who think in military terms, empathy is a first-rate military tool, because it enables us to really understand the enemy and what he is going through.

But we have tremendous difficulty in being empathetic to the Arabs and the Syrians in particular. The fact that Arab intellectuals are usually against us reveals the problem they have, as much as we do. In the rest of the world intellectuals lean to the left, to conciliation and compromise, whereas in Arab countries it is the other way around. This points to the depth of the particular emotional difficulty of the Israeli-Arab conflict, and that there really is no right and wrong here, just two nations who want to live, and those intellectuals get pulled into the emotional turmoil without being able to detach themselves. The intellectuals in those Arab countries have not completely accepted the fact that we have the right to live here. It is an emotional process that will take many more years to resolve. The emotional dynamic of mutual vulnerability is revealed when President Ezer Weizman says, "If Assad doesn't want to, he doesn't have to [make peace]." We will wait for him but will not pursue him. Weizman represents the insult we all feel. The Syrians say, first give back what you took; then we'll talk about peace. They demand a prior commitment to leave the whole Golan Heights before they will enter negotiations with us and agree to a meeting of the leaders. Since the issue is an emotional dialogue, it is hard not to compare the political relations to the world of childhood. It is true in this case as in many other cases. One child says, "first give back what you took and then I'll play with you," and the other says, "first play with me and then I'll give it back." It is true that Assad and Barak exchanged mutual compliments and both sides understand how important it is to change their emotional attitudes, but that is just the beginning. The same cruel Syrian enemy who tortured our prisoners and whom we always viewed as the worst enemy of all, has always kept its agreements to the last detail, and never unleashed terrorism from its territory. Therefore, it is hard to accuse it of manipulations or conniving, just plain pain.

To define the depth and complexity of the necessary emotional processes, let us examine the fact that A-Shara denies that the Syrians fired at Israeli settlements from the Golan Heights before the Six Day War. That lie stings us, and we would be well advised to understand it. The Syrians have a hard time admitting that they wanted to destroy us. That desire was more open and declared in the past, while today they are letting go of it and mourning it. That clear lie shows us that the Syrians cannot even admit to themselves the change they have undergone and recognize the significant aggression they directed toward us in the past. The emotional recognition that because of our strength they will have to concede, that because of our strength they are talking peace with us today and asking us to give back their territory, is difficult and painful for them. We should know how hard it is to admit that we only understand force! We will have a Palestinian state because we were forced to; we have left the Sinai and will leave the Golan only because we have no choice. It is hard for the child to admit that his parents, who forced him to do something, were right. That is identification with the aggressor. We recognize the desires of the other and justify them only because he forced them upon us. Indeed, what begins with identification with the aggressor can end with a real recognition of the other. Both we and the Syrians will have to go through a long emotional process to work through these difficult emotional conflicts and understand how to live with them. The Syrians declare that their choice of peace is strategic, that is, not a tactical local manipulation, but the expression of a deep realization and a new way of thinking. We understand now that it is not only a conscious choice, but unconscious emotional processes that require bringing information into the conscious mind and working through it. The Syrians have to ask themselves, *In what way have we changed, and how, and why?* Only such an honest and deep exploration will allow them to truly recognize us.

But we are going through a process similar to what the Syrians are going through. Are we telling the truth about the way in which we forcefully exiled the Palestinians in 1948? And what is the emotional meaning to us of the lies we tell ourselves and others? For us, just as for the Syrians, the emotional processing of that lie rather than its repression is vital for a process of peace. Because only through that painful exploration can we understand what the other side is saying and feeling. *Raising the question about what the other side feels is the basis for recognizing the other, which is so missing today in the peace process.* Then, only then, can we ask ourselves how far we are willing to go to meet their needs. We know from therapy how important it is to understand the processes of change and learn from them, and not just to get swept away by them.

The Syrians are afraid of getting lost in a peace process that disarms them. One reason is that we are more developed and stronger than they are. Therefore they defensively demand that we declare in advance, prior to negotiations, that we are willing to withdraw to the June 4, 1967 borders. For the same reason they object to a meeting of the leaders at the beginning of the negotiations. They are expressing the fear of being drawn into a peace process where they would lose their power and resistance. It is an experience familiar to our right, of which it accuses the left, of allowing itself a kiss of death in the peace process.

But we focus on the marginal details instead of the main problem, on pieces of land and not on the peace process itself. In therapy we often see a client obsess over a particular detail out of anxiety and miss the bigger picture. Why is it so hard for us to accept the Syrian demand and make it conditional on the fulfillment of all our other demands—questions of water, security, the meaning of peace, and the future of the settlements? After all, each of those points will have much more of an effect on the future peace than another piece of land. In a while we will not remember exactly how much and why we gave it up, and will remain only with the peace process with the Syrians, and the question of whether it is moving in the right direction. What matters today: Taba or the entirety of peace with Egypt? The peace process, as I said, is measured by the emotional change it effects and by its direction, and not by one detail or another. That is where our focus should be.

Where then is our emotional difficulty? It is in understanding the Syrians and recognizing their pain. It is hard for us to understand that their demand for us to withdraw to the June 4, 1967 borders is not a manipulation; it is a real and painful demand upon which they cannot compromise, at least not now. It is no accident that someone spread the rumor that the Syrians want Kibbutz Ein Gev too, a rumor they later denied. Our "shudder," that I already discussed, is what motivates us more than anything else. Who could give up the place we call our "eyes?"

Another testimony of our great sensitivity is in public reactions to different wordings of poll questions. The questions, "Are you for or against a withdrawal to the Sea of Galilee," and, "Are you for or against a withdrawal from the Golan Heights" get opposite answers from many people, even though the difference is not clear. Our sea of existential anxieties floods us and we sink in it. Still, conceding our grandiosity, compromising, which is deeply against the emotional message of any religion, is very hard for us. The operative map is the inner map of each person's soul, the borders of his ego, to the extent that they are nurtured by grandiose and uncompromising religious sources that conceal anxiety, and to the extent that they can accept a more relative way of thinking that sees the other without feeling existentially threatened. The question is also whether we are mature enough for the mourning process that will allow us to stay smaller and with all of our domestic problems without looking for someone to blame from without. Therefore, we as a people continue swinging between the two poles of all or nothing, with nothing in the middle. Our two emotional options are grandiosity or anxiety, which always go together. In such a mental state, it is no wonder that we cling to details, miss the bigger picture, and are unable to agree on a border.

In therapy, as in life, each day is a new opportunity to revisit the pathologies and emotional rules that motivate us all. Those emotional mechanisms do not change quickly, and if there is something stable and permanent in our world, it is the *emotional rules*. The assumption that Assad is avoiding peace because of a "Ceausescu syndrome" is just part of the story that has to be better understood. The question is whether Assad is afraid of processes of openness that could lead to his bitter end like what happened to Ceausescu in Romania. The Syrians, like any pathological personality, want to extract themselves from their pathology. They really do want peace. Sometimes the pathological personality does not know what peace means and is not familiar with the feeling of life without war, but in the depth of his unconscious, everyone wants peace, even if he never experienced it. Indeed, Assad is unsure of his ability to give up his militant posture, and has given some signals that are typical of a process of change.

In this process we have to be aware of the risks Assad is taking, risks any belligerent and non-democratic regime takes when it chooses a foreign policy of peace, which will undoubtedly have domestic implications. Being open to peace actually means giving up force, which is a very difficult emotional position for Assad. It is no doubt that we feel Assad is trying to overpower us, to twist our arm, and to force us to accept his conditions of withdrawal to the Sea of Galilee, conditions we see as humiliating. We have to understand that he is making us feel the way he feels, submissive, humiliated, and threatened (in therapy we call it "projective identification"). He feels in this peace process that he is gambling with his life, his son's life, and his Alawi community's life.

Assad also humiliated President Clinton in Geneva by meeting him without handing him any achievement. He is acting that way not just against us, but against the whole world, and moreover, out of defensiveness. The intensity of his insistence on not meeting Barak, on discussing full withdrawal rather than security arrangements, and in general, the stubbornness of the Syrian position throughout the years, reflect the intensity of *his fear of what might happen to him*, because otherwise, he could have been more flexible.

The question we have to ask ourselves is as follows: Are we fighting against withdrawal to the Sea of Galilee because it is humiliating—the humiliation Assad is making us feel because that is how he feels—or do we have other reasons? Do we experience accepting a Syrian condition as surrender, and are we thereby party to Assad's game of humiliation? Our experience shows us over the years that we always err in the same direction, which is conceding too little because of our anxieties (whoever thought we would give back all of Sinai, the Golan, a unilateral withdrawal from Lebanon, a Palestinian state, etc.). It is time to take the risk of erring in the other direction, or to phrase it better with therapeutic tools: it is time for us to be aware of the feelings of insult and anxiety that motivate us, and of the empathy we have to develop toward the Syrian position.

So What Solution Does Therapeutic Understanding Offer Us?

A-Shara refuses to shake hands with Barak, does not look at him or talk to him. *The conflict is mainly emotional, not cognitive, and it comes straight from the impulsive world of children.* In such a relationship it is no wonder that we focus on the details instead of the totality. As I said, we argue over one more or one less piece of land and miss the peace process itself and the atmosphere in which it should take place. In a state of anxiety the first casualties are creativity and freedom of thought. We know from the clinic how an anxious person seizes the details as if they were everything, just like couples who run accounts against each other, who did what to whom, when, and where, and are unable to think in terms of their emotional bond.

The piece of land around the Sea of Galilee, that very stumbling block, can turn into a symbol of peace and a positive and life-giving experience if, for instance, we think of joint projects that can be done there. Maybe a giant water park for Israeli and Syrian children that becomes a symbol of peace. We are so short on symbols of peace (we are loaded with flags, anthems, symbols of nationality, and symbols of war). The peace process should and can be, absurd as it may sound, a process we enjoy rather than suffer through. Apparently neither we nor the Syrians are ripe for this kind of thinking, but it should be promoted. We could decline to give the Syrians that piece of land by the lake and remain with a cold peace, but that is not what we want. We can give it to them and still get a cold peace. What matters is not the details of the agreement, but the quality of the process and whether it is moving in the right direction.

The same is true for the settlements; they must become symbols of peace. We have already suggested that we could settle Palestinian refugees in them, and that would be our modest contribution to this difficult problem, or possibly construct joint tourism projects to turn those places into resorts, or we could give them to the Syrians as a gift. Everything is possible except for destruction such as we had in Yamit. That is the logic of a peace process, that it means joint construction and not destroying something just so the other side won't get it. The logic of the peace process requires that textbooks in the schools and the media be supportive of the process. The spirit of the process and the emotional attitude toward it will be the main testing stones, as we know from therapy. In therapy we do not only look at what a person does, the surface level, but go deeper and try to understand his feelings and what motivates him, and make the change there. That is because we understand that a person is motivated by her thoughts and feelings, beyond her particular behavior or signing one agreement or another. Therefore we should be insistent, but about the *right* things—tangible expressions of emotional bonds.

A-Shara's refusal to shake Barak's hand and talk to him need not scare us. Rabin did not want to shake Arafat's hand throughout the peace negotiations, and it was only at the signing of the Oslo Accord that he gave him a warm heartfelt handshake. That is another sign of the low point at which this marital therapy began at, and how much patience we need in the long growth process toward peace.

If the problem is water, it has to be solved by joint agreements and by the joint construction of desalination plants, and the same goes for other problems. That is the quality of a peace process, where you turn the greatest points of dissention and difficulty into levers and symbols of peace. A disputed piece of land can turn into a project of cooperation for years. Therefore we should insist more on quality than on quantity, because that is what matters in growth processes. But we are still at a stage where opinion polls are decided by such impulsive responses. The public is asked, Should we withdraw to the Sea of Galilee or not? This teaches and invites the most impulsive thinking, black or white. It is not asked, "Are you for real peace or not? Are you for growth or not?" To that people would surely answer with a resounding "yes." Understanding ourselves and our feelings, understanding that emotional processes take time and that this child cannot grow up all at once, that is what we see in our daily work with patients, and that is our story as a nation. The transition from war thinking to peace thinking, which every child goes through, the reversal that at first seems impossible, but later seems inevitable, takes a long time and a lot of effort.

True, the Syrians demand that we give them the whole Golan all the way to the lake, and have insisted since the Six Day War, without ever changing their position, that our withdrawal has to be exactly to the borders of June 4, 1967. We have to understand why they cling to that line so strongly. The Six Day War was a terrible trauma for them, a horrible humiliation, and they want to correct that experience. They want to turn the wheel of history back and erase the humiliation. A withdrawal to anything less than that line would be etched in their memory as a humiliation for generations, and they cannot tolerate that. That was also the emotional dynamic that led Sadat to demand the return of the entire Sinai. An erasure of the humiliation. I would not rule out responding to these Syrian emotional needs, as long as the direction is peace: joint projects, different education, different statements by them to the media, and a real understanding by us that peace takes time.

We have to emphasize to Assad that he must convince the Israeli public. An emotional bond takes time; there are no shortcuts. We need time for the public to be convinced that this is real peace, and then it will be ready to make concessions. Such an agreement has to be supported by a large majority and will have value only if it is made by a national unity government. It is time that we understand that such agreements cannot be forced on almost half the public. It is an attempt to speed things up and skip over vital developmental stages of the peace process on both sides. It is like when a patient grudgingly agrees to talk to his wife, and feels he is doing her a favor, because he is still full of anger and hatred he has not worked through, softened, or integrated with other parts of his personality. Bashar Al-Assad can visit Israel and address the public as Sadat did, and convince us that he wants peace. We know that convincing someone else is the best way to convince yourself, and in the case of the Syrians is a process that cannot be skipped.

That is the strength of our democracy, which invites us and others to undergo a deep emotional process of recognizing all of the voices and forces within us until they reach integration. (It is no accident, as I explained in the introduction, that psychotherapy is common only in democratic regimes. That is because therapy is emotional democracy that allows different voices to come out and reach a balance.) Besides, we have to adapt to the idea that peace cannot be made "in one stroke." It is a long emotional process, at least if we want warmer peace than we have with Egypt. Therefore, any peace agreement has to take into consideration the emotional developmental process. But we are like a first-grader who does not believe he will ever reach second grade, and cannot even imagine what that would be like. Conversely, we are like the child who prefers one candy now over two later. In therapy too we set goals for ourselves and go on an adventure with the patient toward growth and peace. In therapy we remind the patient and ourselves that change depends on us, but it takes time. If the patient shouts, as they often do, "I have an opportunity now, and if I miss peace now, it will never come again," we reassure him and tell him that not only will there be many future opportunities, but growth is a process and not a one-time event. Therefore, we have to think in terms of process.

We need a peace process that takes a few years, where at each stage we give them another part of the Golan Heights, and our ties with them grow at the same time. We can declare the final goal in advance—a return to the borders of June 4, 1967, and full peace. Yes, we need to be sensitive to the Syrians' difficulties; they are threatened by us, by our economy, and by our power. They may experience open borders as an existential threat. The question then is whether we are going in the right direction. We can compromise over the pace. The only condition is that the partners on this journey, the Israelis and the Syrians, are ready to go on this adventure, and moreover, believe that the end will be good. That is a necessary condition for any therapy or process of emotional change. You cannot promise a person that all will end well. They have to believe in their own power to end the journey successfully; otherwise, they will never take the first step.

Lebanon

Introduction

This section was written in three stages at different times. The first part was written at the end of 1999, when the question of a unilateral withdrawal from Lebanon was in the air, and Barak promised he would take the Israeli army out of Lebanon. The second part was written over the first four months of 2000, when the debate over the withdrawal was heated, while I am writing this introduction in June 2000, a month after the withdrawal, with the Israeli-Lebanese border quiet.

This is an opportunity to take a look at two conditions of consciousness that seldom meet, "before and after," before the withdrawal and after, like a child in second grade who can hardly remember how he felt in first grade, even though it was not so long ago. But the emotional processes remain, and that is the message I want to put forward in this book as strongly as possible. If you take a look at them you become a self-aware person and are much better off.

This emotional exploration is critical since it allows us to learn about emotional processes and how they can often predict the future. If not accurately, they can still indicate the right direction, because growth processes are subject to universal emotional laws. It is not enough to note that the border is quiet. We must study the emotional dynamic that took place and apply our understanding to the future difficulties and deliberations that face us. Going in the right direction of growth does not mean that everything will be OK and that we will only have successes, and indeed there may be future problems on the Lebanese border, but it does mean that the direction of growth is correct and it may even be the only one possible.

Part One

The question, Should we withdraw from Lebanon unilaterally? is worth examining with an understanding of emotional growth processes. There are two different ways of thinking that lead to opposite results: *war thinking* and *peace thinking*. War thinking is a kind of thinking nurtured by thoughts of threat. It is military thinking that opines that we should not withdraw without a signed agreement and a clear commitment from the other side to keep the border quiet. Such military thinking is reluctant to take risks, because it perceives both sides as fighting for their existence to the end, like two animals fighting each other. The feeling is that the enemy has only one goal, which is to destroy us. If we are convinced that this is true, and the enemy's main goal is to destroy us, than surely there is no point in helping him vanquish us by withdrawing. That kind of thinking attests to a very frightened emotional stance of someone who feels that only power speaks and there is no one to talk to. Our state was established and survived based on that way of thinking, because we were strong. That is the thinking that motivated us to try to eradicate terrorists in the Lebanon War by force. The logic was the same: "If someone rises to kill you, rise early and kill him first." That threatened emotional stance dominated human history and was personified by the various religions, kings, and totalitarian regimes. Throughout history, religions, for instance, stood for the absolute lack of compromise with each other. They tried to conquer each other and to impose themselves on people.

Yet changes do occur in the lives of individuals, in our life as a people and in Western culture in general. The growing child goes from the paranoid stage to the depressive stage. In the first stage he is threatened, sees the world as very militant, and is fighting a life-and-death war. In the later stage, the other is given the right to live, and a dialogue ensues. The world has developed too, and international relations are different today than they were in the past. In the past, when kings and religions reigned dictatorially, belligerent thinking was correct, because it guaranteed survival. Although even then, attempts at dialogue were always valuable. I would like to argue that even in the toughest situations there is some value in leaving open the possibility of connecting with the other, a germ of future emotional development and growth. We too have changed in the last seventeen years of our occupation of south Lebanon. The peace process moved forward and further agreements were signed with Jordan and the Palestinians.

Let us look into ourselves for a minute and examine the process we are going through. Who thought a few years ago that a unilateral withdrawal was possible? The prevailing strategy was to vanquish terrorism and defeat it by war. That militant view reached its peak in the Lebanon War and in the thought that we could conquer Lebanon, then make peace with this Arab country. And now we consider the possibility of being the ones who make the first concession as a gesture toward conciliation and peace. So what happened to us as a people? When I check myself, and my countertransference, as I do as a therapist, I discover that I had not considered a unilateral withdrawal before, but only the need to vanquish the terrorists by force. *What changed in me?* I think at one point I must have been afraid, and today I am less afraid. Indeed, we were all afraid of the terrorists in the past much more than we are today, and this is a change. The change has two sides. On the one hand, we learned that force did not work. We tried to defeat terrorism by force; we promised the public we would win this time, but the cheers of triumph slowly faded out. The other change was from a militant to a peaceful way of thinking, from military thinking to emotional, developmental thinking. The peace process moved forward on several fronts at the same time, and that is just the kind of combination that allows a child to grow and move from the paranoid to the depressive stage. The mother is strong and the child cannot overcome her, but he can talk to his mother and she can be understanding. In this way the child is less afraid.

Suddenly we realize that we actually have agreements with Hizbollah of which we have not been aware. It is no accident that we repressed those agreements from our consciousness. There was a seldom-violated agreement that they do not shoot our civilians and we do not shoot theirs. And suddenly the coin dropped, as the saying goes, and what once seemed bizarre to many of us, making agreements with an enemy who says they want to destroy Israel, became conceivable. We repress what does not fit our feeling, our anxiety that they want to destroy us. Then someone says they never even attempted to cross the border. Now it turns out Hizbollah has red lines of its own. It opposes our occupation of south Lebanon, but understands if it attacks the Galilee we will have no choice but to strike it and Lebanon hard. By signing an agreement with Hizbollah we admitted, although not completely consciously, that our presence in south Lebanon is problematic, that we recognize Hizbollah's wish to resist that occupation, and are prepared to pay the price of our dead soldiers without escalating the war. They may not have promised anything in exchange for our withdrawal, but their behavior till this day speaks louder than any promise. Then Nelson Mandela came to Israel and said that Iran wants peace with us. Again it sounds strange considering the many statements from Iran wishing for our destruction. Does that mean that even the cruelest enemy has different voices? Does it mean that Iran has more than one feeling, one desire, and one goal—destroying us? Or are they like any other people, and does even their uncompromising religious position have different shades? The voices from Iran are not uniform and change with time. But our hearing changes with time too, and today we are able to receive wavelengths we could not pick up in the past. This all means that we have an effect on what happens, and we ought to respond appropriately.

We all agree that we are in Lebanon temporarily and only for self-defense. So what does it mean on an emotional basis, that we are withdrawing unilaterally to the clear and agreed international border, that we do not want to occupy land that is not ours, but that we know how to defend ourselves from our territory? *The emotional message is of a distinct and clear separation.* It is the message of someone who knows what is his and what is not. When a parent gives that message to an aggressive child, the message will eventually sink in, even if the child initially declines to commit to anything. We also know that this child is not only aggressive; he is also very hurt and is suffering. That is how the Palestinian refugees and their descendants feel. A mature message of separation is not always answered positively, but we know that it bears fruit in the future, because such a message invites the other side, sooner or later, to take a more mature position. The clear separation of one side always encourages the clear separation of the other side. The merging and dependence of one side draws the other side to merge and to be dependent. Even in war there can be an emotional dependence on the enemy, like a child who is provoked and feels that he has to react instantly to every provocation. In the last years of our presence in Lebanon we said that we would react at the time and place of our choice, because we are independent and separate. And since we have been occupying south Lebanon for seventeen years, and have not tried to convey this mature message, but conveyed the opposite message—we will not withdraw as long as you continue the terrorism—it is time to try. Based on pure military considerations there is no reason to withdraw when our security is not guaranteed, and there is no reason to take a risk. But based on our understanding of emotional processes we know that only a separate and mature position on our part will encourage the other side to eventually take responsibility. The solution of the Lebanon problem has to come more from an understanding of the emotional dynamics than from military considerations. It is only a shame that the emotional aspects get lost in this case, as in our other problems here.

The analogy to parent-child relations is obvious. Because for all the pain the terrorists cause us, they do not really endanger our existence. When a child hits a parent, the parent is advised not to hit him back, but to hold the child's hands or to react in some other balanced way. In that way the parent conveys a message of restraint that filters first of all into the child' unconscious. When a child is very aggressive, it is important for the parent to be able to look ahead and understand that the child can change. When the parent sinks to the child's level, that is a problem. The parent's advantage is that he is not that threatened by the child and can think in peaceful terms. That is the whole difference.

I am aware of the difficulty of the comparison with the parent-child relationship. First of all, children do often want, consciously or unconsciously, to kill their parents. Second, this child is changing throughout the peace process. And finally, I am not saying that they should not be paid back for their actions, but that our reactions have to take place with an understanding of the emotional processes taking place here. Occupying some of their territory and not getting out until they promise to behave is like giving a child punishment in advance. It is not a reaction of ours to their aggression. We are actually saying, "We will take something of yours and give it back only if you promise to behave." But this child is not yet able to make promises, and neither side knows anymore what came first, the chicken or the egg. No parent would punish his child in advance. If we let go of the child's hands and he attacks us, we will respond forcefully and firmly. That way he will connect his actions with our reactions; otherwise we will always be seen as aggressive. Actually, the unfolding of events was like this: first the child was hurt when he felt we were taking away his home. Then he tried to kill us and was hurt again. But if we hold the child's hands all the time, or put him under permanent punishment, he does not have the necessary option and space to change his position. He has a reason to fight us all the time. True, when you let go of the child's hands you are taking a risk, but you also get a chance to find out that even when his hands are loose he is not trying to hurt you.

After holding their hands for so many years, we should try loosening our grip a little. In a state of total threat there is considerable value in preventive or preemptive strikes. But what might have been true for the past, in a state of pure military thinking, has to be reexamined in the state of peaceful thinking. It is no accident that the organization "Four Mothers," whose members are women, is leading this line. Women have a deep understanding of raising children and initiating contact when your partner is hurt. It is unfortunate there are not more women and women's thinking in politics, as I noted before, because if the peace process is a process of emotional growth, and I think it is, then where are the mothers?

Let us take a closer look at the emotional changes we have undergone during our stay in Lebanon. In the past we believed we could solve the Lebanon problem by force. Both right and left thought we could defeat terrorism by force, and particularly the terrorism in Lebanon. The Labor government's Litani Operation and the Likud's Peace of Galilee operation are examples of that way of thinking. We embarked on the Peace of Galilee War (the choice of name alone shows how hard it is for us to think of the other side) to defeat terrorism, to drive the Syrians out of Lebanon, and to make a peace agreement with Lebanon. Those were the three goals defined by Minister of Defense Ariel Sharon and Prime Minister Menachem Begin, and all three failed. In this case, the statement, "the Arabs understand nothing but force" was a projective statement that was primarily true about ourselves. We understand nothing but force and only after we suffered heavy losses from terrorism we realized, through the depressive emotional stance, that we had to make peace with Syria to solve the Lebanon problem or withdraw unilaterally. We understand nothing but force, as I have explained, because Arab force has made us recognize the Palestinians, view the Egyptian and Syrian demands as legitimate, and so on, like any paranoid person, who can take an honest look at himself and budge only when he hits a wall or an insurmountable obstacle. Indeed, we are in an emotional process of growth where different parts of our consciousness as a nation are brought up to our awareness and finally integrated. The Lebanon question touches upon another national repression, where we went through a process of bringing repressed material from the unconscious into the conscious. The unconscious in this case is the recognition of the limits of our force, our weakness, our "shudder," which brings with it the recognition of the other side. The cognitive error that we could defeat Lebanese terrorism by force, joins the cognitive errors or national repressions that led to the Intifada, the Yom Kippur War, and the general belief that we could defeat terrorism by force. The "shudder" I discussed in the chapter 2 is responsible for our difficulty in accepting the fact that it will not work by force, because without force we feel helpless, and we find that intolerable.

If we think back to our reactions from the beginning of the Lebanon War, after each traumatic event in Lebanon, like the death of a soldier, we would immediately launch a retaliatory attack. Our verbal and operational message at the time was to "react instantly." There was something soothing about that instant reaction. That is because after the death of a soldier it was very hard for us to contain our feelings and stay with them, with no reaction. When a person is under grave pressure there is a clear tendency to be pushed into action. Actions supposedly have a soothing effect that eases pressure. This is well known and we know how hard it is for a child who was hurt to restrain himself. In the clinic it is called "acting out," and it is an action directed outwardly, because the person cannot contain his feeling and consider his reaction.

In those days our prevailing wisdom was that this time we would teach them a lesson and put an end to terrorism once and for all. Slowly we started internalizing the change. Politicians and the public stopped believing those boasts, which were repeated endlessly, that this time we would put an end to terrorism; the reaction changed to, "We will react at the time and place we choose." Those were the first signs of an ability to separate and weigh our actions, which came from the depressive emotional stance that recognizes our powerlessness. We are no longer dependent upon the enemy and can make our own rules that suit us, rather than reacting automatically. We know that sometimes waiting for the punishment is worse than the punishment. How do the residents of Kiryat Shmona feel when they wait in their bomb shelters for missile attacks? But besides, the ability to delay one's reaction is a very important developmental achievement. It shows an ability to contain one's feelings rather than being motivated by them. The ability to restrain oneself has become more and more factual and politicians are no longer afraid to say that only a peace agreement will solve the problem. Public figures have not been afraid to restrain themselves and admit that there is no appropriate reaction except dialogue. Saying after one of our soldiers is killed that only a peace agreement will solve the problem is an impressive developmental achievement in its ability to contain feelings and show restraint, an achievement we all share as a people. Indeed, today we have arrived at a new thinking about a unilateral withdrawal.

The Gulf War was a good example of the power of restraint and of the fact that we do not always have to respond. Our lack of reaction prevented an escalation. It also projected a powerful message of restraint, separation, and wisdom.

The Hizbollah terrorists may not be ripe for peace yet, and they might continue attacking us. Then we will have to respond as we have to do when we are hit, forcefully. But there is no doubt that a unilateral withdrawal is a clear and brave invitation to a peace process where we take the first step, as Sadat did in 1977, without being sure he would receive a positive response from the other side. Our peace message will have its effect, if not immediately, then as cumulative evidence that Israel really wants peace. It would be an eminently valuable step emotionally and morally, both domestically, by showing our soldiers that we value their lives, and outwardly, by showing the Arabs and the world that we want peace. The historic reversal, by which the French foreign minister and Mandela are telling us not to withdraw without a peace accord, and that it would be foolish, while we are considering such a move seriously, is worth exploration. That reversal is not new, and for a time the international community, headed by the United States, has understood that we do not need to be pressured, because we want peace more than they do. For peace we are prepared to take risks they would not dare ask us to take. First of all, I believe a person and a state usually know better than others what is good for them, especially in a growing process of working through emotions, that can be followed and understood. Beyond that, this is a new message to the Arab world, that we can be empathetic toward them and understand their problems as well as any other country. We are not just the cruel enemy who exiled the Arabs from their land; we also feel their pain.

So if we do withdraw, it is important for us to understand why. That understanding will serve us during the rest of the peace process. It is true our main motive is the blood of our soldiers, but that does not detract from the fact that in this case there is also a hidden recognition that we are occupying land that is not ours and holding onto it for years. Hizbollah is confused by this step and is having a hard time welcoming it. Of course it is connected to the intense hatred its members feel for us and their difficulty in believing that we are taking a step based on trust and a desire to rely on them. But only with such freedom that we are offering them can they grow in the direction of taking more responsibility. Hizbollah attacks Israel because it was emotionally hurt by Zionism. Its feeling is that if it were not enough that we exiled many Palestinians from their homes, now we are occupying Lebanese soil. Our unilateral withdrawal will help them overcome their injury and see that we are not so terrible. If our withdrawal entices them to continue attacking us, then they really are not dialogue partners. It would prove that they really still want to destroy us and have not given up that wish. I do not think that is the case. It was the case in the past, but it is time to examine whether there has been a change. They might restrain themselves more following our withdrawal, and that will be another sign, along with the previous signs I enumerated, that there are dialogue partners for us in Hizbollah. We have to be like parents who encourage every little sign that indicates that the child is moving toward greater independence.

It is nothing to be ashamed of that we were chased out of Lebanon by Hizbollah. Similarly, the Palestinian state was created by the Intifada children. Their feeling that they beat us in Lebanon and caused us to withdraw is important to the Palestinians and to Hizbollah members whom we have injured. That feeling of victory can be translated in the future into peace. We know this from Sadat, who only after the Yom Kippur War, after the pride of the Egyptian people was restored, turned to the peace process. We know how important it is to the Palestinians to feel victory, pride, and independence, like anyone else. We also know that an adolescent who does not feel like a winner will not be able to reconcile later in life. It is important for us to give the Hizbollah fighters the respect they deserve for their struggle. Without their feeling that victory, there will be no peace. We must not give the Syrians such power over us that they become the ones to see to our well-being in south Lebanon. There may be no choice but to reach a temporary agreement with the powers that de facto rule Lebanon—Syria and Hizbollah. But the final goal I will discuss later has to be encouraging the growth processes of independence and separation of all the parties in the region: Lebanon, Syria, and Hizbollah. If not, we would be collaborating with a militant and exploitative pathology. From the viewpoint of understanding emotional processes, it would not be correct to ask the Syrians to do the work for us in Lebanon, and if they do, they will pay a heavy price. In the past we expected Jordan to do the work with the Palestinians and to control the West Bank. We expected Egypt to take patronage of the Gaza Strip and to put it in order. Today we are expecting the Syrians to straighten out Lebanon for us.

Hizbollah represents Iran, Islam, and the growing Iranian nuclear arms industry, and we have no choice but to reach an agreement with them. We must not close that option even if it presently looks fantastic. There is no reason, emotionally speaking, for such an agreement not to be signed in the future.

An Addition from the First Four Months of 2000

As therapists, we are trained to listen to strange, unusual, and dissonant sounds, and to try to clarify them with the patient. There are more than a few such sounds in the peace process with Syria and Lebanon, which demand us to apply clinical listening. We are about to withdraw unilaterally from Lebanon, and oddly and surprisingly, the Arab countries opposed such a withdrawal, at least initially. What does that mean?

Surely, some of them corrected themselves later and said, rightfully, that they could not possibly oppose the Israeli army's withdrawal from Arab land. But Hizbollah, for one, did everything it could so that the IDF would not withdraw from Lebanon. It declared that it could not promise anything and would not commit to a certain behavior after the withdrawal. Then it brought up demands on the refugee and Jerusalem issues; as far as it was concerned, the withdrawal would not promote peace. Syria acted similarly. At first, the Syrians were against a withdrawal and threatened that if the IDF withdrew from Lebanon unilaterally, they would see it as a declaration of war. The reason was that they did not want to lose their bargaining chip called "Lebanon." But they could not even conceal their pathology. Our withdrawal would be a declaration of war to them? It is hard not to notice what some people call "contrary think-ing" and I say that is the emotional pathology we see in sadomasochistic rela-tionships. How can we explain a statement, especially by the Lebanese govern-ment, that they will oppose our withdrawal from their land and our handing back of land everyone agrees is theirs? They are asking us to be involved, in fact participants, in their pathology. The same goes for the other Arab countries who opposed the withdrawal.

The Hizbollah actually told us in its own way that it prefers us to occupy Arab land where it can fight us. It said, "Come, attack me, occupy me, and then I will attack you back and fight you." That is what sadomasochistic personal-ities do. They can be in one of two positions, victim or aggressors, have a very hard time maintaining their separateness from others, and draw others into their internal conflicts. An experienced clinician can read that from Sheikh Nazrallah's serene smile when he speaks in belligerent and satisfied tones about the tactics his organization is planning to employ.

Simple logic says that every Arab should be glad that Israel is withdrawing from Arab land. But it turns out that an act of separation confuses the Arabs. Arab mentality calls for mixing with the other and a lack of separateness. The very structure of their families and governments contains elements of forceful invasiveness or warmth and intimacy, but both contain a quality of lack of sep-arateness and blurry personal boundaries. Obeying authority out of fear, both in the family and in the government, encourages dependence and a difficulty to formulate a separate identity. A look at the structure of the Arab clan shows how hard it is in such a social structure to rebel against authority and to form a separate identity as we have in our culture. It is no surprise then that the Arabs have a hard time understanding a step such as a unilateral withdrawal, which is based on a mature separateness with clear boundaries.

Getting back to Syria for a moment, the very thought that we can have quiet in Lebanon as a gift from them rather than seizing it by ourselves for our-selves, is a pathology of playing someone else's game and agreeing to their con-trol of Lebanon (the music would sound something like, "let me, I will take care of Lebanon, and you sit still"). The Syrians are saying, "We are the land-lords in Lebanon, and you cannot even do anything good in Lebanon without our permission. Since Lebanon is ours, you will treat Lebanon the way we tell you. And if we want you to continue occupying it, you have to do so." Un-doubtedly this reeks of exploitation and the militant pathology of a sadoma-sochistic relationship. It brings to mind certain societies where to this day the father decides whom his daughter will marry. Sometimes the father is paid money for his daughter. Syria is telling us, "You may not stop beating up Leba-non without our permission. To stop beating it up means breaking all the rules and violating your relationship with us." It is important for us not to assume the role of the partner in this severe pathology. It is a sadomasochistic relation-ship not only between Syria and Lebanon, where Syria uses Lebanon for its purposes and Lebanon accedes, but also between us and the Syrians, who invite us to a turbulent and militant relationship. "If you do not take the gift I am giving you," they say, "there will be war!" (We have to learn the music of that sadomasochistic relationship, where the caress and the blow are rolled into one.) Looking at it a little differently, it is like one child ordering his friend to hit another child, thereby rolling the victim and the aggressor into one in the mind of the friend, namely Israel. The sadomasochist personality knows no other kind of relationship, and has a tendency to draw everyone around it into the same kind of perpetual conflict. Therefore, mature separateness is the name of the game for us.

It is good that things developed in such a way that we are withdrawing from Lebanon unilaterally rather than having the Syrians guaranteeing our peace and security in Lebanon. That way we are not cooperating with the pathological assumption that Lebanon cannot stand on its own feet, and is like a mistress, whose quiet is bought for an agreement with the Syrians.

The defense pact between Lebanon and Syria is also pathological, in the sense that Lebanon asks Syria to make order in its territory, and thereby recognizes that without Syria's help it cannot stand on its own feet. We must not intervene in that pathology, at least not in the first stage, even though we are paying an indirect price for it, which is our inability to arrive at a separate and independent peace with Lebanon. We do need to say that we are hoping and waiting for the moment when Lebanon can stand on its own feet and be independent without the presence of Syria in its territory. But it would not be wise to try to take on the entire pathology all at once.

Sometimes our feeling in Lebanon is of a child sitting at a movie and having somebody hit him from behind. The child turns around and does not know who did it and whom he should blame. In Lebanon we are in a similar situation. The Syrians, the Lebanese with all their factions, and Hizbollah, are all mixed together there with no separateness, so who is the boss in Lebanon and who should we be negotiating with? The goal should be a sovereign Lebanon, but sometimes, when there is no choice and you cannot speak to the child, you have to talk to his parents, that is, Syria and Hizbollah. However, we should remember the final goal we are striving for, a peace agreement with Lebanon that Lebanon can keep. Hizbollah too uses Lebanon to fulfill its pathological needs, that is, the need for constant confrontation. Our demand for a peace agreement with Lebanon and Syria only on the condition that the latter withdraws from the former and only on the condition that Hizbollah leaves Lebanon, may be rational and correct, but is premature in terms of the developmental stage of each party in the pathology.

Before we do an exercise in therapeutic listening to a statement by A-Shara to illustrate Arab thinking with sadomasochistic traits, let us say a few more words about such relationships. We are no strangers to them. We noted the sadomasochistic traits of our relationship with God. When we say that we deserved all the disasters that happened to us, that they are a punishment from God, and that even if we do not understand why they happened we know we deserved them and God is always right, we are in such a relationship. A central theme in sadomasochist relations is that the strong party is always right, and the weak and hurt party is guilty. In other words, the victim brought the punishment upon himself and can only be angry at himself. An old joke illustrates the difficulty of untying the sadomasochistic knot, and how each side invites the other to provide their pathological input. The masochist says to the sadist, "Hit me." The sadist answers, "No!" We know those mutual invitations in the cases of battered children, who often ask their parents, in various ways, to hit them, and over the years become battering parents who adopt the complementary side of the pathology. That is because they do not know any other way of relating.

To reinforce the understanding of the sadomasochistic relationship to which we are invited, I will quote the pro-Syrian Lebanese daily *A-Safir*, which quoted A-Shara:

> Syria prefers the status quo rather than a faulty peace (said the Syrian foreign minister, raising doubts about a unilateral Israeli withdrawal from Lebanon). If Israel adopts the road of defeat, is it trying to draw the enemies of peace in Lebanon and other places to fight against it? And what shall we tell our children when they ask why we should negotiate over the Golan if we could fight and win as in Lebanon? (Therefore, A-Shara said,) Israel is going to leave Lebanon while inflicting heavy blows on it. Israeli agents might fire Katyusha rockets at the Galilee in order to provide Israel with the pretext.

For us to place Israeli agents in Lebanon to fire Katyusha rockets on the Galilee? Where did that come from? Does he think we are masochists?! Is he crazy? Clinical listening can provide the answer.

That passage has to be read several times in order to listen closely and to feel the emotional tone it represents. First of all, why does Syria prefer the status quo over a faulty peace? We know that every peace process is complex and inherently represents ambivalent feelings, and surely feels like a faulty peace, because we have to mourn what we wanted and did not get. So that in peace, as in any growth process, there are more than a few disappointments, and there is no perfect peace. The status quo in the case of Syria, on the other hand, is a condition of ongoing hostility. Syria, says A-Shara, prefers continuous hostility over the painful emotional process of peace. The Syrian foreign minister is saying something important that we know from ourselves, about how hard it is to endure the pain of a peace process, and how it sometimes seems as if a state of war gives you the feeling of more power and less vulnerability than peace.

"If Israel adopts the road of defeat, is it trying to draw the enemies of peace . . . to fight against it?" The opening "if" provides the attuned ear with the general sentiment of a logical exercise that is emotionally out of touch. Syria views a unilateral withdrawal as a defeat. Our weakness, says the foreign minister, invites them to attack us. So why are you inviting us to attack you, asks A-Shara? In other words, he says, we can only make peace with a strong Israel. That is because in our militant world you can only make peace between strong parties. Up to here there is no sadomasochistic invitation, but rather a description we should listen to, by the Syrian foreign minister, of their view of the emotional processes that cause war and peace (you could say our right understands that emotional dialogue better than the left).

Therefore, A-Shara goes on, "Israel is going to leave Lebanon while inflicting heavy blows on it. Israeli agents might fire Katyusha rockets at the Galilee in order to provide Israel with the pretext." Since you could not be choosing the road of defeat because of your weakness, this must all be nothing but a manipulative exercise aimed at allowing you to strike Lebanon even more forcefully. You will pretend you are being hit, you will even send agents to fire at your country, and then you will have a reason to strike Lebanon. Such thinking is the definition of the sadomasochistic relationship and its dynamics. One side pretends to be the victim for a short while, and assumes the role of the weak and beaten only to have a reason to hit the aggressor back twice as hard, only to go back to the position of the victim after the other side strikes back, and it starts all over again. That way, the apparent weakness of either side is nothing but a device to draw the other side to strike at it, and the aggression of either side is aimed at allowing the other side to strike the aggressor. The foreign minister attributes to us their pathological thinking and behavior, where the victim and the aggressor are an undistinguishable pair that collaborates. He is saying, "You are not withdrawing out of a desire for mature separateness and peace, but in order to draw us into a confrontation with you."

Therefore it is very important for us to know how to listen to these messages with trained clinical ears and to know what they are inviting us to do, and that is how we will know how to avoid falling into those traps. Besides, that way we will also know how to explain our position to the Arabs, because it is very hard for them to understand us and our intentions.

The Palestinian Refugees

Understanding the deep historic roots of the Israeli-Arab conflict is just as important as understanding a patient's past and how it effects him today. But just as in therapy, the patient is not always eager to pick through the wreckage of his traumatic past, and asks, "What's the point?" The therapist may try to explain the connection between the past and the present, because after all, nothing started today, and if we can understand how things developed in the patient's childhood, it will help us understand today's difficulties and overcome them. The painful discussion of your past is not a theoretical therapy exercise, the therapist will explain to the patient, nor is it done to establish guilt. Yet it is vital material for the understanding of your inner experience as it unfolds today. But this patient, Israel, has a hard time opening the painful wound that was created during his birth to clarify the emotional problem that started at the beginning of his life and has been with him since then—the problem of the Palestinian refugees. Our patient has been desperately trying to erase that chapter from his past since he was born. Yes, it is astonishing how some patients can erase their pasts, and when the therapist asks them to talk about their childhood, they begin with their military service, for some reason. Only in extensive therapy do the difficult experiences slowly emerge, and then the reason why they had to be so systematically suppressed becomes clear.

We may remember, or maybe not, how during our childhood we never got a full explanation of what happened here. The fact that the establishment of the state of Israel was based on the expulsion of hundreds of thousands of Palestinians and the appropriation of their lands and homes was repressed and denied fully and deeply in the history of modern Israel. It was not discussed either in school or in the media, and not by accident. Our guilt feelings reached levels that did not allow us to discuss the subject. It is like a child whose mother died in childbirth, or whose sibling was neglected because of his own birth. Naturally such a child, whose existence and life came at the expense of someone else's, will feel such heavy guilt feelings that he will try not to touch them. He will have to recognize the difficult truth that his very existence and life are acts of aggression against someone else. He was born as an aggressor who hurt someone else, and what can he do about it? And now the child who was thrown out of his house when the new child was born is shouting that the younger child has no right to exist. The jealousy of an older brother for a younger brother can be cruel and sometimes last a lifetime. The older brother is deeply hurt over being ousted from his central and important position and losing the exclusive attention he got. In our case, it is not a matter of parents giving more attention to the newborn, but of the older brother actually losing his home as a result of the younger brother's arrival in the family. These are not emotions that can be argued over, and there are no parents who could tell the older brother (although they had better not) that he is just imagining that they love the younger brother more. In this case the dispute is over bread. The older brother lost everything he had and was exiled to another country. Actually, this already happened to us once before, when Sara convinced Abraham to banish Hagar and Ishmael to the desert.

We need tremendous fortitude to discuss this issue. Our deep fear can pull us into depression, and then we will have to ask whether our lives are worthy. Do I have the right to live and choose my life, if it comes at the expense of someone else's life? It is those hard questions and feelings that account for our age-old repression of the question of the Palestinian refugees. The recognition that "there is room for all" is not true here. In our tragic case there is not room for all. At least not at first glance, at least not within the Green Line. Rightfully, we oppose the return of the refugees to their homes, because that would be our end.

The first-century sage Rabbi Akiva can help us on this matter. If two people are walking in the desert, he posed, and there is enough water only for one, does that one have to drink the water and let the other die? Rabbi Akiva's answer is yes. You cannot fault someone who wants to live and tell them that they should have chosen death. Nobody has the moral right to make such a claim.

The Jewish people do not have to apologize for their desire for an independent life and their own state. But neither do they have to deny the suffering it caused others. Therefore, we have to do everything possible to compensate the others. Of course we cannot give them a full compensation, because that would mean letting them come back to their homes, but a partial compensation is surely possible: adopting a moral position that recognizes our responsibility, expressed by helping the Palestinians establish their state, from a sympathetic emotional position, and by helping them economically as much as possible. We have to admit, as hard as it may be, that we owe them a lot, without saying that we can turn the wheels of history back and change it. Nor are we sorry about what happened, and if history could repeat itself, we would probably repeat the inevitable action of expelling hundreds of thousands of Palestinians so that we could have independence, because we are allowed to live a national life. But it is hard to recognize ourselves and another at the same time! How would we feel if someone else erased us for their independence because they had no choice? It takes a lot of emotional maturity to admit it, if at all. Therefore, we have to appreciate and understand the courage it takes the Arabs to recognize Israel. It is not easy for them.

The question should not only be why it took them such a long time to recognize us, but perhaps, how some of them recognized us so quickly and forgave us so easily. It is an important question because it allows us to understand them and to enter their shoes. If we ask that question we will be more objective about the peace process, and can see their side more clearly. We will see how they became poor refugees because of us, and have to accept the fact that we had no choice because we were fighting for our very existence. Therefore, the Arabs in general and the Palestinians in particular need to reach a level of emotional and developmental maturity where they recognize another's life as no less legitimate than theirs, and that is a developmental stage that requires tremendous maturity and a lack of egocentricity. We are asking a lot of them.

We have to deeply acknowledge our responsibility in regard to the refugee problem. It is a long emotional, therapeutic process of taking responsibility as a people. That is what happened to the Americans in relation to the Native Americans. It took many years for them to be able to openly discuss what they did to them, to be empathetic toward them, and to publish books that expressed their perspective of the tragedy that occurred. We have extenuating circumstances; we are fighting for our lives. That was not the case of the white man fighting the Native Americans. But it is important to keep in mind that the least relevant question in this case is, "Who is right?" The constructive question is, "Why is there so much suffering in this conflict, and how can it be changed?" I do not belittle the importance of the moral aspect, but in so many vital matters the question, "Who is right?" does not promote solutions. The question behind that question is, "Whose fault is it?" Looking for someone to blame, in many cases, does no good. In therapy, attempts to understand the patient's past and how it all started are sometimes blocked by the patient's reluctance to blame his parents or himself for his difficulties. And we tell him that his parents usually did their best, and there is no point in placing blame, as he was just a child born into that family, and that it is not his fault either, that we are just trying to understand what happened there. We see how hard it is to talk about years of suffering without asking who is right and who is to blame! In deep developmental-emotional processes it is important to understand rather than blame, because understanding moves you forward while blaming blocks you. Life is not just a court of law (in a relationship between partners too it is more important to understand each other than to determine who is right).

Therefore, a clear statement of our responsibility and part in the tragedy, even if we had no choice, is very important. Empathy to the suffering of the other, and a declaration of willingness to help them as best as we can, are the key to the deep historic conciliation. Whoever wants a hint to the value of gestures and declarations should recall the visit by Jordan's King Hussein in 1997 after seven Israeli girls were killed by a Jordanian soldier at Naharayim. That is why we love Hussein so much. He could not bring back the dead girls, but he displayed incredible humanity. That is how Benjamin Netanyahu acted when he expressed regret for the deaths of two Palestinians who were shot as a result of a misunderstanding at a roadblock when Israeli soldiers thought they were trying to run them over. Netanyahu expressed his regret for the tragedy, and such emotional expressions are the essence of the peace process.

Now we have an opportunity to peek into the Palestinian emotional experience in the face of our continuing to build settlements in the West Bank. For them it is a reconstruction and re-creation of past traumas, a continuation of their expulsion and banishment from their land. If what we are trying to do is seize as much land as possible to feel powerful, then we may just ignore the Palestinians' feelings. But if we understand that there are a few other things that are important to us as a people besides the size of our territory, then we should consider their feelings.

Every time the Arabs mention the right of return in the negotiations, we are astonished. Why are they mentioning this? Don't they understand that we are not about to commit suicide? We assume that whoever brings this up does not really want peace. Thus we leave them with the power to surprise us and to bring it up again and again, because we repress the matter and do not explore it deeply with ourselves. When I talk about national repression I do not mean that the subject comes up here and there. Lately the repression has loosened up a little. But it is only the beginning of a deep existential and moral discussion of the harsh fact nobody can blur, that as a result of Jewish settlement in the Land of Israel in the last hundred years, the Palestinians lost their lands and their homes.

The question is how we work through our aggression toward the Palestinians, which fills us with guilt feelings. Just as we say the veteran Ashkenazi public in Israel has a responsibility to discuss the traumatic integration of the Mizrahi Jews and to familiarize itself with their lifestyle and their experience, in order to develop understanding and identification, so we have a duty of learning and studying what happened to the Palestinians who ran away from here and where they went and what happened to their families. It is a journey back to our roots that we must take. That is because only by learning about the Palestinians who lived here, and by studying their lives and their fates, will we be able to work through our trauma over what we did to them out of our distress and lack of alternatives. Alongside that study, we have to give them and their problems attention and try to help them as best we can. It is a process of mourning, where we will have to gradually relinquish our pleasant experience of being righteous and pure, while seeing the others as absolutely evil. It is an emotional process of coming into contact with what we did to others. It is an eminently important emotional process, without which we will not have a real conciliation. We have work to do to counteract the tremendous emotional force that repressed what happened here for years. It is time for us to take the initiative for this educational process because it is mainly in our interest to work out this emotional matter for ourselves.

The transition from a threatened and hateful emotional stance toward the Palestinians to a caring and loving stance is the root of the matter. This can happen only if we stop repressing and start asking what happened here. Indeed, we were born in sin. Our school system has not dealt well with that difficult past, and out of fear of expressing political positions or asking painful questions, it does not permit the discussion of political matters. So where can our students find openness to other opinions and ideas? The curriculum has to have a central section about the emotional complexity of the peace process, because the peace process is primarily an emotional process. So perhaps a more sympathetic attitude toward the Palestinians by the Israeli bureaucracy or even a holiday gift for the Palestinian refugees and their families (just an idea, for better or for worse) are not inconceivable. Do such gestures mean that we recognize our responsibility for their suffering? The answer is yes. We were a party to this tragedy, and we recognize it. Does that mean that they are going to come back to their homes or receive compensations we cannot afford, and blackmail us? The answer of course is no.

American students today learn about Native Americans, and they publish moving books about their fate. Americans have reached a stage where they are not threatened, and therefore they can be empathetic to the suffering of the Native Americans. That is where we need to arrive sooner or later in our development as a people, and hopefully sooner rather than later (I know there are many differences between our story and the Americans', but I want to stress the ability to take responsibility for someone else's suffering, in which we had a part). We cannot underestimate the importance of our moral and emotional responsibility for the legitimacy of their pain in the peace process. Our commitment to help them build a state is an outgrowth of that responsibility. We will not allow them to apply terrorism, even though we caused them pain, but we will help them out of our responsibility for what happened, and it should be out of love. Because that loving feeling is what was lacking in the long years of hatred. The peace process needs love desperately.

But love does not mean concession. We may be afraid, even unconsciously, that if our guilt feelings come up we will not be able to be firm with this child. This often happens to parents whose guilt feelings prevent them from setting firm and clear boundaries for their children. And perhaps the Palestinians will interpret our guilt feelings as permission for them to carry out attacks and to demand whatever comes to their minds. How can we maintain our sanity and mental balance in the face of such a rough past, which motivates and navigates our thoughts and actions and often pushes us in undesirable directions? Indeed, the peace process needs psychotherapy urgently, as a child does who had a traumatic childhood, and it needs people who understand emotional processes to contribute to a process that is essentially emotional. Does empathy toward others, and taking moral responsibility for our part in what happened, necessarily lead us to make compromises on things upon which we must not compromise, such as our security? The answer is no. Because such concessions would hurt both them and us.

It is like a parent who has a disabled child. The parent feels guilty, naturally, and sorry for the child, and feels like relenting toward this child. A good parent will know where to relent and where not to. He will not compromise on the child's need to grow despite his disability. If guilt directs and determines his actions he will not be a good parent. It is hard for a parent who feels responsible for everything that happens to his child not to feel guilty in such a difficult case as a handicap, even if he has nothing to be guilty about. In the same way it is hard for us, who chose our life at the expense of the Palestinians' in this country, not to feel guilty, even if we should not. The good parent will not ask the child to get out of the wheelchair and start walking, or to reach a high cabinet he cannot reach, but he will set up a low cabinet so that the child can become independent. The handicapped child does not need to get discounts on his tests. What would be the point? But he should be given comfortable access and an appropriate place in the classroom. A good parent will not allow the handicapped child to pick on him or attack him with unbridled tantrums, because he is nobody's punching bag. But he will respect the child's desire for independence and push him in that direction. In the same way we must not acquiesce to terrorism, but we must help the Palestinians in every way to build their state. In simple words, we must not be thrown off by the guilt we feel, or be directed by the mercy we feel for this child. The child has to grow, there is no other way in the world. The truth is that this is the correct stance toward the growth of any child. The comparison I made with a handicapped child was meant to emphasize the guilt of the ordinary parent, which corresponds with the repressed guilt we feel. Our attitude toward the Palestinians has to be identical to the attitude of a parent toward his child, warm and loving, with the ability to set limits and impose order (I am aware of the resistance this comparison can arouse, but nonetheless, in a way we are the ones who can help them grow, and therefore this emotional dynamic is valid).

As happens in therapy, only after guilt feelings are brought up is their sting neutralized, and they can no longer move us in undesirable directions. Only then will we be able to help them more than we are doing today, wholeheartedly, in everything that can promote their independence and separation from us and help them overcome the trauma of their expulsion from their land and homes. Then we can also be firmer with them than we are today on things that do not promote peace but regression toward aggressive actions. Our guilt toward them hurts us in both directions. We dismiss them as a reverse reaction to our guilt and responsibility, while what would be correct from every aspect would be to help them grow. And we do not set firm limits to their aggression, again as a result of our guilt, while it is clear that we should not make concessions on that.

A Palestinian State

Here I will begin with a discussion of the problem of Jerusalem, which illustrates the religious nature of the conflict and the personality types that religion represents. After we are impressed with the emotional depth of the conflict I then present two different and complementary ways to deal with that difficulty. I will then stress how important it is not to jump straight to the end of the emotional process and the need to affix and anchor it in daily reality. The believers' need to eat is the best guarantee of sanity and the avoidance of being carried away by magnanimous dreams. I will then present the need for channeling the powerful impulsive-religious libido from hatred to love. In the last chapter, after we have mobilized sympathy for the emerging Palestinian state, I will discuss the emotional stance integrating left and right, which we should adopt.

Jerusalem

The problem of Jerusalem reminds us again that the peace process is essentially an emotional process, and needs to be treated as such and resolved with emotional-therapeutic tools. The difficulty in recognizing that Jerusalem can be the capital of two states is rooted in a deep religious insult, an insult identical in its intensity to the recognition of another god. In the 1996 elections candidate Shimon Peres was attacked and accused of intending to divide Jerusalem. Peres became defensive, apologized, and promised he would not divide Jerusalem, but to no avail. The right had touched upon the root of Jewish narcissism, released the genie from the bottle, and let it loose. That is not the only showcase to our souls, to see what really motivates us and how our political positions are unconsciously guided by primal drives and impulses. Jerusalem is often described as the nation's heart, and who could divide the heart?

Consider too the rumor that was once spread, that Peres's mother is an Arab. Or the settler who said on television that the soil is like a woman, who cannot be loyal to two husbands. We need no further proof to understand what really drives us and why we need psychotherapy. The conflict between us and the Arabs in general and the question of Jerusalem in particular translates into the deepest and most turbulent conflicts in emotional life: family loyalty, betrayal, incest, murder, and so on. A word like "betrayal" is used both for political situations and for family events, just as we talk about defiling Jerusalem and defiling a woman's honor. The motif of land as a woman is a deep and familiar motif that has already been mentioned, mother earth that is sowed and plowed. The people of Israel are often described in the Bible as a whore who is unfaithful to God. The understanding that spirituality, like our age-old longing for Jerusalem, is nothing but a sublimation of impulses, is evident in the Bible. In that book the primal impulsivity, laden with sex and aggression, is well packaged by a big authoritarian father who maintains order. Belief in god and his rules helps man not fall apart under the tremendous pressure of the drives and impulses that fill him. In our society it is obvious that the more impulsive public (religious and rightist) cares more about Jerusalem.

In the 1999 elections Barak was cautious of the storm of impulses many of us harbor, and promised to keep Jerusalem's unity. It may still be too early to touch those impulses of the Jewish people. There is a threat that any politician who thinks otherwise will lose public support, or in the worst case will be seen as a traitor who is dividing his family, selling his wife to others, and so on. The Likud knew that and used it against Peres, and Barak defended himself from such attacks as early as possible. In fact, both left and right say today and said in the past that Jerusalem will always remain united under Israeli sovereignty.

The involvement of religion in our conflict with the Palestinians is obvious. The uncompromising debate over Jerusalem and the difficulty of parting from the territories of Judea and Samaria are tightly connected to religious feelings. We are aware of the fact that it is no coincidence that most religious people will not compromise over territory in the West Bank and tend to vote for the right, and often for the extreme right. Previously we noted that there is no significant difference between the national religious and the non-national religious on this matter. The same religious feelings, and particularly the religious personality, motivate them all, and therefore it is hard for them to recognize the existence of another. That is the fundamental, historic nature of religion (except for more progressive religious people, who are, unfortunately, few), which is impulsive, primal, and primitive. According to religious feelings that have no boundaries, and such is god, there can be no compromise over the Greater Israel, which is an experience of wholeness and purity. That is the nature of absolute religious messages.

The borders of reality and democracy are completely erased for the benefit of the religious experience. A peek into the religious soul is very important because it can help us understand the difficulty we all have in the tiresome journey from religion to state. Religion is at the root of all absence of compromise in our world, the authoritarian father who is the only one who is right and who decides everything, whom we created to satisfy our emotional needs. Of course it is not the religion but its believers who created it and observe it. This creation tells us what its believers need so desperately, and how hard it is for them to accept the modern world in the last centuries, a world of relative thinking, both in science and in the arts, a world of recognizing the other and especially of less projection and more separateness. The infantile-religious stance leaves its believers dependent, like a small child with omnipotent wishes, upon parents who need to protect him against acting as if everything were possible. The haredi public, who do not go to the army or make a living, are dependent upon us. The settlers are dependent upon us and upon our stopping them. What would happen if we did not stop them? If we were all settlers? The same thing that happens to a child who does not have parents to take care of him—we would all die. That is what happens to anyone who lives in an imaginary world that is detached from reality. In the clinic it is called "paranoid-grandiose psychosis," and if we do not take care of the patient, he will come to a bad end.

When I argue that the conflict is fundamentally religious I mean that it is driven by the paranoid-grandiose personality structures religion has represented so well throughout history. The personality profile of the person who argues against returning territories for security reasons is identical to the personality profile of the person who uses religious arguments. Neither are driven by logical arguments—even though the security argument is presented as if it were—but by impulsivity. The evidence is the question of Jerusalem, which is not a security matter, but purely an emotional one. Therefore, when I say that the conflict is basically religious, I am referring to the impulsive-driven nature of the conflict, which includes people who may not define themselves as religious, but whose extreme positions have clear religious personality traits.

But since we are aware of the tremendous forces of the religious personality structure, and we are still far from the separation of religion and state that will weaken the power of religion, on both sides, we must deal with religion from two opposite but complementary directions, which I will detail in chapters 5 and 6. In chapter 5 I will show that there has to be an anchor of sanity in daily reality, as if to say, peace grows from the bottom up. That is because believers on both sides need to eat and feed their families. In chapter 6, about solving the child's first masculine conflict, I will discuss the possibility of channeling the religious libido from hatred to love.

Peace Grows from the Ground Up

Barak is wrong in rushing into a permanent settlement with the Palestinians. That is because these are growth processes that take time and cannot be rushed. Our conflict with the Palestinians is different from our conflicts with the neighboring Arab countries because the former is a fight between family members living in the same house, and the latter is a fight with more distant relatives who do not live in the same house or see each other every day. A fight inside the immediate family, with parents, partners, brothers, and sisters always stirs up strong emotions, because it touches our deepest conflicts. We and the Palestinians are like impulsive children, but under a grown guise, who need a clear daily routine to keep them safe. The child does not know what time it is, when we eat lunch, or when and how his clothes will come back from the laundry. The child clings to the details and facts of daily life, the details of the here and now, the routines vital to his survival that his parents set out for him in order to counterbalance the driven, chaotic inner world in which he lives.

Therefore, in our conflict with the Palestinians, which is fundamentally a religious conflict, in its contents and in the force of its emotional import, we must first of all establish anchors of sanity in reality. Peace, as with children, grows from the bottom up, from the concrete activities of each moment, which are often stronger than any drives. We call those forces the "ego forces," the forces that relate to reality, restrain drives, and are vital for survival. A parent who sees to the family's livelihood is connected to reality. On the other hand, the religious forces are disconnected from reality and express a world of primal instincts. The Palestinians, like us, need to undergo long and difficult processes of separating religion and state. Their various religious streams are even stronger than ours. Their religion also reflects an impulsive, primitive world that drags its believers into regressions in the name of god. We are much like them in terms of those internal structures, except for the fact that we have a large public that is developed. There is no doubt that we must help them build as developed a state as possible. A thriving Palestinian state is our best guarantee of peace.

It has often been said that bitterness and frustration are the fathers of terrorism. Peace can only be made with someone who has something to lose. People who have nothing to lose tend to commit suicide in the name of god and to unleash their hate and rage upon those they deem guilty. We have to start from the bottom and slowly anchor sanity in the fragile reality and simply wish the

Palestinians well. I am saying nothing new when I say that what is good for them is good for us. The economic development Peres speaks of is an anchor against religion. All our adult lives are based on the ego forces joining reality and clinging to it against the chaotic and impulsive world. We are familiar with the people who do not work, do not do army service, and just study the Torah. For them the Torah represents a spiritual world, but we understand that they actually live in an impulsive world of passions, without realistic boundaries, which places religious restrictions on itself for balance. Undoubtedly, if those ultra-Orthodox people worked and were more connected to reality, their political views would soften accordingly. When we talk about the extremists on both sides who harm the peace process, we are talking about religion. Indeed, religion and everything it represents, absolute justice, absolute truth, and absolute narcissism, there is only place for my god and so on, is the main obstacle to peace in the Middle East.

Barak's leap to the end of the road, namely, the final status agreement, comes from a lack of understanding of the depth and extent of the problem. When partners get married they do not leap to the question, "Will it be like this forever?" because it is very frightening and threatening. They build a relationship in the "here and now," from the details of daily life, and avoid generalizations till life's end. You can move from the particular to the general. That is how a child grows, by trying many things before he grows up. In the case of the peace agreements, we could begin with the safe passage from Gaza to the West Bank, for instance, or the Gaza seaport, and change the economic situation, make warm confidence-building statements, and stop the settlements, which re-create and revive the trauma of the Palestinian past of exile from their homes and the loss of their land.

The Palestinians, for their part, cannot speak about peace and holy war in one breath. Their textbooks cannot incite and encourage war. They have to take full responsibility for stopping terrorism, and not remain indifferent when there is Palestinian violence. Those behaviors show how divided the Palestinians are in this peace process, and we have to help them firmly to integrate those different parts of themselves. For the child to reach integration it is important first to anchor him in sane reality, against all the impulses that flood him. Ignoring those belligerent declarations means accepting their emotional fragmentation and not demanding that they grow toward peace.

Surely we cannot decide now where the border will go, because each side's inner conflicts are so big that it is impossible to define the border. The principle of separateness says that for us to agree among ourselves where our border should be, there has to be a minimal level of inner integration between the forces working inside our country. It is true both for us and for the Palestinians. It can be expressed in another way: Our immaturity because of our inner rifts makes us dependent parents who encourage the dependency of their children. A mature and separate parent encourages his child to maturity and separateness.

Our difficulty in letting the Palestinians grow and build their independent and separate state is obvious. Our emotional condition as a nation does not allow us to help another nation grow. Religion, which divides the world into clear and uncompromising good and evil, represents the fragmenting and extreme forces on both sides. The state poses an alternative to religion on both sides. The region's transition on the political level from religion to state or on the emotional level from impulses to recognizing the other, is the real task. But it will be a long time coming. Meanwhile, peace as a growth process has to come from the bottom.

Positive experiences and successes have a tremendous value in the growth process. Therefore, we have to begin with what works, just as in an exam you should start with the questions you know instead of wearing yourself out first with the hard ones. If we build our relations with the Palestinians correctly and gradually, we can reach a warmer and more sympathetic atmosphere later and it will be easier later to agree on the border. Is the most urgent thing for us now to draw a border or to develop good relations with the Palestinian state and help it get built? A first-grader cannot imagine himself in the eighth grade. The truth is that where the border runs is not the most important thing in the world, but what relations we will have with our neighbors is. We and the Palestinians are like two small children playing an associative game, which is a game that does not have agreed rules. You cannot plunge them into games and rules of the latency age. In the oedipal stage, before latency, play is more associative, impulsive, and devoid of boundaries. During play each child talks to himself more than to the other child. The children do not play with each other, but parallel to each other. That is how we and the Palestinians are today. Each religious position talks to itself about itself, and what does it care about other religions? That is egocentricity personified. People need to understand that we cannot solve everything now and that some things have to be left open for the future, and that we should trust our children and leave them some of the work. Why not? People need to understand that that peace is a process and not try to jump to the end because of their impatience. That is why it is too early to speak about the fate of the settlements, for instance. Those issues should be left for the distant future and be incorporated deeply into the network of relationships that are created in the region. Then everything will be simpler and more appropriate than trying to decide these things prematurely.

How the Child Resolves His First Masculine Conflict

At the end of the oedipal stage, the son does not attack his father or take his wife away from him. He bonds with him through identification, love, and male brotherhood. The son longs for his father, wants a relationship with him, wants to be like him. The feelings for the father have a very important role in this male brotherhood, which we know well from friendships between males, such as in the army. The peace between father and son is the peace of the brave or the heroes. That is why Arafat's term, that Barak sometimes uses in regard to our relations with the Palestinians, is so true. This peace requires courage because you have to join the father you were going against, and not be so afraid of him. This peace requires courage for another reason; the child has to give up something he thinks he cannot relinquish, the desire for his mother to be his partner. In the homosexual pathology it does not happen, because the father remains frightening and threatening and cannot be joined. In the clinic you see the tears of love pour out, and realize how desperately the child misses the father who rejects him.

The same is true in the case of girls, who have romantic fantasies of marrying their fathers in the oedipal stage (kindergarten age), and gradually identify with their mothers by realizing that that is how they can obtain someone like their fathers when they grow up. Those romantic fantasies are repressed during the school age, and bringing them up or remembering them usually makes the girl feel shame. So that the girl too goes through a deep unconscious process of moving from rivalry and hatred toward her mother to the desire to identify with her and be close to her. So girls too know the reversal we are discussing, but in this section I will stress the boy's developmental process, because it better represents the necessary transition from the powerful murderous drives (the boy's oedipal stage is like our relations with the Palestinians) to brotherhood and peace.

When one of our national leaders announces with tears and emotion that an Arab child is like a Jewish child and that there is no difference between them, it must not come from an indifferent leftist stance that recognizes human rights, but from deep emotional identifications that the public can identify with. It has to come from the ability to turn hatred into love, just as the child turns his first war into the victory of brotherhood and love. That is how the child settles his first war against his father. We too need a tool of masculine identification to solve this problem. The Palestinians would accept this approach with love. True, they hate us now and have good reasons, but the real change in the course of history can happen only from a different emotional stance, a loving stance. How can it be done? We can learn from the child. We have each gone through it already with our fathers. We changed the threat and war into love and identification. The Palestinians need us very much, and if we present a loving emotional stance we can change history. An Israeli national leader has to settle the Israeli-Arab conflict with love, through emotional statements that convey a message of partnership, togetherness, male brotherhood, and the peace of the brave. We need to feel tears choking our throats when we say, "an Arab child is like a Jewish child," or, "we must protect the rights and honor of the Palestinian workers who work for us," or "Israeli Arabs should have full equal rights." Because it is those tears of identification and understanding that turn war into intimacy and love. Without those tears there can be no emotional bond, as any child knows. We and the Palestinians really are brothers living on the same soil with a common fate, with a joint history. We both know what it means to be homeless refugees, and are both trying to build our homes, although some of us are at a more advanced stage than others. We can understand them better than anyone else, because we have been and partly still are there. We are like two adolescents, or like a father and a son who resemble each other and understand each other, except that one is older and has gone through more than the other. So why not use our own experience of male bonding; why not use our psychological know-how; why not use our emotion to understand the essence of this emotional process called "peace"? The fundamental quality of the process has to change from a business negotiation over bits and pieces of land, to an understanding of the emotional dimension of the need of two brothers to live together in this land. Just as friends call each other "brother," which is also what Arafat called Peres, the solution has to be through mutual identification, mutual concern, love to the point of tears, and a desire for closeness. The question is whether we understand the emotional logic of the process, a logic that requires a heartfelt emotional statement of our historic commitment to help the Palestinian people live in dignity.

Great statesmen brought great emotion into their leadership. Deep conflicts, as we all know, are settled on the emotional level more than on the rational, cognitive level. Therefore, we have to be attuned and open to emotional peace with the Arabs. This conflict cannot be resolved by any agreement if it does not have emotional depth. The family model I have adopted throughout this book points to such an emotional stance. Relations inside the family are primarily emotional relations. That is how they should be seen, dealt with, and resolved. The Palestinians and Israelis have the same problem. We are both homeless refugees who want independence and peace. Sometimes you can see us as brothers with similar issues. Sometimes we are the parents and they are the children. Those feelings come up when we behave like adults who already achieved the independence the Palestinians want so desperately. Whichever model we use, male bonding and the peace of the brave are the correct emotional solution.

The child needs to mobilize great strengths to turn hatred and war into love. He has no choice because there is going to be some emotion between him and his father. The child can love his father or hate him, be for him or against him, but he cannot be indifferent toward such an important figure in his life. And if the child says that he is indifferent to his father, this must come from pain. Similarly, there has to be emotion between us and the Palestinians. It would be hard to imagine indifference or a lack of emotional involvement or a lack of caring between two brothers who live in the same land. In this case there are cold and alienated feelings that show emotional distance. That is the model of the cold peace with Egypt, which is possible because we have a clear border between us and physical distance. But two brothers living in the same house, the Palestinians and us, intermingling, with Israeli Arabs within the Green Line and Jewish settlers in the West Bank and Gaza, in such physical and emotional proximity, in cold peace, are in a state of war. If there is going to be emotion, it should be love rather than hate and war. Because in a family, just as between us and the Palestinians, there cannot be an emotional vacuum. That is the essence of the difference in our relationship with the Arab countries and in our relationship with the Palestinians. It is like the difference in relations with a distant relative and relations with an immediate family member, such as a brother, a parent, or a child. The deep emotional dependence between us and the Palestinians, as opposed to our ties with the other Arab countries, arouse powerful feelings. We can choose which ones.

We need a national leader to show us the way. The public should be able to identify with such a leader and with his emotional solution that people understand from personal experience. It will surely be easier for the right to turn enemy into friend, because the right is more emotional. It is interesting that the phrase "peace of the brave," which is the emotional resolution of our conflict with the Palestinians, was coined by Arafat. He was also the one who called Peres "my brother." Indeed, the Palestinians are closer than we are to their emotions. Therefore, they are able to sum up the complex problem between us in one simple, emotional statement, taken from such a primary model, the family.

Any Israeli national leader who declares that a Palestinian child is like a Jewish child, who speaks passionately about equal rights for Israeli Arabs, and who calls for giving respect and social benefits to the Palestinians who work for us, would find openness on the other side. That is because there is an oedipal constellation between us. They are very eager to identify with us because we are the ones who can really help them. Just as in relations between brothers or parents and children there are past wrongs and the possibility to forgive and move on. The question is whether we can create a corrective experience through mutual identification, mutual crying on each other's shoulders. The question is whether we can encourage the process of male bonding between us and them.

If we translate the child's developmental dilemma to the political arena, we will understand that we need a dramatic religious conciliation between Judaism and Islam, a conciliation that turns separate insults into a joint victory, which rechannels the divisive passions (Jerusalem is only ours) into a unifying direction (Jerusalem is the symbol of peace). Such processes of identification can have an incredibly positive effect on the peace process. The most important part of this transition from hatred to love is that fear disappears and concern and affection for the other side remain. The child replaces his fear of the father with an experience of intimacy and togetherness. The child is no longer afraid for his existence. Peace also needs symbols, as does war, and Jerusalem offers us the opportunity of turning the most problematic place in the conflict into a symbol of peace.

It is like a child who disrupts class to get attention. We try to help him, to channel his wish for attention and recognition to constructive directions. We know it is too early for him to understand what motivates him, and relax. We also understand that as long as there is no separation of church and state on either side, as long as the tremendous religious passions rage, which they will for a long time to come, we cannot fight them, but should use them by rechanneling them to desirable goals. Therefore, our options, like the child's, are love or hate, and at this point there are no other choices (e.g., empathy, which is a partial identification with the ability to keep a distance).

Jerusalem is the Jewish people's narcissistic wound. It is the essence of the statement, "my god is greater than anyone else's god." But just as a growing child turns his weaknesses into advantages and power, just as we all can use life's wreckage to open a new chapter, just as a patient turns his vulnerability in the course of therapy into sensitivity and power, and just as a child turns his war with his father to a warm peace with him, so Jerusalem can lead to a deep historic conciliation of peace.

With the same emotional force we feel toward Jerusalem when we say, "a united Jerusalem under Israeli sovereignty forever," let us say, "Jerusalem the capital of peace," "the symbol of peace for Jews and Moslems," "the symbol of world brotherhood," and so on. We have to help the public translate its deep hurt and insult into an emotional investment in the constructive direction of peace. Powerful feelings such as "a united Jerusalem under Israeli sovereignty forever" cannot be stifled; they need a different emotional channel. Therefore, the religious conciliation has to be dramatic. It cannot be a romantic peace. That is why we need a dramatic leader to call for the historic conciliation of the two religions.

I am talking about a child's growth process, where he has a framework that holds him together, just as peace grows from the bottom up, in addition to the identification processes that let him channel his emotion in the right direction. Indeed, the socialization of impulses is not easy. It requires a framework and boundaries of reality while channeling the impulses in the right direction. Therefore, we must change our fundamental attitude toward the Palestinians, and go from a state of hostility and hatred to a state of warm and supportive parental responsibility toward their future and their fate. We have to take a leap, but we have the emotional strength to take that turn. The language of the Middle East is dramatic and passionate. Our relations with all of our neighbors are based on that impulsivity: the peace between Begin and Sadat was a dramatic peace, in keeping with the personalities of the two leaders; the warm peace with Jordan's King Hussein (an extroverted warmth is impassioned, as are hatred and war); the exchange of complements between Syria's Assad and Barak, with Barak calling Assad "a strong leader," and Assad saying Barak is trustworthy; the cold peace with Egypt's Hosni Mubarak, who often addresses us with insults and anger ("If the Jews ate broad beans they would be smarter,"

"Netanyahu hurt the Egyptian legal system," etc.); and lastly, Arafat's "peace of the brave." We see that every step toward peace in the Middle East, like every step toward war, uses the language of passion and drama. This is not Europe, a world of repressed impulses. Here we wear our hearts on our sleeves.

As I will detail in the next section, an Israeli national leader has to be a dramatic leader. That is because we have a large public that speaks that language, and has to be helped in order to channel its powerful emotions in the right direction. The contents have to be romantic, but the rhetoric has to be dramatic. That is because the left listens more to the contents while the right notices the style. So we need to lead a line of conciliation outwardly and inwardly, between left and right, but passionately. We need to do this until we are able to speak in a less primal and impulsive language. The spirit or style or externalized emotion need to be dramatic, while the content or the goal are romantic. In that respect all of the nations in the area are alike, including us.

Religious people on both sides need to be helped so that they can translate religion and all of its values into terms of peace and conciliation. It is also the only way to reach peace, or at least to alleviate the tension with extreme Islamic countries. An address in dramatic language, which gives respect and space for Islam and recognizes its importance, is absolutely necessary. How would we Jews feel if an Arab leader honored our religion, quoted from it, and relied on it! What pride would we feel and what love would we grant that Arab leader! What if that Arab leader expressed his opinion as to the special qualities Judaism has given the world. What would we feel toward him? It is hard to describe. Therefore, with the same libidinal energy with which we cry, "a united Jerusalem as the eternal capital of Israel," thereby hurting Palestinian feelings, we could declare, "Jerusalem the capital of peace forever," and thereby respect Islam and the Palestinians. When the motivating force is love, suddenly we cease to understand how afraid we once were for our survival, and how preoccupied we were with the question of whether they do or do not have a parliament in east Jerusalem. That is because our whole way of thinking changes. That is what I aim for, a deep change in our way of thinking.

The problem is difficult because there is no deeper insult to one religion than recognizing the existence of the other. Religions have not compromised with each other in human history. God is by definition one and mine, and there is no compromise on that. There is nothing as total as religion, which allows, by definition, only a fight to the death with other religions. One God has never been tolerant of other gods. But maybe at the start of the twenty-first century it is time to promote the idea that the two main religions of the Middle East can live here together. Because if you think about real conciliation, you cannot circumvent the religious feelings involved in the conflict, and you have to think in religious terms and speak that language, which is the language of the Middle East. A dramatic call for conciliation between Judaism and Islam can be promoted by a religious dialogue, where the subject is not politics but rather that each religion will introduce itself, its faith, and its attitude toward strangers that live among it. It would be an introductory meeting. The psychological effect can be incredibly powerful, because the passions involved invite love and not just hate. A call for a meeting between the Ayatollahs and the rabbis would change our whole way of thinking, and plant a seed that would bear fruit in the future. Therefore, it is very important to encourage the clergy to take part in the peace process. They should be encouraged to take responsibility, rather than leaving them out as an extremist minority. We know how children change when they take responsibility and become parents. We also know it from some of our own leaders who moved from the opposition to the coalition and took responsibility for the country, and we see how that responsibility makes them more moderate. Therefore it is important to include the religious perspective in the peace talks and for religious people to participate in the process and to take responsibility for it. It would mean a lot to the public on both sides, for people who may not be extremely religious, but who care a lot about their religion.

In the religious-emotional stance we are in today it is no wonder that we feel every concession means conceding all, and we are seized with anxiety. If partners treated each other that way they would not live in peace. Such black-and-white thinking—we either give back everything or nothing—requires a long process of therapy so that the patient can define what matters to him more and what less and what are the things on which he can compromise. In other words, the patient has to discover his truth, and we have to discover our truth. *Beyond the sea of our anxieties there is truth.* This truth will become clearer and more accessible to us out of an emotional stance of identification and love for the Palestinians. As soon as we are not so threatened, things will suddenly clear up. We know this well from a child's growth process. When the child is not threatened it is hard for him to remember what he was so unsure about. He is in another state of consciousness and is no longer afraid. Partners can surely understand from their experience how frames of reference and ways of thinking change when the relationship shifts from war to love, and how the same reality and the same facts can be perceived completely differently.

In therapy we know the problem often is not technical, and it is no accident that the patient cannot see possible technical solutions. That is because his emotional stance limits his thinking and does not allow him to consider other possibilities. We have trouble deconstructing the word *sovereignty* and discovering that it has many elements that are of no importance to us anymore, for instance, controlling the Palestinian population of east Jerusalem regarding education, health, welfare, and so on. So what is left of the slogan, A United Jerusalem Under Our Sovereignty?" It's mainly a feeling, which really is hard to divide. Perhaps we can avoid dividing the city, but manage it jointly, viewing it as a mixed city with Jewish and Arab residents. And what about two mayors working together? Is an Arab parliament in the east side of the city an emotional insult, or perhaps a symbol of coexistence and peace? It is not hard to find technical solutions that respect both sides when emotional attitudes allow it. Perhaps there is room for a council of Jewish, Christian, and Moslem religious figures, who would sign a commitment to peaceful coexistence, and try to find solutions to the city's religious problems. Such cooperation, including a religious declaration of conciliation between the faiths, can have an incredible emotional impact. After all, two parliaments in the same city would be symbols of real peace. Jerusalem has to be a symbol of our changed thinking, like the reversal children undergo in their growth process. Then it would be clear that there is room for two.

So that we do not repeat the mistake of the Intifada, we have to remember that the Palestinians are stronger than we are and much more motivated to fight for their capital, Jerusalem. That is because our motive for keeping Jerusalem under our control is a narcissistic motive, while they have yet to realize their desire for a capital. We are fighting out of fear that what we have will be taken away from us. They are really fighting for their lives and for their independence. Therefore, as in the Intifada, as in an adolescent's rebellion, they are stronger and their cause more just than ours, because they have nothing. We had better recognize that as soon as possible. Would we give up our capital? It may sound banal in its simplicity, but the message is profound. Jerusalem is the biggest stumbling block in the peace process, because it really touches our deepest emotional recesses. And herein lies the singular opportunity to turn the war into peace.

We should notice the direction of the process. Once we thought that giving up the Sinai endangered our security. We thought that a Palestinian state was an existential threat. We thought that a withdrawal from the Golan Heights was inconceivable. Once nobody thought we could withdraw unilaterally from Lebanon. All those were narcissistic injuries we learned to live with, as a child learns to recognize the existence of the other, in a long and painful process. It is not a process of endless erosion, as some among us fear. It is a process of seeking our inner truth, what we can give up and what we cannot, and how we live with the other. But identifying with them out of love means extracting ourselves from our current state of reacting to a reality imposed upon us by them, and shifting into a situation where we lead the process. Until now we have been led, and it is time we lead the process. We can also enjoy the process of allowing the Palestinians to grow alongside us. Today it sounds absurd. But yes, we can enjoy our relationship with them, and not just squeeze our eyes shut in fear and pray to God that they stay weak. Instead of being the kind of parents who let their children grow and identify with them, we are parents who are afraid their children will grow up and threaten them.

An Israeli leader who declares how much he appreciates Arafat for his steadfast struggle over the years for Palestinian rights will be highly esteemed by them, and will be in a position to promote the peace process. What esteem we would feel for a leader of theirs who praised a leader of ours, or made statements to the effect that he understood our existential fears. Such an Israeli leader could talk about the fact that we too employed terrorism in our struggle for independence. He could say that we are not asking who is more right, but asking how the suffering we are all living in can be eased. Our leader could speak to the Palestinians as equals about our common tragedy as two peoples living on this soil. He could admit that we recognize that we exiled Palestinians from their land and homes and caused them much suffering. But we want to live too, and we will not give up our lives or apologize for them. Therefore we cannot let the refugees return to their homes, but compensating them with money is certainly a possibility. Our leader will say that we have a moral responsibility for the fate of the refugees and an honest desire to help them as much as we can. Yet, we will not put up with any terrorism. Such an emotional statement, which comes from identification and love, which contains the whole emotional logic of natural processes of growth and development, can change the picture in the Middle East. And I have not said anything new here, except that such a statement can only come from someone who is no longer defensive.

The day will come when church and state are separated, and then religion will weaken and those primal impulses will be repressed. When we reach that emotional place, each side can be empathetic to the other. Empathy is a later stage in a child's development, and he cannot get there right away. The child has first to experience the two poles of love and hate, and distance and identification, before he can find a place that is not too far and not too close, before he can partly identify with the other and understand what he is saying without entering his shoes. He has to believe there is room for two. That is a developmental stage that European states are at.

But as long as church and state have *not* been separated and religion is still strong, we have to work both from the bottom, by changing reality, as I described, and from the top, with the dramatic language of the Middle East, like parents who place limits and boundaries upon the child, but who can still identify with him and with his needs in a warm and constructive way. The parent's caring and concern for the child are a necessary but insufficient condition for the child's positive growth. The parent should know how to treat the child, and how to combine the parent's wish for the child to have a good future with the need to set clear limits. That is where we are in relation to the Palestinians, and what the next section is about.

Integration of the Political Left and Right

The optimal Israeli leader would be someone who can solve the nation's problem of split identity between left and right, and unite them under one complex identity. I will now discuss the necessary integrative position between left and right regarding a Palestinian state. I will begin with a detailed explanation about personality development.

The condensation of the emotional stances of left and right into one entity is a significant developmental-emotional achievement in a child's growth process, as it is in the development of a nation. In the previous chapters we discussed the developmental aspects of voters for the left and the right, the difference in their emotional attitudes, and their different languages. Indeed, we as a nation are deeply divided between left and right, and each camp represents different developmental aspects of the soul. The left represents the yearning for peace, the longing for a bond that in its extreme form is embodied in the romantic image of a calm, new Middle East, and a brotherhood of nations. Therefore the left represses and denies the existence of aggression and ignores it. That attitude is resembles the depressive experience, where aggression is directed at oneself. In the new Middle East, in that paradise, as I noted, there is no aggression. The right represents security, the militant position that believes in struggle and standing our ground, the clear separateness between ourselves, the good guys, and the Arabs, the bad guys, which in its extreme form is the paranoid position. Therefore the right emphasizes the experience of aggression coming from the outside and feels it is as pure and innocent as a newborn baby. These are two complementary developmental aspects of the growth process of a child or a nation. One is represented by the yearning for peace, the other by the emphasis on security.

A child whose parents give him a lot of empathy, warmth, and love, but little by way of clear limits and firmness in the growth process, will have problems. Perhaps the parents do not set limits because they are afraid of their own aggression and feel guilty when they are firm. We know children need clear limits in order to feel safe. A child who does not come against parental firmness in the right places will be restless and unable to calm himself. The child feels guilty because his parents are "good," permit him everything, while he is the bad one who runs wild and does things he is not allowed. Therefore, the absence of parental firmness leaves the child feeling that he is bad and his parents are very good. The child does not understand that his parents are simply weak, and therefore he casts himself as bad and feels guilty. The child who does not have limits may impose upon himself harsher and stricter restraints than his parents, in an attempt to protect himself. The parents conveyed weakness to the child, and told him in their own way that they do not believe he can accept borders or live within them. A parent who has a hard time accepting the role of the "bad" guy may not understand that it does not really make him a bad parent but a good one, even though at certain moments the child will view the parent as bad. This happens when the parent builds himself a romantic world without anger or struggles, thinking you can live without anger, without limits, and without firmness. The parent becomes exhausted. There is nothing worse than a parent who cannot take care of himself, because the child needs the parent to be strong for him. A child who does not have limits blows up until he bursts. In his experience he can do anything and deserves everything and will get everything. Such a child cannot tolerate frustration, which is a necessary part of life. Such a child cannot stand disappointment or recognize his own or his parents' limits. The child and parent develop an omnipotent experience, as if they can do anything. They forge a false alliance based on the parent's weakness. Only clear and benevolent limits, without anger, out of a recognition of the parent's right to live and take care of himself rather than being an eternal victim, only such limits can bring peace, conciliation, brotherhood, and true togetherness. Because without such borders there is only an imaginary intimacy, partnership, brotherhood, and a new Middle East. The parent has to ask himself what his borders really are, and we, as a nation, have to ask ourselves what we are really able and willing to concede. I think there is a pretty clear national consensus on what we can concede and what we cannot.

The left has given the Arabs a lot of empathy, which was partly fake and came from a longing for a bond and a refusal to recognize the aggression directed at us. The left was less aware of the importance of aggression in regard to Arab terrorism, and was often swept into a romantic relationship out of unrealistic fantasies of a desire for intimacy, bonding, and peace.

Other parents err on the side of excessive authoritativeness by imposing restrictions and limits that are not necessary and prevent freedom. The child's thinking might stay restrained in stiff limits out of a defensive stance. He will experience the environment as aggressive and persecuting, believe he has to be cautious, and have difficulty building trusting relationships and believing in change. In its extreme form, which is the paranoid emotional attitude, that sets a clear boundary between inside and outside, which in the child's experience means he is good and the outside world is bad.

But the right has found it hard for years to believe in peace, to believe in change, to soften its threatened attitude, and to believe in a better future. The right has been very preoccupied with Arab aggression, and has had a hard time absorbing the changes it was seeing around it, and changing its position.

The child who grows in the optimal environment will find a correct balance between those two central forces of growth. In the growth process, the representations of peace and security are intermingled into one entity. The parents of such a child know when to set limits when it is necessary, to help him relax and experience inner order, but the child will also have an experience of freedom, openness to the world, and hope for change. Some say true freedom can be found only within boundaries. In marriage, for instance, an individual may experience more freedom than outside of it. Secretary of State Warren Christopher said, "Only a safe Israel can make peace."

The emotional condensation of peace and security into an entity that has inner unity rather than conflict, like two sides of a coin, is what our nation needs today: a parent who is authoritarian and sets limits, but who also allows the child to take off, hope, and be optimistic about the future. That emotional combination is not easy and cannot be taken for granted. It is no wonder that there is no such leader today, at least not in the position we need. We know this from therapy, that fragmenting forces are strong and regressive and pull us toward the extremes. And what hard work is needed to integrate the different, opposing perspectives within the soul. Most of us strongly identify with the left or the right and have difficulty understanding the other side's positions or identifying with it, even for a short while.

The optimal leader would be the nation's therapist, and like any therapist or great leader he has to speak out of emotion and speak to emotion. In the previous chapters about a Palestinian state I discussed how important it is to be connected to, and aware of, the impulsiveness of the Middle East, and stressed that we have to know that dramatic language and use it. We said that a religious conciliation between Jews and Moslems has to be dramatic because of the tremendous emotional charges it carries. The optimal leader has to give an answer not only to others but to ourselves, to the public's difficulty in merging supposedly conflicting points of view into one harmonious entity. He has to give the people the feeling that peace and security are the same thing. He must not fall into the crack between the two. Therefore, like any unifying force, the optimal leader has to be dramatic both inwardly and outwardly. Arafat is able to make that synthesis when he uses the phrase "peace of the brave," and thereby unites those two aspects of the soul. He also speaks of peace dramatically, and condenses peace and security into one unity, just like a parent who sets limits but gives freedom. The Likud's phrase "a secure peace" is more integrative than the left's peace. The Likud began with an exclusive emphasis on security, but gradually was able to add the word *peace*. The therapy the nation needs, like a growing child, is to unite the rift in the image of a leader with whom the people can identify, who will unite and personify both security and peace as one entity. Possibly Ezer Weizman stands for that, more than other leaders in recent years with his dramatic striving for peace. That is why he is very popular. The more mature we become as a nation, the rifts between right and left narrow, and the chance for an integrative resolution increases. It is already easier to identify with a unifying leader than a divisive one, and the rift is narrowing to the dimensions that exist in more developed countries.

An example of the required balance between security and peace can be found in the question of Palestinian terrorism. The Palestinians want to grow and achieve independence, and the question is how we help them grow in a way that serves our future need to live with them. The Palestinians have no reason to stop terrorism, because it rewards them. It is hard to imagine that they would have achieved anything without the Intifada and terrorism. That is how an adolescent rebels and achieves his independence. As we know, independence is something you seize, it is not handed out. Only after the adolescent achieves it does he relax. Can we not understand that? Our right always said you can only get a state by armed force and there is no other way in the world. It always said that and it was right. But the right repressed that insight when it grew up and became a parent. This happens to a lot of parents who need to be helped to understand what they were like as teenagers, to help them understand their children. The only thing that stopped the terrorism by the right, by Etzel and Lehi, was the establishment of the state. Again and again we see people who were extreme rightists, such as Begin, Sharon, and Yitzhak Shamir, become moderate when they sit in the government. We know what will happen to those rebellious adolescents in a few years, when they become parents and start pushing around a baby carriage. They will become much more moderate when they become the authorities. We also know it is better for the adolescent to win his rebellion, because that is the only way for him to grow, feel equal, and not be subdued, and make peace with the parent from a position of strength and security.

What is the connection between the important balance between peace and security, or the integration between left and right, and the love we should feel for the Palestinians? The answer is in the child's growth process. It is hard for Arafat to fight terrorism. He can promise us the world but not keep his promise, as long as no better alternative is available to him, just as a child needs a better alternative for him to abandon violence. If he sees he can excel in school, for instance, or succeed socially, and win his place without using violence, then, and only then, will he be willing to replace one way of attention-getting with another. A child will never give up his weapon, which gives him power, attention, and many other gains, if limits are set but no better alternatives are offered. The firm rightist position against terrorism has to be bolstered by an alternative to terrorism. The correct alternative is a state, so they have something to strive for. We have to tell them that they will get a state, and that we will help them build it, if they stop using violence. Only then will they have a deep emotional reason to fight terrorism, and no other way will work. This is the right's mistake, that it has not given the adolescent the hope of a better future.

The left, on the other hand, did not understand that the child needs to be helped to grow not only by making promises to help him, but also by placing firm boundaries. Just as children may unconsciously beg for firm but benevolent borders, so does Arafat ask us for them because it is hard for him to stand against the Hamas alone, and he needs us to tell him, as parents tell a child, "you can do it, and there is no choice, the aggression that comes from you is your responsibility, and will hurt you first." He needs us to tell him that to grow and receive independence and rights means also keeping your commitments, meaning controlling your aggressive drives. We will not compromise over that. Only now does it become clear how wrong the left was in thinking that terrorism could be defeated by kindness. In other words, we would give them optimism, which the right does not give them, we will give them hope, and they will do their part. When Rabin said, "we will fight terrorism like terrorism, and continue making peace regardless of terrorism," he absolved Arafat from the responsibility for his aggression, and helped that adolescent shirk his responsibility for his actions. Rabin actually said that we will handle this aggression as if it were not yours, and continue being warm and supportive toward peace. We know from therapy that that is false empathy, which avoids dealing with the aggression and encourages the soul's divisive forces. In the same way that is an erroneous attitude toward children. Children need limits. Understanding that combination is the key to progress. It is hard for us too to fight the terrorism of the extreme right, and we repress it, as I have stated. We feel that they are doing our work for us, expressing our repressed aggression, just like the saying that the work of the righteous is done by others. If it is hard for us as an independent state to relinquish our repressed aggression, how hard it must be for Arafat, who is not yet able to set up a state. This adolescent, who wants independence, has to grow and take responsibility for his actions.

Clear, firm, and uncompromising limits on terrorism are the order of the day. All that has to come with peace, optimism, and help toward achieving self-realization, which are naturally as important to the Palestinians as they are for anyone else. We see a rightist emotional position that stresses security and a leftist position that stresses peace, and it is clear that they need to merge into one entity in the Palestinians' growth process, so that we can help them grow properly. No adolescent will give up his aggression if you do not set limits and give him a more rewarding alternative. One of the two is not enough.

As explained previously, in the growth process of a child or a nation, without firm security demands, there can be no optimistic message of hope and peace, and without an optimistic message of a better future we cannot make firm demands for order and security. But the left and the right have blurred their correct messages. They have paid a high price for their refusal to integrate each other's correct points. The left has given up tough security demands, and therefore cannot go all the way in offering real hope to the Palestinians. We have to say that we want them to have a state as much they do. It is as much in our interest as theirs for them to be happy. The right was unwilling to give them hope for independence and for a state, and therefore could not demand full security. Our security is as much in their interest as ours. The right and the left have each moved toward each other and toward the center, blurred their correct messages, and failed to move toward an integration that accepts the truth of both messages as well as their necessity to go hand in hand. We demand more, but are also willing to give more.

Evidently, this is a paradox. Only when you are lefter than left can you make demands that are righter than right. In terms of growth and development, only if you delineate a better future of independence and honor will your tough conditions receive understanding and agreement. It is not enough to set limits and demands; alternatives need to be offered for the child to have a reason to want to grow. Therefore we need to issue a dramatic statement that clarifies that it is our job to help the Palestinians grow and to establish an independent and developed state. At the same time we would make a much firmer demand upon the Palestinians to disarm the Hamas and fight terrorism. The message is simple, that we believe this child can grow and stand on his own two feet.

When clear boundaries are delivered with warmth, love, and hope for a better future rather than anger, they are experienced very differently by the child. That is how we should help the child grow. The child needs to receive before he is able to give. Here we recall the message of the previous chapters, of the importance of a dramatic, sympathetic, and loving attitude toward the Palestinians. We have to go through the reversal I described in the child's growth process, from fighting the father to loving him, to the peace of the brave. We have to give the Palestinians the message that we are not against them but for them. Helping them grow has to come with love. That way it will be easier for the child to accept the borders and the limits. I think the public is ripe enough to accept that position today. The tables need to be turned. It is true that the child gives us a lot of trouble, but we will have to live with him, and we have to help him grow correctly, not just continue fighting him. Looking at the Palestinians as someone we need to help grow takes us out of our traditional threatened position to an ability to look at the process with more openness and freedom, which we all need. *Therefore, a dramatic statement is necessary, to the effect that we will help the Palestinians achieve the state and independence they deserve, as long as they keep their commitments.*

Thereby, the whole complex system becomes one entity. What is true inwardly is true outwardly. As for the Palestinians, we have to adopt the warm and loving dramatic attitude that helps them grow and knows how to set limits. While domestically, if we want to integrate left and right, and security and peace, the message has to be in dramatic language but its contents have to be romantic. That is, as I said, the way in which the left needs to convey its messages to the right. The contents are romantic but the way in which it is conveyed is dramatic, because the left listens to the contents, while the right listens to the style.

The question remains of how we respond to the Palestinians when they do commit acts of terrorism. After all, it is clear that we will have to deal with such attacks for a long time to come. In the case of an attack I think we must not impose sanctions on the Palestinian seaport or airport. I would also avoid imposing closures that harm their ability to work and make a living. Because we do want to help this child grow, and therefore our response (in education we prefer "response" to "punishment") has to be educational. We should not punish the child by not letting him go to school or not letting him eat and make a living. We will not harm the things that help him develop, because those are interests common to both of us. But we can withhold agreements that express respect, maturity, and independence, things that have to do with the Palestinian currency, for instance, or their flag, postage stamps, passports, or parliament. We can delay agreements that recognize their sovereignty and independence in matters of trade, tourism. and so on, responses that reflect the fact that they are not yet grown and cannot control themselves, rather than responses that starve them or withhold things they need for their existence. The response has to be associatively connected to the goal we want to achieve. If they do not control their drives, they are still children who do not deserve independence, and do not deserve to be issued travel permits. But withholding work, food, or study are not productive responses but merely revenge. If we need the closure for security reasons, that is one thing. We can close the safe passage that is used for family visits if the Palestinians use it for terrorist attacks. During the Intifada one of our punishments was closures. We prevented the Palestinian children from going to school for long periods and thereby hurt both ourselves and them.

Netanyahu made the opening of the Gaza seaport contingent on their keeping the Wye Agreement and fighting terrorism. His intention was valid; the Palestinians do too little to prevent terrorism, but his response was incorrect. Our goal has to be helping them grow by educational responses, rather than by increasing their bitterness and frustration. We have to respond without vengeance, so that the Palestinians can identify with our responses and understand them. We have to give them a list of things they did wrong: terrorism, disturbances, statements, textbooks, and so on. We must not let them off the hook on these matters. It requires us not only to respond appropriately, as I said, but to be more than honest ourselves. Deceptively building settlements, and covering it with some bureaucratic excuse that does nothing to relieve the horrible offense to the Palestinians, and re-creating the trauma of their expulsion from their land and their homes, cannot coexist with the goal of striving for real peace. We cannot deceive their feelings. We are the big ones; we have to be role models for them, because they really want to be like us, big, independent, and developed. We have to be real models of honesty and trustworthiness, unlike what is happening today in the matter of the settlements or in many other matters, where we are imposing deprivations on the Palestinians. They come from a society that has bribery and corruption, and our credibility could be a role model for them. The real question is, Do we want them to grow or to be frustrated? If we check ourselves and our latest statements, that it is not our business if they declare independence at some point, we will understand what a great opportunity we are missing—to help this child, who we have to live with, grow.

Murderers or Heroes?

The dynamics of the emotional processes between nations are often more regressive than relations between individuals. Therefore, we need to turn to childhood experiences to understand those dynamics. This can illuminate the question of Israel's releasing Palestinians jailed for killing Israelis. In the daily life of normal adults we rarely see sharp splits between enemy and friend, murderer and hero, or good and evil. In the political field the notion that our soldiers are heroes while the enemies are murderers is common.

What process does the patient or the child need to go through in order to merge the murderer and the hero into one entity instead of viewing them as different parts of the soul? In this example, the child feels himself the good hero, while the child he hates in his class is the bad monster. In that way the child projects onto the other child aspects of himself that he does not want to accept. Now the world is "in order." The good is within the self, while the evil is in someone else. Now the child does not have to take responsibility for the less attractive parts of himself. In that way, the child's conflict is with the outside world rather than within himself. In the growth process we hope those splits will modify and the child will become strong enough not to project parts of himself onto others, and understand that it is he who is torn between different aspects of himself. In that way the child will understand that everyone is both good and evil, and he is no different from the other child in his class whom he sees as a monster.

In the same vein, the more self-aware we become, and the more we recognize our own aggression—the murderer within us,—the more we learn to be less afraid of the other's aggression and murderousness. We see in the clinic how, when a patient starts getting in touch with his own aggression, he starts understanding the other and being empathetic toward him, understanding the monster who threatened him and becoming less afraid of him. The more we recognize the suffering we caused the Palestinians, our desire to control as much as possible of this land and to possess the whole country in the name of God without leaving anything to others, the less we will see them as murderers and the more we will see them as hurting, frustrated people. The more we connect with the murderous part of ourselves, the more the other will look to us like a freedom fighter fighting for his land. We will understand that the murderer and the hero are two sides of the same soul, like two sides of a coin. We will learn that in emotional life, behind every hero there is a killer, just as behind every killer is a hero. In other words, people are not only good or evil, but are made of different emotional tendencies.

How do we help a child or an adult become less threatened by others? The process of moving closer to the "monster" has several aspects: first, the patient needs a lot of empathy in order to relax and feel less threatened. He needs to feel basic security. Without that security there will be no progress in therapy. Could we have thought about peace at all in the middle of the Yom Kippur War or in the days before the Six Day War? When we are flooded with existential anxieties we cannot think about peace at all, only about survival. Only after the patient feels the therapist is with him, that he has the right to exist, can the patient slowly look into himself and recognize his own aggression. Because to get in touch with his aggression, the patient has to feel strong. We as a people are going through a process similar to therapy. Over the years, our existential threat has gradually diminished. We do not feel the same anxieties with the same intensity we felt during the Holocaust, for instance, or at the time Israel was established, or during the Yom Kippur War. Meanwhile we are starting to realize what we are doing to others. At first we occupied the Palestinians because Jordan attacked us in the Six Day War and we were fighting for our survival. Today we are gradually realizing that we are occupying another people and oppressing them. This is when our empathy with the people on the other side emerges, and they slowly turn from murderers into people who are suffering, possibly even people whose actions can be understood. Barak said bravely, "If I were a Palestinian I would join a terrorist organization myself." All of a sudden (of course, it is not really all of a sudden, because hidden emotional processes preceded it, but in our minds it seems sudden) we are willing to build a monument to enemy casualties, and to understand that their graveyards also are full of heroes. We see a parallel process of being able to contain our "shudder" and our anxieties and not repress those feelings, while our ability to recognize our own aggression grows. In other words, we are getting to know ourselves better, like patients in therapy. While we get to know ourselves better, the others slowly turn from monsters into people with different sides whom we can understand.

Only after we go through that emotional process can we take another look at ourselves and remember how much we resembled them. We too fought for our independence, and we too had terrorist organizations (Etzel and Lehi). And if we today boast that as opposed to the terrorists we never killed children, there are two answers to that. One is that the intensity of the aggression reflects the intensity of the hurt and insult that motivated it. The second, more important answer is, And so what if we are better and more moral? The peace process is not a contest of who is better, righter and more moral, but on the contrary, is a process of accepting the other, believing he is a person who is not so different from ourselves, who can be understood. The process of changing "monsters" into people is like the growth process of a child who believes in witches, monsters, and fairies. Only after he grows up does he learn that there is a little of everything in each person. Sometimes the parent is experienced as good and sometimes as bad, but it is still the same parent. Yes, the Palestinians' rebellion and liberation hurts us, which is how the parent feels toward the rebellious adolescent. But a good parent does not turn his child into a monster, but understands how hard it is for him and that he is fighting for something dear to him, his place in the world and his independence. Moreover, a good parent knows it is a temporary growth process and in the future, after the adolescent feels he got what he deserved and realizes himself, there is a good chance the two will be on good terms.

We are talking about the long emotional process of peace, but on the question of murderers versus killers we face a new situation, a dichotomous emotional situation. We are asked to release terrorists from our jails. In other words, we have to go from looking at the terrorist as a murderer to seeing him freed and given a hero's welcome on the other side. Is he a jailed hero or a free murderer? When the gap between the two narrows, it is quite a confusing feeling. What can we say about the emotional process that can help us go through this difficult and quick transformation? Similarly, what kind of therapeutic intervention will help the other side change dichotomously? We have to define a certain moment, the Oslo Accords for instance, until which the terrorists can be called "heroes" and be freed. Any Palestinian who kills after that moment has to be seen as a murderer and stay in jail. Again, these transitions are too sharp for our emotions.

We need to use additional emotional mechanisms to help us go through that change. Let us look at the rituals of different cultures, particularly Judaism, to see what solutions people have found to the sharp transitions in their lives. With the bar mitzvah ceremony the child, all at once, becomes responsible for his actions. From hereon his sins are counted against him and not against his father. With the wedding ceremony too the couple moves all at once from one world to another for the rest of their lives. Suddenly they are in a different situation. They are married and committed to being loyal. The ceremony serves and has served in many different cultures to smooth these impossible transitions. The ceremony is a message that touches the personal and collective unconscious and allows for such a transition to take place. The ceremony is joyful and helps repress fears, and calls upon the boy or the couple to rise above themselves, to mobilize their strength and move forward toward a different future. There is no going back, not for the thirteen-year-old child and not for the married couple (at least not regarding their intentions at the time of marriage). The ceremony, with its cultural symbols and the participation of the guests, is testimony to the transition, and gives the person unconscious strength to make it through.

Therefore, I propose that we become the guests, the main partners, and the best men at the ceremony declaring the Palestinian state. Because it is first of all our interest. In this joyful ceremony all of the terrorists will be released, including those who killed until the moment the state was declared. Afterward no terrorist will be released. We have seen that when you want to effect an emotional reversal at a certain moment, you need a ritual that draws strength from the unconscious. Without a ceremony the person cannot draw the strength for that reversal. The Palestinians, for their part, will promise that after they receive their independence they will stop demanding that we release terrorists. The unconscious, associative rationale connecting the establishment of an independent state and controlling one's aggressive drives is clear. The declaration ceremony of a Palestinian state, to which we would be full partners, is more than another peace agreement. It is the final stage of their growth to maturity and responsibility. Indeed, we have to give them everything we can, just as parents help a marrying couple. They give whatever they can, and expect to receive wholeheartedly (I know my terminology and emotional associations can give some people the chills. But the peace process is, after all, an emotional process, and follows those rules). After the wedding, the expectation is of loyalty, and after the bar mitzvah, the Jewish expectation is for the child to be responsible for his actions. This is all possible as long as we are full partners to the establishment of the Palestinian state, and as long as the willingness comes from us. Then we can make the important connection between their growth and our taking responsibility. Then we will be seen as giving adults rather than as someone who needs to be hurt.

The ceremony by which we become allies of the nascent Palestinian state has to be deep and unconscious, and filter into all levels of consciousness of Palestinian society. To do so, we should learn from ceremonies we know. At bar mitzvahs and at weddings, for one thing, a lot of relatives are invited. The large crowd that represents the extended family has a deep effect on us and on our commitment. Before the Palestinians' independence ceremony, they see hurting us as hurting the enemy. After the ceremony, they should realize that they are hurting someone who is raising them, hurting their parent. Another important aspect of the ceremony is the gifts. We find gift-giving to be part of festive ceremonies as far back as the Bible and ancient legends. Giving is a form of recognition and emotional inclusion of the people invited. The guests become part of the support system of the event. Some of those symbols are present in today's peace agreements. The representatives of other countries are invited to the signing ceremony and asked to add their signatures to it. Yasser Arafat, who is more sensitive than we are to the importance of symbols and their effect on the unconscious, and uses them more than we do in his manner of speech, his clothing (charged language, military uniform, his headdress shaped like the map of Palestine, etc.), says again and again that the United States and other countries are guarantors of the agreement. As to the gifts, the United States, and some European countries, have promised financial aid following the agreement. As in the other ceremonies, there is no turning back in the peace process. Indeed, processes of growth and emotional development are irreversible. We can learn from the other ceremonies we know and expand the symbolic, unconscious parts. We can invite the representatives of more countries, maybe even as many as possible, to convey the message of the responsibility of the family of nations and its partnership in this peace process. The gifts, in this case, can help the Palestinian Authority grow. But symbolic gifts are important too. They say, "I too support the peace process." Using differing symbols during the ceremony is important. That is because symbols have direct access to the unconscious, for instance, releasing balloons and doves and reading passages from the Bible. We already noted the central role of religion in the

Middle East conflict. Creating new religious symbols that express peace between the different religions is vital, because there are no such symbols at the present time. Resolving the question of Jerusalem requires forging new symbols of conciliation between the religions. In our history there has never been deep and real conciliation between the different religions, and therefore there are no symbols that represent that collective unconscious of brotherhood between the religions.

I may have compared the Palestinians to children again, and us to parents, but it is clear that in this growth process we are children as much as they are. We too need a transition ceremony to allow us to change our view of the Arabs in general and the Palestinians in particular. Why should we not respect their "Nakba" day (the Palestinian disaster—their expulsion from their land in 1948)? Are we not mature enough to bear the pain of the other along with our own pain? And perhaps we should announce that we are going to change our attitude toward the Palestinians from the moment they announce their independence, just as parents treat their marrying children differently, and begin seeing them as adults with full rights. We too need ceremonies to help us internalize the deep change in our attitude toward the Palestinians. Without the help of such ceremonies or memorial days it will be hard to convey the message in a way that filters to all levels of Israeli society.

As soon as the adolescent reaches independence and responsibility he goes through a process of relinquishing his terrorist aggression. A straight line runs from the child who disrupts class until the teacher gives him an important job to calm him, through the rebellious adolescents who become parents and become mollified by their responsibility, to the stories of the various terrorist organizations that ceased operating when they got statehood. Etzel and Lehi laid down their arms when Israel was established. Ben-Gurion responded to the Altelena ship crisis with maximum firmness in order to make the point that the terrorism period was over, and that now there is a state with one central government. The trauma was engraved deep in our hearts, but it served as the basis for curbing the same drives we expect Arafat to curb today. Many underground organizations laid down their arms when their struggle bore fruit and they achieved independence. It is a difficult emotional transition. On a personal level, the terrorist turns into a person who gets up in the morning and goes to work, relinquishing the grandiosity of the terrorist experience and accepting that the burden of ordinary life is not easy. On the national level, the terrorist organization that is used to carrying out its impulses has to become subject to a state that does everything to control its impulses. But the connection between receiving independence and controlling impulses is appropriate and emotionally correct.

All that requires us, of course, to act like adults and to be responsible for our own aggression toward them. And we have a lot of aggression toward them. As long as we are unable to take responsibility for our aggression, we cannot expect them, the growing adolescents, to take responsibility for theirs. It is simply a necessary requirement for the process. Among us too there are murderers whom some treat as heroes. We too need such a ceremony for the transition. Terrorism by the extreme right toward the Arabs before the declaration of independence of the Palestinian state can be forgiven, but our terrorism toward the Palestinian state after it is established is not heroism but murder.

Our aggression is not our very existence, because we have the right to live and live well. Our aggression is in some of our actions. It is like telling a child, you are not bad, but some of the things you did need improvement. Thereby you do not negate the child's existence or cast him as inherently bad. The child can change his actions. He cannot and need not change his personality and character or negate them.

Therefore, the more we feel we really gave the Palestinians everything we could, and the message that those are our red lines is conveyed unconsciously, the more they will understand that we will not be blackmailed, and they will not get anything more. It can be soothing to know you cannot bargain and get a better deal, because the price is set. We have to be sure that if another Intifada breaks out they will not get any more than they are getting now. Only such an unconscious message from us to them can bring calm and peace. Because it has to be understood that as long as we think in the depths of our unconscious that we have been had, they will also think in their unconscious that they would get more by force. Therefore we have to find our truth, beyond the narcissistic Jewish laws of history, by which, according to the Bible, peace never lasted more than forty years, but from the laws of human history, based on the recognition of the other. We have another opportunity to glimpse the great importance of self-awareness, which has never been a strong point of religions, that self-awareness requires strength of introspection and honesty, and especially the ability to tolerate pain, and not only the feeling that "I am the best and the biggest."

Clarifying our thoughts is a powerful and too-little recognized tool for the peace process. Just like in therapy, each party's unconscious influences the other. If we believe we beat them or set them up in the peace process they will feel it and it can be very dangerous. Moreover, in some situations people might agree to things they should not agree to. It is a question of identifying with the aggressor, like a rape victim who blames herself even though she is not at fault, or a battered child who thinks that is what he deserves. We can be sure that it will all burst out one day and there will be a price to pay. The Palestinians can, as I already said, relinquish Jerusalem in order to receive the economic aid they want so badly, but if they agree to something to which they should not agree, we can expect a sure blowup in the future. Those are the soul's laws, and they are perfectly clear.

In the light of all that, instead of a prolonged negotiation where we feel forced to free terrorists, we should understand the emotional logic of the process. The terrorists' sharp transition from the status of hero to the status of murderer once the Palestinian state is established, and the transition of those who killed before the state was established from murderer to hero, can occur only through a ceremony led by Israel, which touches upon our collective unconscious.

According to this logic, the release of terrorists who have killed need not be conditional upon the Palestinians' fighting terrorism. That is what Benjamin Netanyahu did when he stated, "If they give they will get, if they don't give they won't get." It is a deeper emotional process than a temporary attempt of theirs to behave like good children and to thereby gain rewards. We are talking about unconscious mental processes rather than some kind of tactical manipulations. Netanyahu was drawn into a Palestinian way of thinking, characterized more by bargaining than by drawing clear boundaries (see chapter 5 on "Arab thinking"). It is a matter of their inviting us to a relationship of emotional involvement rather than an absolute truth. Peace, as a process of growth and change, is much deeper than fashions of cognitive thinking, and needs emotional order. We know the rules of growth, and we know it is no accident that there is a legal age of responsibility, which in Israel is eighteen. A younger defendant receives preferential treatment, and rightfully. After that age there are no more excuses.

A parent is not a superman. He may have to learn to try to stand his ground with his teenage child, but he cannot always succeed. If the Palestinians try to extort us to free terrorists in exchange for the release of Israeli hostages they take, we should, of course, try not to give in. But if there are cases where we do give in, that is not the point. Those exceptions do not change the principle of arranging a ceremony whereby the Palestinians are granted independence, with us standing with them rather than against them, and both of us being in a different state of awareness afterward.

Our goal should be to create a new reality where together we seek symbols that express the depth of our commitment to peace. As I said, just as war needed symbols throughout human history, so does peace. Perhaps a sanctuary of peace built on Temple Mount; perhaps a monument for all victims of war; perhaps a joint peace hymn; perhaps a joint flag that represents peace and flies in Jerusalem; a peace statue is also a possibility, like Mount Rushmore, where the faces of presidents are engraved in stone. Anything is possible.

We understand that a child grows gradually as does a relationship between partners, yet we still need ceremonies such as bar mitzvahs and weddings to determine the date when a person becomes responsible for his actions. The ceremony is society's stamp of approval, which the person needs so badly, that from now on he can control his impulses and be responsible for himself. It is a kind of declaration of an end point of something that started much earlier. Both we and the Palestinians need a date from which we will all be responsible for our actions. It is a deep, unconscious experience of order and impulse control. Our emotional nature demands such an event with a celebration and guests, an essentially dramatic ceremony, like the swearing-in ceremony of soldiers. From that moment on life changes. In the peace process the confusing question is whether the person in question is a killer or a hero. That question contains in it a demand for order, as is necessary for any human society. The individual and the state's emotional growth process, which is long and slow, requires many secret preparations before the ceremony. Then the target date arrives. That is the nature of the human development of a child or a state, from chaos and impulses to order.

5

The Arabs and Us—An Intersubjective Approach

Arab Insult

The Arabs should learn to live with our shortcomings but not with our humiliations. I am writing this to increase our awareness of the emotional messages we convey to the Arabs. It might be simplest to begin with Egypt. If we just listen to Mubarak with emotional listening, as we do in therapy, we will understand how much we have hurt the Egyptians. Mubarak says that the Jews used to be smart and he doesn't know what happened to them. He said Jewish merchants used to keep their promises, and today they do not. He added that maybe if we ate broad beans (like the Egyptians) we would get brains. What does he want from us? Why did he even give Rabin a hard time when Rabin pursued the path of peace? And recently, after our elections, whom did he invite first to Egypt? Netanyahu, the loser, not Barak, the winner. He rushed to send Barak a cautionary message that he, Mubarak, is afraid Barak's messages are not going in the right direction. You have to just listen to the insulted tone in which he speaks.

But how can he help it? The Egyptians tried to destroy us in 1948, in 1956, in 1967, and in 1973, but all those attempts failed. If that isn't an insult, what is? Add to that our nuclear capability, which they do not have. Suddenly a younger brother is born in the family, and the older one tries to restore his hegemony and control. But the little one, who was just born, strikes him again and again, throws his older brothers out of the house and banishes them. The elder brother bursts out crying and says, What did I do? All I wanted was to keep what I had, not to have my place taken.

The Egyptians are very hurt by us emotionally, and therefore peace with them is cold, and they take an anti-Israeli position in the international arena at every opportunity. True, they ultimately got the Sinai Peninsula back, but only after they promised to behave, and they have made that promise to the whole world. The reason for the cold peace with Egypt is not mainly manipulation motivated by competition over the hegemony in the region, as many explain cognitively. In clinical work we are trained to listen to emotional contents, and we know well that feelings are the real motives of behavior, more than cognitive considerations. Let us listen to how the Egyptians were insulted by us for years. In the negotiations over Taba, for instance: it was clear to them that it was their land, and we argued over it. True, we do not have to apologize for our existence, but we do need to be tolerant of this cold peace, of Mubarak's double messages, when he speaks of peace but invites anger and intrigue, as when he jailed the Israeli Azzam Azzam on spying charges. If we understand the Egyptians and how hurt they are, it will be easier for us to be empathetic and forgiving toward them. Again, it is like a marriage. An intimate knowledge of our spouse's feelings helps us be empathetic even in difficult moments. That is the nature of emotional understanding: it helps us gain a distance from powerful feelings and look at them from the outside. We see this in everyday situations, where our understanding of the other helps us be empathetic, because we stop seeing him only as an aggressor, but rather as someone who is troubled.

What about the Syrians? It is basically the same story. They rose up against the Zionist infiltrator; they basically did not want a foreign child in the family. And the child, who was just born, beats them in the wars of 1948, 1967, 1973, and 1982. How much humiliation does the older brother need to suffer from the younger brother, who put cannons as close as 30 kilometers from Damascus in 1973, who demolished his air force at a rate of 1:80 in 1982, so that deep insults will guide his thinking? We only need to listen to them, to hear how they speak about their Golan Heights that they long for, just as we longed for Zion. Lately our newspapers carried interviews from Syrian newspapers about how they feel as if they are David and we are Goliath. They do not see themselves as aggressors but as victims, and they can be understood with empathy. It is not only possible but important for us to do that. Only if we understand the Syrians and their feeling of insult, will we not think it is a manipulation when they ask for early warning stations in the Galilee so that we do not attack them. They really are afraid of us. They really do think we are aggressive invaders who expel people from their land. What does a Syrian feel, who lives well below our poverty line, is not allowed to carry a cell phone, is not allowed to

watch international television broadcasts, does not have Internet, and has a security guard on every street corner, when he looks at us? Like David and Goliath, like any weak person next to someone strong, he feels humiliated by the
strong one, and feels that the strong person does not really care if there is peace
(if we are honest with ourselves, a lot of us say the Golan Heights is more important than peace with Syria).

It is no wonder Jordan's King Hussein was the only one who spoke about a
warm peace. It is true he too was humiliated by us over the years and in the
wars, but he suffered more from the Palestinians and was more threatened by
them. He gave up part of his country to them not to us, and the Palestinians
threaten him even in his country. Hussein, it has to be said, was smarter than
we were. He recognized Palestinian rights before we did, and spared his country the disaster of an Intifada. In a sense we became partners in distress. It
seems as if these days, since the king's death, that warm peace too is cooling off.
With the Lebanese we do not have as charged a relationship as with the Syrians, the Egyptians, and the Palestinians. They would have made peace with us
long ago, but Syria does not let them.

Let us do a simple exercise, which every therapist does during a therapy
session. He asks himself again and again what this patient makes him feel. He
uses those feelings to understand the quality of his relationship with the patient. So what do we really feel toward the Palestinians? We feel contempt toward them, their poverty, and their helplessness, and see them as a mob with
no rights, in whom we have no interest unless they are committing terrorist attacks, and we are not really willing to help them. Indeed, only the Intifada
made us view them and their wishes with more consideration and respect. Alternately, we see them as a cheap labor force, lowly workers we can exploit for
our benefit. That is how we feel toward them, and that is the feeling they get
from us, and they are right. If we do not emotionally recognize Israeli Arabs, is
it any wonder we care even less about the ones who escaped in 1948, or lived in
the territories for all those years?

But where did we get the denial we have employed all this time, as if they
do not know how we feel about them and are unaware of it? They feel we look
down on them. Not only did we physically demolish their homes in the past,
but in the present we emotionally ignore their existence. That is exactly what
we have to change, because that is the root of the conflict, our insulting emotional stance that would enrage anyone. Yes, our arrogant stance toward them
comes, like any arrogance, from the emotional hurt we feel, that we are trying
to protect. It is fed by the existential threat we feel. We know it well from therapy, the insult and hurt that are behind pride. We know an arrogant person is
not aware of his arrogance and doesn't know what others are talking about.
After all, he knows he feels hurt, so what do they want? But other people keep
telling him how aggressive and dismissive he is. It takes a lot of hard work to
help such a person get in touch with his emotions, both the insult and the arro-

gance. Moreover, the other party has a hard time seeing the insult to the person who comes off as aggressive. You need a great deal of empathy for that. Being able to recognize the pain of someone who attacks you, and understand the emotions that lead to aggression and to arrogance, is a rare talent. It is hard to expect a Palestinian who comes to work for us and tills a field that could have belonged to his father or his grandfather, but this time does it for meager pay and without rights, to understand how fearful we are for our existence. The same goes for a house cleaner who is cleaning a house that could have been hers. For them we are the robbers of their land and property, who turned them into our slaves and servants. We have to enter their shoes to understand the tremendous rage and insult they feel toward us. Anyone who still needs proof of the fact that the peace process is primarily an emotional process should listen to the Palestinians say repeatedly that we are "raping their land." Just as victims of sexual assault need therapy, so does the peace process require therapeutic analysis.

It is true that even if we help them grow the anger will remain. It will not fade away overnight. But it is the right way, to take responsibility and to change our emotional attitude toward the Palestinians. The obvious question about the UN resolution equating Zionism with racism is not whether it is true or not. Sure, it lacks empathy and understanding of our side, but if we want to learn something from it, as a therapist does from every expression of anger and aggression that a patient utters, then the Arabs and the nations who joined them are telling us how they see us. We have to do everything we can to modify those feelings. It is not necessarily a matter of concessions as much as care, recognition of their sadness, and pain. The facts that we too are refugees who were expelled, were destroyed, and who suffered a lot more than they did are true, but do not help the Palestinians view us in a more positive light, just as a bad parent cannot appease his child or quell his anger by telling the child that the parent, too, had a difficult childhood. The child would want, rightfully, for the parent to understand him and see what is hurting him, and not tell him about his own pain. Only after he receives enough warmth and empathy can the child understand the parent's difficulty, and no sooner, while he is still focused on his own problems. That is why it is so important for us to be careful to avoid insulting statements, and to teach the public to be sensitive and attentive to the Palestinians' suffering and understand our emotional and moral responsibility toward them.

Take for instance the queues at the roadblocks, which are very humiliating. We could easily add more soldiers so the wait would not be so long. We could teach the soldiers to treat the Palestinians with more respect. What if we smiled at them at the roadblocks, installed awnings with chairs and water fountains so they would not have to come to their day's work so exhausted? Is it an accident that the residents of the occupied territories suffer from cruel bureaucracy in every area of life that has to do with us? As they say, for them every clerk is like a prime minister. We need only to look back at our past policies to get the chills. We encouraged the extremists in the territories who opposed the Palestine Liberation Organization to fight them for our benefit. Is the bureaucracy just an accident, or is it that our unconscious, which is trying to humiliate them, is playing its arrogant game here? Is it an accident that the line in front of the Ministry of Interior in Arab East Jerusalem runs all the way down the scorching street, without chairs or water? Something like that would never happen in the west side of the city. How does a Palestinian feel toward the Israeli authorities after standing in a line like that for hours?

We know the emotional value of little gestures, and in this case fair treatment could save lives. Little containers of chocolate milk at the roadblocks, a clerk who would say, "the customer is always right" even in regard to Palestinians, could prevent terrorist attacks much better than the Shin Bet can. In other words, various kinds of economic help, humanitarian help in hospitals, seeing to it that they have water in the summer, and so on. We must take emotional responsibility for every Palestinian child who is shot. I already mentioned the powerful effect of King Hussein's gesture of paying condolence calls. It is a life-changing gesture. Obviously it does not mean we don't have to shoot rioters, but we could also feel for the loss of the family whose child is killed with our involvement. Again, it is not a question of who is right; it is a matter of a human act of sympathy. It is a matter of saying that from now on, a Palestinian child who is killed hurts us as much as one of our children being killed. It is a matter of a respectful emotional stance. Could we not propose a solution for the status of Jerusalem that honors others? Do honor for others and consideration of their feelings necessarily conflict with our interests and our sovereignty? Is their feeling of humiliation necessary or can it be changed? We could say, for instance, that we cannot give up more than 2 percent, but the statement has to come with a feeling of sadness instead of a feeling of triumph. The feeling has to recognize that this hurts the other side and does not satisfy him, without being provocative and saying, "you won't get it." How you say something is important, not just what you say! We know that often the style, not the contents, is the main message. In simple words, since the peace process is mainly an emotional process, I want to focus on the emotional attitude we express, and what we tell the other side, sometimes without words, but let them feel by our various behaviors.

In therapy it is called "acting out," the aggressive behavior manifested by the patient that he is not aware of and that he cannot really understand. The assumption is that if the patient could speak about his feelings and raise them into his consciousness, he would not need those behaviors. A child who can talk about the insult he feels would likely be in less need of violence to quell his insult. The same is true for us. We have to ask ourselves why we are so cruel to the Palestinians, and what unresolved feelings that comes from. Some deep emotional issue is preventing us from looking them in the eye. Is it their very existence that we find so threatening, the fear that they will demand our land, which once was theirs? Or perhaps our erasing them and ignoring them is aimed at preventing ourselves from seeing their suffering, so that we can repress our guilt toward them? Fear and blame are feelings that of course do not cancel each other. In therapy we clarify such feelings and understand them, so that they will stop driving us without our being aware of it. A true examination of our national feelings toward the Palestinians is not easy and has not been done sufficiently in an open national discussion. But only such a therapeutic approach will help us treat the Palestinians more humanely, instead of adding insult to injury.

In the best case, we are like the parent who gives his child every material thing possible (although this is a wild exaggeration, considering all the examples I have given). But that parent gives the child very little from an emotional point of view. In other words, he does not give him warmth and sympathy. We know what serious pathologies such emotional neglect can lead to. Indeed, we are giving the Palestinians land, a port, a safe road, a police force, permission to work for us, and more, but we are withholding from them the warm and sympathetic attitude they need so desperately, the promise that we are on their side, that we will help them grow, develop, and reach independence. Every child knows that this is as important as the material giving. Are we repressing what the United States gives us? They give us generous material aid, but no less important are the repeated statements by U.S. presidents that come from the depth of their hearts, as to the deep commitment of the United States. to Israel's security and well-being. Could we, as a nation, forego the warmth and the love the United States gives us? They understand how important that emotional bond is to us. Whoever finds it hard to love the Palestinians, should think about the fact that our loving them is a first-rate Israeli security interest.

I think that sensitivity and a psychological view of the peace process are in order. We have to demand that they fight terrorism, but you cannot just demand something from a child and call him to order. You also have to ask what you are giving him on the material level, as well as on the emotional level: attention, interest, help, and so on. Otherwise, the child will have to rebel and do negative things to get your attention. Therefore, our demand that they fight terrorism has to be supported by a much warmer and more empathetic emotional attitude. The parent within us has to ask himself why he has been treating this child like this for all these years. Why can't he say one kind word to him? What is it about this child that arouses such harsh feelings, which makes us reject him, not be able to tolerate him, and mainly, not see him, and say that he does not exist? *Are we like parents who are afraid of their children and simultaneously feel very guilty toward them?* Many parents say, it is that aggressive adolescent, it is his fault. But we, as therapists, know how hard it is for parents to take responsibility for the complex relationship they have maintained with their child for years.

A few words about more distant insults. We have to understand the Palestinian identification with Saddam Hussein in the Gulf War and their cheering from the rooftops when they watched the missiles fly into Israel. For a moment they viewed him as the only Arab leader who really cared about them, who was not afraid of Israel, and who was willing to fight for them and restore their honor. At that moment what Hussein did to Kuwait and his own people was less important to the Palestinians. They used him as an anchor of rescue in a reality in which even the Arab states did not care about them. The Palestinians' feelings of insult, hurt, and rage are that strong. It is no wonder they produce suicide bombers. In our own tradition Samson killed himself in order to kill many Philistines, who hurt him and whom he hated. The suicide is driven by deep insult and even deeper rage. That is how Samson felt after the Philistines bore his eyes out. So let us not say that there is no such thing in Jewish tradition and that we cannot understand them at all. But here is the place to note Hussein's sane part, when he said that he would respect any agreement signed between the Palestinians and Israel. Therefore it is important for us to hear that voice too, and understand the deep meaning of an emotional conciliation between us and the Palestinians and how it can reverberate with wider circles of conciliation between us and the Arabs. Hussein is not a madman, even though madmen have human feelings too, which we understand in therapy. Hussein is very aware of Palestinian suffering and identifies with them and with their insult. I suggest not distancing ourselves from anyone by calling him a "madman."

And what about Iran, which can understand religious hatred as well as we can? What do we really think and feel toward other religions? What covert contempt, which is inherent in the exclusive status of every religion, do we feel toward Islam? Add to that the insult they felt from the Jews, the humiliation and the expulsion of their brothers from their land. Why should they love us? The least we can do is respect their feelings and their religion. We could invite them ceremoniously to take part in the discussions and decisions regarding Islam's sacred sites, for instance. True, every religion is extremist by definition, but it does not mean that our actions are devoid of importance and influence (as I write these words, the Hizbollah leader, Nasrallah, has declared that his organization intends to lay down its arms).

Shimon Peres's new Middle East threatens all the Arabs. They are very sensitive to our narcissism, and from their point of view, rightfully. They hear correctly that what we see in this new Middle East is only "how are we going to help those primitive people," and not "what are we going to get from them." Our "generous" giving is experienced by them as another humiliation in the series of humiliations they received from us. The penetration of our "progress" into their markets and world is nothing, for them, but the continuation of our overpowering them, and it opens an ancient wound in our relations with them. They want our help, of course. Who wouldn't want help? But here, the how is important. A good father waits patiently for his child to ask for help, and does not jump forward and show him how big he, the father, is, and how small the child is. There needs to be an appropriate giving that neither floods nor is grandiose, and realizes how hurt the other side is.

But the problem is even more complex. To them, we are the robbers who invaded their home, and now have the nerve to offer them gifts. The idea of the new Middle East greatly insults the Arabs—it contains a romantic message from the aggressor. The robber who invaded their home and expelled them is now talking about love. Our desire to erase everything that happened here and to open a new page, a new Middle East, is very hard and very insulting for them. Would we agree to relations in which our past with Germany is erased? After all, we always stress the need not to forgive and not to forget. It is no wonder that in many meetings between Israeli and Palestinian leaders our leaders come out optimistic and theirs come out pessimistic. Even our optimism insults them, as if everything can be fixed. Therefore we must respect their sadness and their painful memories and our giving has to be subdued. It should be the giving of someone who can restrain himself and control his narcissistic drives. A humble giving, the way the United States gives us.

And here we reach the main point. I think we have to apologize to the Palestinians and declare officially that we are sorry for the suffering we caused them. Not because they are right and we are not. Nobody here is right or guilty; it is a joint tragedy of the two peoples. We too were refugees and wanted to build our home here. We were part of the Palestinian people's tragedy not because we wanted to be or planned it that way, but because those were the circumstances of the establishment of our state and of our war for survival. We did nothing maliciously yet we still caused them much suffering. Therefore we apologize and see it as our moral obligation to help them build a state, grow, and develop, despite our limited resources.

This is where we should undergo a fundamental change in our attitude toward them. They expect us, right fully, to be good parents to them (even if we are very angry at them). After all, we are ten times stronger and more developed than they are. Our intention has to be conciliation, so that we can live together in the future, and so that there will be a good memory of our helping them, and not just memories of expulsion, dispossession, and humiliation, as well as agreements they imposed upon us by the use of terrorism and the Intifada. There are so many ways we could help them but don't. Such a public apology could turn the course of history and cast us as people who helped build the Palestinian state instead of fighting it, as people who helped them grow instead of preventing them from growing!

True, we have to impose uncompromising demands upon them to fight terrorism, but the spirit of our dialogue has to change. It has to be the spirit of a big, benevolent father, who sets uncompromising but kind limits, and mainly, who helps his child grow. A father who understands that it is important for the

Palestinians too to stop terrorism and to control their aggression. We know this dynamic from raising children, how clear and firm borders can go with warmth and love. That is how children grow and become independent. Just as a child carries the memories of his childhood with him for his whole life, and those memories shape his adult relations with his parents, so it is important for us to invest today in building the Palestinian state, so that we can reap the fruits of the good relationship as much as possible in the future.

Arab Thinking

I will begin with a replay of a dialogue between Mubarak and Netanyahu in different languages (Channel One, September 21, 1997), and try to understand that difference. Mubarak is responding to Netanyahu's request to release Israeli Azzam Azzam from the Egyptian prison, where he is held on spying charges.

> (A brief chuckle). After all they have done. And what can I say to the Egyptian people and the Egyptian court system?! He, Netanyahu, smeared the Egyptian legal system. That system is one of the cleanest and most just legal systems. And I say this as a man with experience. So how can I do it (pause and hand gesture of question)? They made a lot of mistakes in handling this matter, and it is their responsibility. I can do nothing. I have not pardoned anybody since I was appointed president.

The interviewer asks Netanyahu, "Mubarak says Azzam Azzam will not be freed from jail because of things you said. Are you sorry you said them?" Netanyahu answers, "It's been a long time since I've heard such an excuse for keeping someone in jail. Azzam should not have been jailed in the first place. He is innocent, and everything else is excuses."

Mubarak's initial chuckle bears examination, because this is not a laughing matter. It is reasonable to suppose that it is essentially a defensive chuckle that is meant to mask the injury that emerges from his subsequent comments, beginning with the first sentence, "After all they have done. . . ." through "Netanyahu smeared the Egyptian legal system," and ending with "I say this as a man with experience," Mubarak is telling us how hurt he was by Netanyahu's dismissive attitude toward the Egyptian legal system, which he, Mubarak, feels the need to defend. There is no reason not to believe he really was hurt by the criticism voiced in Israel toward the Egyptians. We would be hurt too if someone from the outside said our judges were dishonest and could not be trusted. There is no doubt that in this case Netanyahu fell into the trap Israeli leaders fall into all the time, that is, hurting and insulting Arabs. The question is not, of course, who is right, Mubarak or Netanyahu. It is reasonable to suppose that Azzam is not a spy. It is reasonable to suppose that he was "saddled" with something he did not do. It is even possible that Mubarak knows this happened. There were such cases in the work of our own Shin Bet too. It is even possible that the trumped-up charges were motivated by the political motives of hatred and vengeance. Those things happen here too. I am saying this to emphasize our attitude toward the Arabs, which is often arrogant and dismissive, as if to say such things could not happen to us. Alternatively, it is possible too that our Shin Bet did not tell Netanyahu the whole truth, as has also happened before in the relations between our prime ministers and the secret service. But this is not a contest of who is better and who is right. The central question is how to communicate better with Mubarak, how to understand the different ways of thinking between Israelis and Arabs, the difference in our languages, in our emotional attitudes. This will also help us achieve the goal of improving our relations with Egypt and freeing Azzam. And here Mubarak is telling us they were hurt by Netanyahu's contempt for the Egyptian legal system.

The story began with the jailing of an Israeli whom we think is innocent. It is a grave act that greatly upsets us and brings out our feelings of victimization, which may partly be justified. I don't know which specific words of Netanyahu hurt Mubarak, but it does not matter. The very fact that Mubarak was hurt requires us to be mindful of his feelings and the feelings of the Egyptian people. But we reacted out of our insult, out of our feeling of victimhood, as we often do, and responded with a sweeping accusation against the credibility of a whole system and maybe even a whole country. We felt as if the Egyptians acted in malice, as if they are against us and want to hurt us, and we thereby reinforced our perceived circle of persecution. At this point it is already clear that if we had treated the Egyptian legal system with more respect, which it may well deserve, and added a request to free Azzam because an error occurred that could have occurred in our country too, we would have better served our relationship with Egypt as well as with Azzam himself. I want to stress that it does not matter who is right. We have to listen carefully to the emotional dialogue taking place here, when we, out of the hurt we feel, are unable to address the Egyptians from a position of equality and respect. Mubarak ends this statement with the question, "So, how can I do it?" In other words, you tell me, in such a situation of insulting our honor, how can I pardon him?

We have to be aware of the different quality of Arab thinking compared to ours. Mubarak is sharing with us the emotional experience of insult more than any logical structure. When he asks, "how can I do it?" he accompanies the question with a gesture, and waits for an answer from the interviewer or from the audience. He, Netanyahu, did to me such and such . . . so how could I pay him back differently? This is thinking on the emotional level, which is certainly different than Netanyahu's thinking. Mubarak does not ask whether Azzam spied or not, he is not dealing with facts; he is dealing with the *emotional relationship* that has arisen here, as opposed to Netanyahu, who is less interested in the emotional relationship, and who stresses the "objective truth." We, as a state, would never make clarifying the truth and justice dependent on what the Arabs said and whether they insulted us or not. Indeed, each side speaks his own language. Mubarak uses a more figurative, associative language, which is more connected to his emotions, while Netanyahu uses a logical language, which comes from a place of objectivity and is devoid of emotional content.

Mubarak's statement, whose aim is to protect himself from injury and insult—"They made a lot of mistakes in handling this matter, and it is their responsibility"—is a sadomasochistic statement which blames the victim for his suffering. He is both hurt and responsible for what happened to him. In other words, "Azzam Azzam will not be freed and it is your fault, so go eat your hearts out." Indeed, the interviewer responds to the invitation to this pattern of a relationship and this emotional response, and asks Netanyahu whether he is sorry about what he said. And immediately we feel guilty about ourselves and about Netanyahu, and wonder whether we behaved incorrectly and if what happened really was our fault, and we have no one to blame. It is the kind of relationship that if you are not aware of, can arouse strong feelings of guilt and shame. It can lead to repeated thoughts that had we acted differently, had we spoken differently, what happened would not have happened. It can set us off in search of the appropriate statement that would appease the other side. That pattern repeats itself often in our relationship with the Arabs, and it is worth understanding in depth. At question is a very elementary mechanism in the developmental process, called "identifying with the aggressor."

Identifying with the aggressor, as I have already explained, is an existential need for battered children. They identify with the parent who claims it is their fault, and cannot stand up to that parent and say they deserve better treatment, which they do not know at all (that is the problem). The parent swallows them emotionally, that is, forces them to agree with him, and does not allow them a separateness that could be expressed by the child's anger directed at the parent. Those children often invite the battering, because that is a way to join the parent and get attention. It is also the dynamic often seen in cases of sexual abuse, where the girl is not only hurt, but she also feels guilty and responsible for what happened. Our relationship with God too has a sadomasochistic element, like any passionate relationship with a stronger power that often seems to be arbitrary. The religious explanation for the Holocaust, for instance, is that we apparently sinned, did something wrong, and deserved it. We may not quite understand why we deserved such a horrible punishment, but God is always right and knows what he is doing, so that we can have no complaints.

The same is true for the Jews' exile from their country, the persecutions they went through, and so on. In all of these cases we were getting the punishment we deserved from God. This is definitely a relationship of identifying with the aggressor and sadomasochistic relations with an imaginary figure.

Training animals is another example. When we train an animal we demand the animal's absolute obedience and identification with its master, while completely giving up its independent wishes (identifying with the aggressor and a sadomasochistic relationship are similar emotional structures. That is because the person who identifies with his aggressor agrees and justifies him, and in that way derives pleasure from the aggressor's actions). Indeed, the Arabs often say that the Jews' role is to suffer, be beaten, and humiliated. The Jews should, according to those speakers, who usually come from religious Islamic circles, accept their passive role with submission and understanding, because that is Allah's decree.

Identifying with the aggressor is also a kind of relationship where the aggressor discards all guilt and the victim feels he deserves the punishment he got. It is a kind of relationship where the strong one is right, and the weak one is guilty and responsible for what happens to him. When the right says that the Arabs understand only force, it really means that the force used against them will make them understand that they are wrong (give him two slaps and then he will understand you are right). Such an attitude invites such a relationship, except that in this case we are in the sadistic position. A child often perceives the parent as right because the parent is strong, and therefore the child concedes to him. For no other reason. From a certain point of view you can understand that the growth process starts from that point, and the fear of punishment is a very powerful motivator in education. As adults, when the blow is terrible, we are thrown back to our feelings of weakness from childhood, and we identify with the aggressor because we don't have the strength to stand up to him. That identification soothes us. When a disaster comes, for instance, we often accept it with resignation, because the alternative is bitterness and anger toward the higher power. We understand that identification with the aggressor is a primary developmental mechanism that exists within all of us. When we say the refugees are to be blamed for their fate because the Arabs started the war against us, even though that is factually true, that is a sadomasochistic position where we are placing responsibility for what happened on the victim and removing it from ourselves. Or when we say we are lucky, since the Arabs are so stupid that they brought all the troubles upon themselves. Every time they refused a partition plan or initiated a war against us we gained and they lost. That statement is often made with gladness, as a result of our relief from absolving ourselves from responsibility and guilt.

We can find an identification with the aggressor in Israeli Arabs who vote for Zionist parties, especially the ones who vote for Likud. Collaborators who identify with the Jewish objectives also identify with the aggressor. We should listen to those quiet notes that are found in all of us, that brief gladness that we quickly repress when a disaster happens. When one of our soldiers is killed in Lebanon, for instance, we get a fleeting feeling that quickly escapes our consciousness, that we got the punishment we deserved. It is a feeling of some satisfaction, like scratching an itch. As Job said, "The Lord gave and the Lord hath taken away, blessed be the name of the Lord." After Rabin's assassination some people said he brought his punishment upon himself. Whoever really thinks like that is suffering from some pathology. But we should learn to recognize our whole range of feelings, and sometimes the most extreme among us can help us listen to ourselves more correctly. The importance of listening to those repressed feelings is to know the feelings that guide us and the Arabs and to understand our emotional dialogue with them.

The structure of the Arab family is fundamentally authoritarian. The father heads the family and the wife and children are his subordinates. This family structure invites feelings of identification with the aggressor. Indeed, the connection between femaleness and masochism is well-known. The son growing up in such a family will grow up to resemble his father in demanding that others identify with him and with his aggression. The more impulsive and primitive the society, the greater the impact of those feelings. That is how people identify with totalitarian regimes. In such regimes, as in traditional families, fear and power shape the patterns of emotional communication. It is no accident that clinical psychology, as I have mentioned, exists mainly in democracies. The ability to understand impulses, to look at them from the outside, and to take an objective look at subjective experiences, cannot be taken for granted, and can exist only in democratic regimes and societies and in egalitarian families, where the other is recognized. In Israel the right is more impulsive than the left. Therefore its psychological mechanisms are more exposed, more accessible, and are more likely to motivate behavior than in the left. In that respect the right is correct when it says that it understands the language of the Arabs better than the left.

Identifying with the aggressor is just the end of the road. The most extreme emotional act that can be done when one is threatened by force is to join it so as not to feel fear and anger. An intermediate condition between identifying with the aggressor and rebelling against the aggressor is being afraid of the aggressor and not rebelling. We separate from him and retain our anger toward him, but do not rise up against him. Our relationship with Israeli Arabs, Palestinians, and Arabs in general is characterized by those three emotional stances.

We have to understand the emotional meaning of the insult the Arabs have received from us. When the insult is strong enough and the Arab feels he cannot stand up to us, he might say he deserved that punishment. That is because it is hard for him to tolerate separateness and to tell himself that he wants to protest against that punishment. That is why it took the Palestinians so many years to stage their uprising. It is also the reason why they did not rehabilitate themselves as refugees for so many years. As if to say, what I got is what I deserved.

For the same reason, Israeli Arabs have not rebelled. They think, not entirely consciously, that they deserve their punishment, expressed in their disadvantage compared to the Jewish sector. They may feel they deserve the punishment because they collaborated with the Zionist enemy rather than fleeing like their brothers, the refugees (see the section "Israeli Arabs"). That might just be an added factor, and they might have identified with us, the aggressors, in any case and not rebelled. Their voting for Zionist parties is an example of their identifying with the aggressor. Even in our secret polls, behind the screen, a high rate of them vote for Zionist parties. After all, Israeli Arabs with their numbers could get more seats in the Knesset and increase their strength, but they choose not to. In the interim condition the Arab waits for an opportunity to rise up and rebel, is aware of his anger, and does not repress it as much as in the case of identifying with the aggressor. Again, the repressed anger of Israeli Arabs and the Palestinians in the territories these days, which might burst out in an Intifada, illustrates that emotional position. And finally there is the rebellion itself, the Intifada, where all the repressed feelings come out to be seen by all. Developmentally, that is the natural direction of the growth process. Repressed feelings wait to burst out, and that is why it is so important for us to be aware and alert to those processes.

Identifying with the aggressor is a primitive mechanism that contains a great deal of anger, which will burst out the moment the identifying person has more of an ability to be independent and separate, when he wakes up one day and says he does not deserve to suffer. Alternately, the identifier might feel the aggressor has weakened while he got stronger. Then too the identification with the aggressor loosens. We can see, therefore, two dangers—one, the emotional growth of the Arabs, both the Palestinians and the Israeli Arabs, who will ultimately demand their honor and place, which they deserve, and two, their feeling that we have gotten weaker and the balance of power has changed. Then their identification with us will weaken, and their fear of us will fade away. A long-term relationship cannot be based on identifying with an aggressor or fearing him; that is clear. This is the source of those sayings to the effect that if you turn your back on an Arab he will stab you, and that we must always be strong. If we examine those statements from the emotional point of view, we will understand that someone who stabs you from the back is afraid to stab you from the front. That is how the Arabs feel. To say the Arabs feel weak and afraid of us is an empathetic statement. To say they will stab us in the back emphasizes their treacherous nature. Clearly, the empathetic view, which we so lack in relation to the Arabs, is more constructive than the critical view.

Saying we must always be strong has some truth to it, particularly in a relationship with a more primitive and impulsive society. States are often born in struggle (in personal life it is hard to find such extreme examples of the idea that if we are not strong we will not survive physically, which is an indication of the primitiveness and primariness of the dynamics within the family of nations compared to interpersonal relations). Nevertheless, we must remember that to this day the Arabs have kept the agreements they signed with us. But we add insult to injury, humiliate them, and stoke the militant confrontation, with the idea that somebody has to be up and somebody else has to be down, which is at the basis of the emotional experience they know so well, as if they were battered children who grew up with fear in their eyes, and we treat them brutally, hurt them and reconstruct the relationship they know from the past, rather than helping them build a new relationship. We humiliate them under the guise of our intellectual, Western, democratic values, rather than doing so with the open impulsiveness they know, thereby increasing the injury. They stand in front of us like children, without words. They feel our propaganda machine has silenced them for years, and prevented the world from being aware of their pain. For them, there is no difference between what Saddam Hussein did to Kuwait and what we did to them. And they don't understand why the world did not react against the Jews the way it did against Saddam. They feel as if the Jews have magical powers, which invite them to repeatedly examine those powers by confrontation. We have to understand the emotional reaction that results from the humiliation of a primitive society. This is a situation that needs to be changed, of course.

The fact that Arab society is primitive does not only work against us, as Arab intellectuals throughout the world, who are most strongly against us, can testify. Because they are primitive, they are also warm and tend to be forgiving. We don't have to look too far; we know this dialogue from the relationship between the Israeli left and right. When we say that the Arabs tend to exaggerate, that their promises cannot be trusted, that they are liars, flatterers, and traitors, statements that come from racist attitudes, we forget that each one of those words has a positive side. The emotional attitude of the Arabs may be childish and impulsive because they are less developed. But if they tend to exaggerate and not cling to the truth, they also tend to forget and forgive what they feel we did to them. They are less vengeful and willing to reconcile and turn a new leaf, just like children, who fight and make up quickly (that is our problem, that we have yet to learn to appreciate Arab forgiveness). If they are flatterers, that is because they feel weak, and the same is true for their treachery. Loyalty and not flattering require power, and if the Arabs as a society feel weak compared with us, which is the case, then this is our opportunity to show a benevolent and loving attitude, and help them grow. In this racist list of attributes I listed childish tendencies that are evidence of the weakness of ego forces, which invite us to create a warm and close relationship with them, and provide an opportunity to somewhat correct past traumas. I am not sure we would be better off if we were facing European countries that were neither treacherous nor flattering, who kept their word, and whose hatred was also long lasting. Exiling people and seizing their land would not be more quickly forgiven in Europe. The evidence is their long history of wars and hatreds. The real question is whether we are able to see the good and the positive in our lifetime partner in the Middle East, and even love him and want to help him.

Let us examine the dynamics of our emotional relationship with Egypt. We are very careful in our relationship with Egypt because we are afraid, in the depths of our unconscious, that it will retract the peace agreement it signed with us. Because it was the first Arab country, and for years the only one, which signed a peace accord with us, and because it is a strong Arab superpower, we have treaded and continue to tread gingerly with Egypt. With a slight exaggeration, we have taken the attitude of a shy child or a bashful bride standing next to her groom, or the attitude of someone who is getting a favor they do not deserve. There is a mixture here of the elements of identification with the aggressor—this time from our side—self-flagellation, feelings of guilt and shame, and an attempt to appease the other side. There is abundant evidence of compliments we offered the Egyptians for their contribution to the peace process, while the Egyptians treated us aggressively for all those years. Rabin, for instance, complimented Mubarak even though Mubarak attacked him repeatedly; Barak's Sharm A-Sheikh agreement gave Egypt the honor of hosting the peace process and being a partner to it, while they showed antagonism toward us at every opportunity; for years our leaders made repeated comments about Egypt's contribution to the peace process, while the Egyptian leaders maintain a cold peace with us. They refuse to visit Israel, while we run to them at every opportunity. We maintain such an emotional relationship with Egypt out of a feeling of weakness and a desire to please more than out of honest appreciation of their contribution to the peace process. Indeed, the Egyptians invite us to a militant confrontation out of the insult they feel toward us, as was just noted.

We have to be careful here. I think we made a mistake on the matter of Azzam when we insulted Egypt. That was unnecessary, but it still does not mean we have to appease Mubarak at every opportunity. As opposed to our relationship with the Palestinians, we do not humiliate the Egyptians today actively and continuously, nor do they need us the way the Palestinians need us. The Egyptians are inviting us to a game we must not enter: a game of power, aggression, and hurt. Only by knowing these emotional games can we avoid falling into their trap. We do not have to hurt them, but we need not flatter them either. It is an invitation to a sadomasochistic game where the Egyptians hurt us and invite us to hurt them back, and then they will surrender for a moment, only to wake up from the hurt even angrier. In this power struggle to which Egypt invites us we have two choices: to surrender or win.

Mubarak's emotional dynamic was revealed again when he complemented Netanyahu at the beginning of his term, when he said that Netanyahu is credible and we can make peace with him. It is hard to understand what moved Mubarak to pay such complements to Netanyahu, which were surely very premature, and looked strange to many of us who knew Netanyahu's positions. It can only mean that there was something about Netanyahu's position, his militancy and charisma, which drew Mubarak to identify with him. The same was not the case for Mubarak's relationships with Barak, Rabin, or Peres. The awakening was not late in coming. Mubarak dropped his illusions and a fierce power struggle ensued. Mubarak used insulting language again when he called Arafat "son of a bitch" when Arafat did not want to sign the Oslo Accord. He laughed at Assad together with Peres when Assad failed to attend the funeral of Morocco's King Hassan, out of fear he would meet Barak there. He invited Netanyahu to Cairo after he lost the election, and not Barak, who won. He sent a message to Barak saying his positions arouse his concern.

In all of those examples there is an invitation to a lack of separateness and an accession to a humiliating relationship, emotional processes that are familiar in the clinic between therapist and patient. Just as in therapy, the goal is to be aware of what we are feeling and what the other party arouses in us, because it is only awareness that can prevent our being drawn into the tumult of emotions. That is Mubarak's emotional reaction to the primal insult the Arabs feel from us; it is the emotional reaction of an impulsive personality to insult; this is the emotional volatility, the game of emotions that has to do with Arab thinking, which we have to study and come to know. It is expressed in changeable and confusing emotional attitudes, which at one moment give a feeling of peace and intimacy, and in the next deal a blow (an emotional attitude we will later find in Arafat, which makes the blow even sharper). If we give him complements he does not deserve and actively involve him in the peace process, but at the same time we insult him, we will be serving the continuation of the same sadomasochistic relationship to which Mubarak has invited us. Only full alertness to the emotional message Mubarak is conveying to us can help us react appropriately.

The developmental achievement of a person who can contain his feelings, who is not easy to set off and cannot be taken to places where he does not want to go, is called "separateness." Just as in the case with Syria, the name of the game is "separateness" (see chapter 3 when we discuss Lebanon, in regard to A-Shara). Mubarak's inappropriate responses should surely be protested, nor should we give him prizes he does not deserve. Yet we should still maintain his dignity, which we are falling short of doing now. Egypt is not the desirable model of our relationship with Arab countries. Letting Mubarak mediate between us and our neighbors is a bad unconscious message. The late King Hussein would have been more suitable.

If we go back to the example at the beginning of the chapter, Netanyahu answered Mubarak logically and rationally that he hadn't heard such an excuse for holding a man in prison for such a long time. In other words, there is logic, there are rules and norms, and you don't keep a person in jail simply because of something I might have said. But Mubarak, who in the manner of Arab thinking put emotions at the center, is busy with something else, his emotional relationship with Netanyahu. In his response, that "objectivity" is appropriate; Netanyahu is missing the correct listening to Mubarak, the listening to the game of feelings: hurt, insult, and an invitation to a dependent sadomasochistic relationship. Netanyahu insults Mubarak again by using the word *excuse*. Now he is right inside the game to which Mubarak dragged him.

The tremendous importance of alertness to the emotions that move psychological processes comes from the same logic as that of therapy. We know that if we are aware of our feelings, we are less unconsciously motivated by them, and have more control of the situation. If we listen well to our insult, we will not be activated by it. If we listen well to the Arab insult we will be able not to intensify it and to escalate the conflict. Being aware of the sadom-asochistic play of feelings allows us not to fall into that trap and not to feel ourselves as either victims or aggressors. Therefore it would have behooved Netanyahu to apologize to Mubarak, who was hurt, because Netanyahu had no intention of insulting him or the Egyptian judicial system or the Egyptian people. Netanyahu would surely agree to that. Still, only an apology would serve the self-flagellation Mubarak anticipates in this sadomasochistic relationship. Therefore, it would be appropriate to say clearly that there must have been a mistake here, one that could have happened to us too, and that it should be corrected.

Arab thinking is different from ours, and we have to learn to know it. It is the kind of thinking that in therapy we actually encourage. It is more associative, figurative, emotional, and impulsive. In that way they make it easier for us to understand how they feel. Often, their statements are closer to their emotions than ours. Arafat speaks from his feelings and ignores the details. Hussein showed demonstrative warmth. Mubarak repeatedly adopts an attitude of hurt and insult. Assad conveys strong rigidity and frugality, and is decidedly unemotional. That too is a kind of emotional statement, a very defensive one. Each of the Arab leaders usually has his own style of a clear emotional statement. They are less committed to orderly logical thinking and more committed to emotional, symbolic, and associative thinking. Therefore we should listen to them as a therapist listens in the clinic. The therapist asks himself how the patient's words make him feel. He focuses on feelings and tries to help the patient identify his feelings. The therapist may listen less to the details and the logical arguments, which often serve as defenses against the feelings that are behind them. The therapist will ask the patient what it reminds him of, or what it arouses in him, and will follow his associative flow, that is, what reminded him of what, to help the patient identify his feelings.

We are often very critical and derisive of the Arab lack of credibility. When Egyptian radio announced in the Six Day War that the Arabs were winning on all fronts, it was a joke. We are a democratic state with a free press. That is not the case for the Arab countries. There is no doubt that it is a significant developmental difference. Democracy in psychology means allowing the different voices within us to express themselves. But in Syria, as I said, there is no Internet, no cable television, no mobile phones, and there is a security guard on every street corner. In Arab countries the leadership may not feel it is its duty to tell the public the truth. That is really a different way of thinking that we should try to understand. The militancy of such governments has a lot of impulsivity that perpetuates a regressive emotional stance and childish thinking, motivated by fear. Understanding the worlds of childhood and clinical psychotherapy helps us understand Arab thinking. We call it "primary thinking," which is more associative than secondary thinking, which is based on ego forces, order, and logical structure (dreams are the best example of primary thinking). Still, it is important to note that the years-old fear that we could not sign an agreement with the Arabs because they would not keep it, did not materialize. Time showed, to our relief, that it was untrue. The Arabs are not that regressive, and the agreements signed with the Arab countries—disengagement agreements with Syria and peace with Jordan, Egypt, and the Palestinians—usually were successful.

Let us try to understand the psychological dynamics of the Arabs' lies, their well-known lies on different matters in the media (I cited one example in chapter 4 in the section on Syria concerning A-Shara's statement that Syria did not shell Israeli settlements from the Golan Heights before the Six Day War). In the past, for instance, they were not in the habit of reporting their defeats in battle. A kindergarten child can say that he saw a dog as big as a donkey. He is not lying, he is telling us how he feels, that he saw a big dog. In the latency period (roughly age 6–12) we know children tend to lie. We call it "holes in the superego," thereby saying that their conscience is insufficiently developed. Such lies appear, for instance, in games when the child wants to win very badly or at other moments when the child is having a very hard time, and cannot resist changing reality according to his emotional needs. At the clinic we see adults who are pathological liars, not because they want to be liars, but because they are defending themselves against a reality they cannot bear. We say therefore that any lie can be understood, and that, more than it seeks to distort reality, it expresses a deep emotional difficulty in accepting an intolerable reality. The Arabs' lie is a kindergarten-age lie, a latency-age lie. They know the truth, but it hurts them and they are not strong enough to tolerate that pain and tell the truth. Indeed, the Arab media has focused for all those years on the aspects which are easier for the Arab viewer to accept. It is easier to be strong and right than weak and guilty.

We too lie, although in a more sophisticated and covert way, as befits someone with more developed defense mechanisms. Such is the case on the matter of the refugees, the matter of the uprooted residents of the villages of Ikrit and Baram (who have not been allowed to return to the villages they left in 1948, despite Israeli promises to let them); such is the case of the long-standing discrimination against the Arabs in Israel and in the territories, and such is the case of the frequent corruption cases in our country. When we lie, we have reasons, arguments, and mainly rules. We can prove with numbers, on paper, that the Arabs are not disadvantaged, that the refugees fled voluntarily, and that there is some problem that prevents us from letting the uprooted villagers have their homes back. Since our thinking is more advanced and our lies are better argued, they are also less accessible to us. That is, we are like paranoid people who are convinced they are right. It seems as if the Arabs are more aware of their lies than we are of ours. They take themselves less seriously, and that has advantages.

Let us address for a moment the cases in which we say the pure truth while the Arabs lie. In psychotherapy we know the limits of the kind of thinking that supposedly tells the whole truth and is scrupulously faithful to it, but often misses the main point, the emotion and the emotional context. We can insist upon the truth and the details and be the most right, while at the same time conveying a lot of aggression and lack of trust, which hurts the other side. We know well from the clinic that objectivity, which negates subjectivity, logic that does not recognize feelings, is a defensive emotional stance of someone who is not ripe for a human relationship. How hard we therapists work in the clinic to help that defensive, right person grow and recognize his feelings, while a whole world hides behind his defenses. So perhaps we were right about that point, but A-Shara was insulted. If instead of saying that he, the Syrian foreign minister, was lying, we said that we understood the Syrian insult whereby they felt that the land they experience as part of their homeland is under foreign control, and that we would consider giving it back to them if our needs too are fulfilled, *such an approach, focused on the emotional message rather than on the "lie," could promote peace.* At the same time, we would be glad if the Arabs could understand how hard it is for us to admit what happened with the refugees. We wouldn't want them to catch us lying and wave our lie in front of the whole world. We know how important emotional understanding is, and how stuck everything is if you ignore the emotional dimension and focus solely on the cognitive dimension of lies and absolute truth. We expect adults to be able to integrate their objective and subjective parts, to recognize two ways of thinking, the emotional and the cognitive that complement each other, and not to develop one at the expense of the other. The Arabs tend toward subjective thinking that speaks from emotion and experience, while we tend toward intellectual, objective thinking. We feel that their position is inferior, though we do not need criticism, but rather understanding of the difference.

Observing the bargaining process allows us to learn about the difference between us. Israelis, for instance, are less inclined to bargain. There is an absolute truth that may be experienced as rigid, cold, arrogant, or insulting by the other side. Arabs are inclined to bargain, and the price is more flexible. We might look at bargaining as a manipulative and disrespectful stance, which invites extortion and arguments and leaves you feeling either exploited or exploiting, that you either won or lost. The Arab stance invites you to emotional involvement. But whether this is a power struggle or a warm, pleasant game, depends on the quality of the interaction between the sides. The Arabs have a hard time with emotional distance and separation; having a separate self is hard for them. It starts with emotional processes inside the family, which is why objectivity and democracy are hard for them. The salesperson opens with a high price, and if you agree you may come out feeling like a sucker. The salesperson expects this and invites you to an interaction of bargaining over the price. That is the essence of our relations with the Arabs. They spark in us those elements that we usually interpret as humiliating or humiliated. We have a hard time experiencing or interpreting bargaining as an invitation to a warm and intimate interaction, because such emotional mingling threatens us with its regressiveness. We may avoid entering negotiations with that salesperson, which is not possible in our area. We can pay him the price he requires, and again, that too is an unwise step in our situation. We can bargain over the price and try to humiliate him, but that will do us no good in the future either. There is only one option left, which is to treat our partner to the process with warmth, despite the differences between us, while checking what price we are willing to pay. We should do our homework well, be aware of ourselves, and define our red lines in such a way that we neither exploit them or give up our interests. Then we should go to that salesperson and say, this is the price we are willing to pay, no more and no less. If you are interested, it is a deal. If not, not.

I believe over time the Arabs will learn to respect such a direct approach. We do not have to get involved in a game that suits them but not us, but a warm and sympathetic attitude has to come across. The main rule is that what you do does not matter; how you do it does. We can bargain with them, or decide not to get into that game, but in both cases it has to be done with a warm and intimate feeling.

We have to understand Arafat's double language, where at one moment he speaks of Jihad (holy war) and at the next of peace. The same goes for Mubarak and for other Arab leaders. Those are very confusing emotional relations. One moment we are glad Arafat is making a peaceful statement, and the next moment we receive a blow we did not expect. It is a childish emotional stance, motivated by shifting moods and emotions of the moment, which do not have enough ego strength to ground themselves in reality.

Arab thinking is distinguished by its fluidity, the quality we see in the clinic in certain personality disturbances, which use denial rather than repressive mechanisms. Repression is a more advanced mechanism that allows us not to split the experience. Splitting by denial is characterized by feeling good one moment, and the next moment bad, without any connection or link between them. The repressing person has more ego strength to deny pain and distress than the denier, whose feelings are externalized, and who does not have the ability to pack them in a more orderly manner. These are more hysterical and manic kinds of thinking than ours, which is more obsessive and grounded in rules. In our case it is not a personality disorder, of course, but a more primitive way of thinking, a more childish one, which has difficulty making internal order and overcoming pain. Arafat's shifty statements stem from a combination of primitive Arab thinking and the insult and humiliation the Arabs receive from us. The interaction of that insult and their weak ego forces create that labile thinking.

Let us take a brief look at some of the central elements of Arab thinking that make it primitive: *Magical thinking:* that is a kind of thinking typical to childhood. It is the belief that words have the power to change the world, for instance. The child who curses his mother, wishing she would die, may be afraid he will really make it happen. Superstitions, magic, miracles, blessings, curses, and charms, are all examples of magical thinking. We have only to remember how the streets of the West Bank cities were empty during the solar eclipse. The Palestinians were afraid to be outside in case something bad happened to them; the Arabs' were afraid of fighting at night, which the Israeli army took advantage of for years; the conquest of Jaffa by Etzel was assisted by a loud boom that was generated to make the Arab residents flee. Their magical fear of the Jews and their abilities assumed unreal dimensions over the years. We were often perceived by the Arabs as demonic creatures and aroused within them primal fears. They ran away from us out of fear, for instance, without even engaging us in battle. And in a sharp cut to the present, when Peres talks about a new Middle East, the Arabs are alarmed and afraid we will take control of them in this new Middle East, this time under a benevolent guise, just as they feel we have taken them over, and their land, and their homes for years. The Arabs' magical fears, nourished by archaic fears of overpowering and swallowing (the Syrian soldiers who fought the Yom Kippur War were ordered to eat the flesh of the enemy), in this last case, have a basis in reality.

Primary thinking based on drives: the Egyptian defense minister compared Arafat to a stripper who every minute gives the Jews another item of her clothing. The minister added that the difference is that strippers are beautiful but that Arafat is ugly. This illustration of Arab insult—Arafat's passive female submission to the Jew who is raping him—is the experience speaking from the mouths of the Syrians, against which they are defending themselves. As in any primary thinking, the impulses are on the outside and you can look at them (here is an opportunity to take a rare peek at the deep sexual drives that motivate the relations between the two peoples). The promise to the Egyptian soldiers at the start of the Six Day War, that they would be able to rape Jewish women, and the sadistic torture of Israeli prisoners of war by the Arabs, are further examples.

Absence of ego forces: many Israeli Arabs (compared to the Jewish population) do not pay municipal taxes. It is hard for them to internalize order and organization beyond their primary, egocentric needs. The proliferation of traffic accidents in the Galilee, which comes from the Arabs' failure to follow traffic rules and signs, is well-known. The many cases of corruption in the Palestinian

Authority come from the same difficulty, that is, the absence of ego forces that help curb drives and install order in their associative feebleness.

A child who alternately laughs and cries is asking for attention to what hurts him and amuses him, not for both to be ignored. When Arafat calls for holy war, or when his wife, Suha, blames Israel for poisoning the air of the Palestinian territories, we have to take up these issues with them. We cannot ignore them. The inquiry will not be easy for us. Their magical, associative thinking contains a germ of truth. Maybe we did not contaminate their air purposely, but perhaps Israeli factories disposed of toxic waste there, as happens in Israel, and contaminated water sources, as they do in Israel, or dumped toxic chemicals that contaminated the soil, which, again, happens in Israel, but in this case with greater abandon, knowing those are Palestinian territories. The Palestinians are not always able to explain themselves as well as we can. It is also hard to argue with a paranoid person, who spends his whole life proving to the world he is right. It is true especially if he is inclined to childish, primary thinking. After all, a child is always right, and whatever he feels toward his parents is always true, and we have to listen to him empathetically and understand what he is saying, because he is always saying true things, that hurt him, straight from the heart. But there are parents who tell their children: "What you feel is not true." We therapists try to teach them to be empathetic toward themselves as well as toward their children, and simply listen better to what they are saying. In therapy, we would not ignore anything the patient says, because it reflects his feelings and his inner world and is no accident. At home, we should not let our child swear and say anything that comes to mind, even if he is right. That is what the peace process is, a process of emotional exploration, a process of understanding what is hurting the other side, and exploring whether their pain can be relieved by a mutual peace process. Our serious attention to Arafat's every word is the only thing that will eventually install order in his dramatic, associative, inconsistent language, which leaves us confused.

We cannot remain complacent when an Arab leader calls for Jihad or supports the Arab boycott against Israel or persuades other countries not to make political ties with us in an era of peace. That is a kind of terrorism to which we must respond. Everything we said about terrorism is also true about verbal aggression. Such aggression must not remain fragmented, external, unintegrated, and without the Arabs taking responsibility for its occurrence. I am referring to the Arab way of thinking that requires our clear but benevolent boundaries. Rabin erred when he said we would deal with terrorism as terrorism, and continue the peace process separately. He made a mistake no good parent would make, by ignoring his child's aggression and absolving him of responsibility. Again, our reactions have to be educational. We cannot deny them food, health services, or schoolbooks simply because they spoke inappropriately. But we can hurt their symbols of independence, sovereignty, and honor, which are very important to them because they cannot control their impulses.

It is necessary, as I have stressed, to declare with warmth and love, "you will get a state because you deserve one, but only if you keep your commitments and show independence and maturity." The connection between receiving independence and controlling impulses is natural in the growth process. Ignoring verbal aggression is simply a failure to understand that it comes from the same place in the soul that physical aggression will soon come from. The question of our love of the Palestinians may draw the ridicule of people who cannot understand that kind of developmental solution in emotional life (see chapter 4 on how the child resolves his first masculine conflict). Only if we love them and honestly help them can we demand that they stop the doublespeak. As children relating to parents, they will have a reason to identify emotionally with our demands, because identification comes through love. I am referring to the love we will give them, as if they were our growing children. We can help them develop their democracy, that is, help them move from primary, impulsive thinking to thinking with rules and laws. *We created the refugee problem, and we have a moral responsibility to help them.* If we can ever look them in the eye, it will be because we took care of them, and not only dispossessed them. But we are like parents who say, "This child (who may be only three) does whatever he wants; we have no control over him; we have lost hope." In therapy we try to show the parent that he has a lot of influence and power over his small child, even though he doesn't believe he does and feels helpless. Ultimately, even the parent understands that the child needs his love.

Let us look at the difference between us and the Palestinians. Their impulse control is curtailed by fluid, associative thinking, and by the lack of sufficient ego forces. We give our aggressive urges organization, order, and "reasoning." They, as children, are less firm in their demands (this was more evident in the years when they did not rebel), and it is hard for them to be consistent. We are more consistent and stubborn, as befits people whose defenses are better crystallized and whose thinking is better organized. We have to remember that the difference between us is not in the quality of our urges, but only in our defenses. Ours are better developed. Our urges are clothed in a democratic, Western wrapping. When we do not keep our word, we have a "reason." They are less inclined to require reasons. When we lie, it is first of all to ourselves, because we have sophisticated repression mechanisms, and because we do not see what we do not want to see. When they lie, they are more aware of it, because they are more externalized; everything is open and accessible. They are less self-critical, which has positive and negative aspects. Self-criticism is very important to development, but excessive self-criticism has to do with a rigid superego (the conscience), which arouses excessive guilt feelings. Indeed, we are inclined toward guilt, while the Arabs are inclined toward shame. Shame has to do with more developed repressive mechanisms (e.g., from the oedipal stage) while shame has to do with more narcissistic, primal elements. The Arabs are aware of this and take themselves less seriously than we do. If we dig under our Western intellectual wrapping, we will find all of our repressed feelings and sharp splits. In our deep unconscious, both sides want the same kind of peace, a childish peace, a religious peace, where only our God exists, and where we deserve everything. Our democracy represents the forces of ego trying to wrap up the sea of impulses storming beneath. Such is our Knesset with all of its fragments and factions, a container about to burst from its internal pressure. We all come from the same impulsive world, and we are all motivated by its strong forces. Just as you help a child grow, we have to help the Palestinians to ultimately speak in one unified voice. But for that, as I have said, we have to be good parents and role models. In this emotional relationship we have to be as credible and clear as possible, self-aware, in control of our impulses, and not giving double messages; in other words, all the characteristics of a good parent, so that we do not confuse them further when they are already so confused.

Now we can easily answer the question, Should we try to free Azzam Azzam by quiet diplomacy or by massive media exposure? Since the idea of conducting a quiet diplomatic effort comes from the desire not to aggravate the Egyptians, and is a way of cooperating with the relationship to which they invite us, in which we are afraid of them and feel ashamed and guilty, it is undoubtedly better to take the course of open diplomacy that opens the issue to the whole world, and where we do not cooperate with those feelings. Otherwise we are playing a part in a sadomasochistic relationship with them (they are saying, "Keep quiet and we will take care of things," and putting us in the emotional position of a child asking for help and protection, rather than an adult insisting on his rights). The many years of trying to bring Soviet Jewry to Israel with quiet diplomacy did not work and proved to us that there too we cooperated with a relationship characterized by a *lack of separateness*.

Speaking to Arabs

How do you talk to an Arab? Some Israelis say they know how to talk to Arabs. There are people who say they know the Arab mentality and that helps them communicate with them (Yitzhak Mordechai, prime ministerial candidate in 1999, made that claim in comparing his qualifications to Barak's). This question bears clarification. As always, the best place to start is with ourselves, our feelings, our gut. What happens to us when we talk to an Arab in the street or in the grocery store, or with construction workers? What happens to an Israeli soldier who addresses a Palestinian at a roadblock, to a Jewish employer addressing an Arab worker, a Jewish woman addressing an Arab cleaning lady? If we examine ourselves closely, we will find that we do not talk to Arabs in the same way we talk to Jews, or even in the same way we talk to Americans or Britons. We are secretly aware of the invitation to emotional involvement in this case. Often the feeling is fear, but not always. We are just as likely to develop a warm relationship characterized by an emotional involvement and a lack of separateness.

Let us start with the fear. When we pass a construction site with Arab workers who stare at us as we walk by, we feel fear. It might be weak, almost imperceptible, but it is there nonetheless. Do we turn our heads away to avoid looking them straight in the eye, or do we look right back at them? At that point we already are in a war, a war of stares. Any soldier who patrols an Arab city or stands at a roadblock knows the power of staring and the expectation that the Arab will lower his gaze. Indeed, when we meet an Arab we often think there are only two choices: to rule or be ruled, to win or surrender, to intimidate or be intimidated. Those really are the only choices between an occupier and a subject. Ruling over somebody implies inequality, which is just waiting for an opportunity to burst out in the form of a violent rebellion for liberation. An occupier is always afraid, and has to repress that fear and hide it, especially from himself, so as not to panic and lose control, and let the other become the ruler. That invitation to be either an aggressor or a victim in every daily encounter of ours with the Arabs is at the root of the problem of the peace process, on both the personal and the national levels.

What we forget is that in their impulsive, primitive society, which invites that emotional involvement with which we come into contact, there is another repertory of behaviors, namely, warm and intimate relationships. The Arab usually demands either absolute identification or nonidentification. You are either with me or against me. Many Ashkenazi Jews are familiar with this from their encounters with Sephardic Jews; the emotional solution into which a member of a Middle Eastern culture is likely to invite you: a warm and loyal friendship, backslapping, and a willingness to do almost everything for your friend, all out of complete identification and lack of criticism. This loyalty exists in the family or tribe, with the Oriental warmth we have forgotten in the midst of all this fighting.

Let us examine our feelings when we encounter Western, American, or European culture. We can learn from those feelings how the Arabs feel toward us. I am referring to the feelings of a member of a primitive culture in his encounter with a member of a more developed and advanced culture. Many Israelis see Americans and Europeans as cold, alienated, and distant. Israelis who live abroad often miss Israeli warmth and view the Americans, for instance, as cold and impersonal, as people with whom it is hard to develop real friendships. What looks to Europeans or Americans like a correct, appropriate relationship, can be experienced by an Israeli as an intolerably cold relationship, which needs to be colored with more emotion in order for them to feel comfortable with it. Absolute justice, objectivity, and order, all those can be experienced as something very impersonal, distant, and arrogant. That is how a child, and not only a child, feels when he is waiting in an orderly queue, and does not believe his turn will ever come. That is how an Arab merchant may feel when we refuse to bargain with him, or how an Arab may feel if he asked us for a favor and we refused. That is how the child often feels toward his parents, who do not seem to understand or consider his feelings.

If we think about the inferiority we feel toward European standards of order and justice, we can begin to understand how the Arab world feels toward us. Objectivity can be experienced as coldness, alienation, and arrogance, and we should remember that well in our relationship with the Arabs. True, there is no other way to grow but to enfold the sea of impulses in a wrapping of ego forces. We too, in our desire to resemble the West and not the Third World, have to overcome the insult that every child goes through in the growth process. Democracy, equality, the ability to recognize the other, and the objectivity we still lack in many areas of our lives, are often very insulting during the growth process. We have to be aware of the difficulty our neighbors experience in following our demands that they keep agreements, not use doublespeak, and so on. We would demand the same of a child too, but we would soften our demands with love, because we know a child needs unconditional love. Anyone who has close relations with Arabs or Mizrahi Jews or children knows the importance of the warm and accepting foundation for those relationships.

It is clear how it all started. Undemocratic regimes often emerge in societies where women do not have equal rights. In such societies generations of children grow up without equality between people. The husband controls his wife who is inferior and who serves as an object to fulfill his needs. That is the image of the mother in Arab society. Similarly, we find authoritarian and forceful Arab parents, and less equality between parent and child in their society. Again, physical strength counts. The nature of government in Arab societies reflects the family relations. It is no accident that in this book I bring many examples from the first and most important group into which we are born—the family. This is the first place where we experience interpersonal relations. The transition to international relations is merely an extension from the family to the family of nations.

We Israelis, with our power and our might, serve as authority figures for the Arabs, like a big parent who can be close or distant, be generous, or inflict pain. In our relationship with the United States, for instance, which we need in every area, there is an invitation for a parental relationship, only luckily in this case it is warm and supportive. We feel toward the United States the way a child feels toward a teacher, whose every word can elevate or deflate him. An Arab laborer, who earns NIS 500 per month and who needs a permit to work in Israel, sees us, right fully, as people who can change his life from one extreme to the other, provide his needs or deny them, all with the bat of an eyelash. If we add to that the humiliation we have inflicted on the Arabs, and the fact that they are a primitive society, where the level of passions, projections, lack of objectivity, and lack of separateness is high in relation to any figure, then it is hard to expect them to see us in a more balanced, objective light. Since the father in Arab society is an omnipotent authority figure, we, as authority figures, serve as the objects of many projected feelings: longings, fears, needs, and so on. It is our choice whether we register in their consciousness only as insulting, hurting, and frustrating parents or also as warm parents who give them something for the future. We all know how powerfully childhood experiences stay with us throughout our lives. Today, at the dawn of Palestinian independence, they are shaping their experience of us. They will always remember how we treated them in their national childhood.

Warmth, to be seen and to be helped, are what the Arab wants from the soldier at the roadblock, and what the Arab cleaner wants from her Jewish boss, or what the Arab worker wants from his employer. That is how the poor feel toward the rich, the weak toward the strong. That is often how our political right feels toward the left. They want a childish emotional involvement, and if they do not get it, they feel insulted and hurt. Everyone feels that way toward authority figures, especially if he is emotional, impulsive, and childish. We have to remember that the Arabs feel longing and needy toward us the way a child feels toward a parent, or the way a member of a primitive culture feels toward a member of an advanced culture. So far, most of our encounters have ended with the Arabs feeling hurt and insulted. But since these are childhood experiences and primary needs, and we are still at the beginning of the life of the Palestinian state, the optimistic message is that it is not too late to correct that.

An encounter with a member of a primitive society carries inherent instability that is typical of children. Their weak ego forces are not yet ripe enough to establish a permanence that endures the changes of time and shifting emotional states. Such a shifty relationship, like a child's growth, requires regular nourishment, and an ongoing response to their feelings and hurts. Parents get no time off and no holidays. In a certain respect, the same is true for our relationship with the Arabs. We have to accept the fact that there are a lot of ups and downs in store for us. It will take a long time for this child to be more stable and crystallized so that he can be trusted. Being alarmed by his aggression is like a parent being insulted or hurt by a child. We do not expect a parent to be hurt by his child as if he were his friend. We expect the parent to be able to see the child's hurt that is behind his aggression. True, this child is full of aggression toward us, and we understand why. It does not mean that we will throw him out of the house or beat him up. It does mean that alongside a warm and sympathetic attitude that will help him grow we will also set firm and clear boundaries. That is the correct parental attitude toward a child's aggression. It is not a rejection of the child or a descent to the child's level or age, but unconditional love, with a clear statement that there are some things we will not tolerate. But we often behave like the parent who says the child is doing whatever he wants and we cannot control him. In therapy we try to show the parent how desperately the child needs him and is thirsty for his love.

Let us get back to the first question, Are there really Israelis who know better than others how to talk to Arabs? Did Begin get along with Egypt's Sadat better than Golda Meir? If he did, it was because of their shared mentality and dramatic language, which is why he was the one who made peace with Egypt. Psychotherapy offers an answer to what it means to speak correctly to any person. The correct way to speak to anyone is to be aware of the feelings they arouse in us and not to repress or deny them. That is how we should talk to the Arabs. It can be assumed that the Israeli left, which represses aggression, would repress the aggressive message conveyed to us by the other side. It can also be assumed that the right is more aware of that power-oriented relationship. Yet, the right might, typically, respond to the other side with too much force and perpetuate the conflict. Begin may have received Sadat with a festive ceremony and let him address the Knesset, but we know that this was followed by a chilling of the relationship between the two, and ultimately there was no great love between them.

It is important for the public to be aware of the range of emotions aroused by our daily encounters with Arabs on the street, because that is the basis of the peace process. Not every conversation with an Arab is a war of survival, even if we are invited to such a horror film. Yet, we should be aware of the invitation to a warmer and more emotional relationship, so that such precious signals are not lost. The greatest difficulty is the attitude of threat, the inability to see someone else. We could still bargain, for instance, but within a warm and sympathetic relationship. Again, what you do does not matter; what matters is how you do it.

Phrases such as "Arabs only understand force" require emotional clarification. There are situations in which that is the only option. But when I encounter an Arab in the market, why do I have to talk to him that way? Why does our daily dialogue with them have to be through warfare? Are we not inviting precisely what we are afraid of and don't want, namely, war? Saying that Arabs understand only force, not only does not allow peace, but comes from our deepest fears that are not always justified. Saying that the Arabs only understand force means I am afraid. And if I am motivated by fear and moved to speak from a position of force, I had better check myself closely. Is this not a self-fulfilling prophecy? How would a child grow if we assumed that he understands only force? Will he grow up to understand anything else, not to mention what that perception says about the parent? In other words, "the Arabs only understand force" is a projective statement. It is hard to admit, but there are more than a few examples in our own past that show that we understood only force. I have already mentioned the Intifada, our need to withdraw from Lebanon, and mainly, the very need to strive for peace, which stemmed from our realization that we are not the strongest people in the world.

The Arabs unconsciously expect us to help them grow. No expectation could be more natural for a less developed person from a more developed person. That is how the Arab cleaner feels toward the Jewish housewife; that is how the Arab worker feels toward his Jewish boss. That is why they will value any person who is not guided by their fears and threats, and who gives them a warm and loving relationship. That is how a good parent operates. A good parent understands the child's feelings, but also sets goals they both have to reach. A good parent mediates between the child and reality, between the place where the child is now and the place the child has to reach. He has to feed the child small, appropriate portions. He cannot be too close and identifying, or too distant, like a cold and abandoning parent. This should be our attitude toward Arab impulsivity. We have to understand it and be empathetic toward it, but also see that it is a point in a long road we have to take. The child will ultimately appreciate this.

The Gulf War is one of the only examples in our past (in the last few years, our restraint in Lebanon is another example) of the freedom in the absence of reaction, the liberty in restraint and the way in which not being directed by someone else's dictates not only does not weaken you but strengthens you and your power of deterrence. But every parent knows that.

When someone says, "Leave it to me, I know how to talk to Arabs," he is really saying that he knows the Arabs' *tricks* and knows how to *outsmart* them. That is an arrogant, condescending, and aggressive attitude that actually perpetuates our fear of the Arabs. How would we feel if someone said they know "how to talk to Jews?" We would be very insulted. We want to be talked to as people, so that we can respect the speaker, and we do not want to be outsmarted.

A soldier checking an Arab at a roadblock is by definition in a position of power. As Jews, even when a Jewish police officer comes over to us and asks us for our license, we feel the power he has over us, as well as the fear and potential confrontation built into the situation. A good police officer, fulfilling his duty to arrest us if we were guilty of a traffic violation or to stop us to check our papers, can sweeten the bitter pill if he is nice and polite, smiles and does the job. That is the lesser evil. Surely, if he approaches us with a threatening glare and a forceful attitude, we will feel humiliated and resentful. But if we asked Palestinians to fill out a questionnaire showing interest in how they are treated by soldiers and how they feel at the roadblocks, we would see an immeasurable change there.

There is no doubt that in every encounter between us, who come from a developed democracy, and the Arabs, who come from more backward and primitive countries, there is a basic inequality that we should be aware of. That gap invites an arrogant attitude on our part, which is a form of abuse of power and aggression by the party that feels superior. Clinical experience shows us that an arrogant person may not be aware of his arrogance and superiority. He will cling to the objective facts and say that they are not arrogant, they are just better, and have objective proof thereof. But we know the question is not who is better. The issue is the emotional message, and how hard it is for the arrogant person to understand how his emotional attitude affects the other person. The attitude of Peres, that we can help the Arabs develop, despite his good intentions, was seen by them as patronizing and insulting. To them, as I have noted, it was another irritation to an old emotional wound, regarding their experience of our taking over their lands and homes and the Middle East in general. Therefore they were not thrilled by those initiatives. Therefore, should we hide our abilities and development, or pretend there is no difference between us and the Arabs, just so that they are not offended? The answer is no, of course. We do not need to blur the truth, that we are more advanced than they are in many areas, but between here and taking an arrogant emotional stance there is a very short distance. That is because they really envy us and the state we built. In this context we already discussed the sensitivity every parent needs to show when entering the child's world. It is important to remember this example in relations between nations that begin with the personal encounter of the Arab worker and his Jewish employer. In interpersonal relations, as in international relations, as soon as a warm emotional relationship is established we are on safe ground and the chances of our being seen as arrogant are minimal.

Our relations with the United States are an excellent example of the way in which the weakness of one side does not necessarily lead to the arrogance of the other. If we want to learn how to give without condescending, we should learn from the United States. They have given us massive economic aid for years, and it is hard and frightening to imagine how we would have managed without it. They have done so quietly, for years, as if they were giving without our noticing. Therefore we really are not aware enough of that aid. They are not suddenly threatening to cut off the ongoing aid they have given us every year. They do not wave that whip. Theirs is a noncondescending giving that is accompanied by warm statements of intimacy and caring, and therefore we are not sufficiently aware of it, which is a shame, because this leads to our illusions of power and might, which have no basis, such as saying that the United States needs us as much as we need them. That is of course an arrogant statement that is not true. The United States does not need us for its immediate existence the way we need it. It is the statement of a child whose parents give him everything, and he can shout that he is as big and as strong as they are and does not need them. Such parents should remind that child once in a while that he cannot stand on his own feet yet, that he needs them, so that he does not get too full of himself, because it will hurt him. The educational problem all parents ask, "To what extent should parents tell their children what to do with the money they give them?" comes up here too. The norm is for the child to decide about the small change, the allowance he gets, but not beyond that. Undoubtedly our ability to be swept away by grandiosity into omnipotent obstacles is nourished by American money. In our case the American parent should be more directive and boundary-setting, because we are still having a hard time on our own. We need the money, but the Americans have to tell us which uses they are willing to fund and which they are not. They are prepared to give us military and economic aid, but not money to build more settlements. It is hard to make the distinction because the money is in the same till. We are able to invest in settlements because we have economic strength in other areas. Therefore, the Americans can tell us there are things they object to our doing. We need American money with the European attitude. It is the attitude of a parent who is protective of the child and who sets organizing and soothing limits. It is the attitude of the parent who helps the child see what is really important to him. Economic development—yes. Swelling our territory and feelings—no. That is how the World Bank acts when it makes its loans conditional on appropriate economic policy. That is how it helps the various countries not to be directed by internal pressures and to grow properly. Every child needs such a parent to help him control his urges. If the United States conditioned its aid on correct economic thinking and not buckling to internal coalition pressures that cause waste, we would benefit from that because we are still struggling on our own.

The question is how we can give to the Palestinians with the goal of helping them grow, while deeply respecting them and showing humility. I think that there is a clear connection between our inflated ego, fed by the Americans, and our difficulty in giving to the Palestinians from a position of humility. Surely our lack of humility hurts us in all areas. The first, most severe damage is to our ability to listen to emotions, because we "can't be bothered." There is a known connection between humility, clear boundaries, and the ability to listen to emotions. A person with grandiose tendencies will not hear the gentle tunes played on the strings of his soul, and surely not on his neighbors'.

What is missing in our desire to help the Palestinians is a change in our fundamental emotional attitude toward them. The transition from feelings of threat and hatred to generous and loving giving is not easy. The United States gives to us out of love, while we want to give to the Palestinians in order to feel strong and able, and therefore we flaunt our giving and hurt the Arabs. That is the summary of the difference between the way in which the Americans give us and the way in which we want to give to the Palestinians. Only a deep change in our emotional attitude toward them will change our giving to them into a benevolent giving, rather than being insulting and hurtful. Therefore I am working so hard to compare our relations with the Palestinians to the relations between a parent and child, to arouse our warmth and concern for them, which is desperately needed in this power-oriented relationship. The advantage of either side, as any parent knows, can be translated into either hurting the other, or into a warm and intimate relationship. The question is which you choose.

But how can we make that difficult emotional change in our attitude toward the Palestinians, and how can we mobilize empathy toward them when they often treat us with severe violence? When a patient comes into the clinic and we have a hard time with him because he is aggressive and does not appreciate what we are doing for him, dismisses us, and so on, we know one of the best ways to connect with him and to feel his pain is to ask him about his past. Because then, when he was small and had not hurt anyone yet, he suffered. That is where we can connect to the root of his suffering, to be empathetic to his aggression, and to understand where it comes from. We can better connect to a battering parent, for instance, if we connect to the suffering he endured as a battered child. We will understand that he carries the trauma of his childhood with him every day and every hour. In the case of the Palestinians, as we have seen, we have to go back to the refugee problem. The one and only way for us to treat the Palestinians with more warmth and appreciation is to understand what they went through in their "childhood" and what great pain they carry with them. Only that way, by knowing their past, through learning about their lives, their travails, and their fate, which we try so hard to blur and whitewash, will we find empathy for them and change our basic position toward them. We know the deep connection between thoroughly knowing a person or culture and feeling empathy toward it. Deep familiarity leads to understanding and love, while distance serves alienation, hostility, and hatred (I already mentioned the importance of the political left learning about the daily lives, past, and heritage of the Mizrahi Jews in order to get closer to them). Then we will want to compensate them and give them the little we can, and this time, from real emotion, not out of arrogance. The essence of the change is our moving from a childish emotional position to a parental position, a transition from a frightened and threatened attitude to a warm, loving, and mature attitude, which takes responsibility and understands the existing emotional situation.

Our difficulty with the Palestinians reminds me, without comparing, of course, of the difficulty between the Germans with us. Our relationship with the Palestinians cannot be ordinary because we caused them a terrible trauma, which we still deny because of our guilt, which is not justified. The Germans, as I have noted, understand today that they cannot expect their relationship with the state of Israel to be an ordinary relationship. The terrible past will always stand between us. We expect them to live with that past and not to make allowances for themselves. There is a big difference, of course. The Germans really should feel guilty, but we should not. We were fighting for our right to live, while the Germans were not. But we have to understand that the Palestinians are going to continue seeing us for many years to come as the people who destroyed both their personal and national lives. If we want anything good ever to develop between us we must not repress the past. Because correct listening to the Palestinians cannot deny the past and the emotions it entails. Just as we take every dignitary who comes to Israel to the Yad Vashem Holocaust Memorial, to explain in the most graphic way what the Jewish people went through, and how our life is affected and shaped by that trauma consciously and unconsciously, so the Palestinians need their own "Yad Vashem." They need a place to take their guests and tell their story, how they lived in their land and homes and tilled their land until they were expelled from it, and that today they are dispossessed refugees. They did nothing wrong; they just did not want the Jews to take over their country. Our real recognition of their "Yad Vashem" along with the understanding that we are *not guilty* requires a high level of maturity and emotional integration. The demand is not to get sucked into the guilt feelings we might feel, nor to erase the Palestinians and their past as a converse reaction to that guilt. But we are still dealing with who is right and who is wrong. That is why we are defensive. *As soon as we realize that we are really not wrong we will be able to give the Palestinians more love.*

The attitude of Jewish building contractors or farmers or housewives toward their cheap Arab labor bears examination. Their very need to come work for us necessarily implies humiliation and inferiority. The current insult is added to the original insult, and they feel fear and hatred toward us. An encounter with authority and power always brings the weak party back to their childhood, where they first encountered an unequal relationship. Therefore, naturally, yearnings for intimacy and warmth arise. And herein is an opportunity for real amends. We supply them with work, and if it were done respectfully and under humane conditions, that would be a real gift. After all, they choose to work for us; nobody forces them. What can we do then, so that this benevolent giving does not get lost in the sea of hatred they feel for us, so that they can appreciate what give them? This emotional situation is very confusing. On the one hand, we rule them, and there is no such thing as humane occupation of another people. Ruling another people is an unequal, militant, and arrogant relationship by definition. Our giving is therefore mixed with the humiliation we cause them, and goes to waste.

Therefore the separation between us and the Arabs (described in detail in the section, "The Principle of Separation") is so important to make order out of all this emotional confusion. Under the cover of the humiliation of the occupation it is very hard to make emotional order and to find out what is appropriate and what is not in this relationship. A humane attitude could be interpreted as weakness. Does a battered child or woman have the possibility of emotional introspection that will help her grow while still subject to the violence? Is it sane to expect the battered child, for instance, to appreciate something good that he got from his battering father, or will he experience that giving as a perpetuation of his dependence in a sadomasochistic relationship, where it is not clear when he will get caressed and when beaten? Indeed, the Palestinians see us as very unpredictable (as do the Syrians, when they ask for early warning stations on the Golan Heights), as they often state when they say that our intentions are not clear and that they do not know where the next blow will come from. And we are astonished and do not understand what they are talking about, because we think we are clear and predictable. That is the fate of anyone who represses his aggression and refuses to recognize it. For the battering father it is just a little slap; for the battered child it is his whole world coming apart. For Israel it is moving a few military bases; for them it is life and independence.

The same is true in the case of a Jewish employer and an Arab worker. Only after the violence of our occupation of those who do not want us ends will the battered child be able to slowly, not immediately, learn the difference between good and bad. We know from therapy how complicated that is and how many years after the battering ends the battered child will continue inviting violence, or acting with violence toward others, and being caught in that emotional trap. Indeed, the necessary separation between us and them, so as to give them independence, is only the first stage in the long, real process they need to undergo. We know from our own experience that the declaration of independence is only the beginning of a long, difficult, and complicated journey toward real independence. Only then can the Palestinians make the necessary order within themselves, and say that "occupying another people is not humane, giving work in general and social benefits in particular is humane, and that not everything is the same." Only after that emotional order is in place and we stop being the battering and caressing figure at the same time, can their deep yearning for a warm parental attitude from us be satisfied, and our giving appreciated, so as to help establish a warm and intimate relationship. But a necessary condition for all that is for us to be able to distinguish between when we are giving and when we are oppressing. Then, and only then, can we tell ourselves the important message: *"It is not our fault, even though it is very hard for the Palestinians."*

6

The Nonconventional Threat

The issue of nuclear, biological, and chemical weapons (called "nonconventional weapons, or "weapons of mass destruction") touches Israel's deepest anxieties, which we suppress. Nonconventional weapons in our region provide our enemies with the actual possibility of carrying out their wish to destroy us, which has been expressed openly and freely. Everywhere in the world that nonconventional weapons exist, with their practical ability to destroy the other, they pose a serious threat.

But the United States and the former Soviet Union, which were engaged in a cold war and a nuclear balance of terror for years, never actually tried to destroy each other. Our region is singular because it has already seen attempts of destruction, and now possesses weapons that make realizing that wish possible. That is surely one of the reasons, whether more or less consciously, why the international community invests so much emotional energy in settling the dangerous Middle East conflict. The matter of nonconventional weapons is a prime example of the importance of understanding the emotional dialogue that is at the root of the peace process. It is no accident that I am addressing this question at the end of this book rather than earlier. I probably repressed this question, as everyone does, out of a desire to imagine a Middle East conflict without nonconventional weapons.

The reason we have to bring this repressed material into our consciousness is that losing this precious material would harm us. Strong feelings of helplessness, which are realistic and represent a correct assessment of reality in the given circumstances, could get lost. Those feelings are the only way we can break out of the paranoid stance we are in. It is no accident that we have repressed this material for years, and it is no accident that when we do discuss it we keep our voices low rather than shouting. Unfortunately, that is reality; Israel is being threatened by nonconventional arms, and that threat, if we do not repress it, can modify our feelings of omnipotence and give space to the more moderate feeling of recognizing the other. That is why it is so important for us as a nation to speak openly and freely about the threat of destruction hanging over our heads.

This chapter will take us on a journey. It begins with an attempt to understand our current situation, where we need a strong conventional army along with unconventional weaponry, and clarifies the emotional reasons why we have chosen a policy of ambiguity. Later the repressed material is brought into consciousness to allow a discussion of our situation from a more depressive emotional stance. In the end we go back to the dramatic language, the language of the Middle East, and translate our insights into that language in a way that promotes the peace process.

Conventional military capabilities give us many degrees of freedom that allow gradual processes to unfold. There is the possibility of winning or losing wars, and the whole range of options in between. Therefore, a gradual negotiation between the sides is possible in this process. In this case, we feel more security that allows us room for deliberation over whether to make a concession or not, to go back if we have made a mistake and to correct it. The nonconventional threat does not leave room for corrections. The experience is total, very frightening, and takes us to one of two places: panic, where we withdraw into ourselves and feel helpless, or a counterphobic response, where we attack. That is how we can understand the comment by Henry Kissinger, that even in the nuclear age an army needs conventional weaponry, to give it the freedom needed to participate in a limited war. Our past confirms Kissinger's hypothesis. The Yom Kippur War, the Lebanon War, the Gulf War, and the Intifada all broke out despite our nuclear potential, which was known to the Arabs. In other words, our nuclear capability did not deter the Arabs from starting a war against us. Our nuclear capability may have curbed their military goals—they may have given up the wish to destroy us in war, but it is hard to imagine how we would have felt in those wars without conventional arms.

We know the experience of the nonconventional threat from interpersonal relations. There are people who lack degrees of freedom, who are inflexible, who feel totally threatened by everyday situations. Those people move between feelings of omnipotence and impotence. They are people who did not feel fundamental security in their past, and they might invite or create aggressive situations. Sometimes they behave aggressively, and sometimes the opposite is true, as they reconstruct and relive familiar situations from the past, when they were victims of violence, they inadvertently invite the other side to attack them because of their behavior and their unconscious reactions. Such a patient tries to draw his therapist into acting the same way. But he needs a stable, separate, and clear therapist, not a frightened one, who invites his aggression, or an aggressive one, which leads to the same result. Only a stable therapist can help that patient calm down. Double messages can drive such a patient crazy. The Iranian or Iraqi personality disorder, like any personality disorder, tries to draw us into its inner world, a religious world of black and white, all or nothing, where either we destroy them or they destroy us. We must not let that happen. That is the essence of the emotional invitation we get from extremist Islam, which wants to erase us and does not allow compromise. We must avoid the emotional pathology of "life hanging between two extremes," an emotional state that is very hard to bear. For that we need both an appropriate emotional stance and a strong conventional army.

Developmentally we are like a growing child who is still unaware of the many sides of his personality or the drives that motivate him. Looking back, we can see that we have been led by growth forces more than we have led a conscious emotional process of peace. Again and again we were surprised; again and again the Arabs were ahead of us; again and again we were compelled to agree to things we did not choose. Indeed, the forces working within us and around us were greater and stronger than we were. Truth be told, it is still hard for us to rely on ourselves, and rightfully so. We are a people who underwent the Holocaust and other disasters through our lives, and are experiencing a real existential threat from our Arab neighbors. As in the case of children, our lack of basic security invites the forces that fragment us to overcome the forces of integration. In the face of the nonconventional threat it is hard to stay integrated. Integration is a state of balance, at an equal distance from the conflicting emotions of aggression and victimhood, fear and courage, between the fear of the major disaster that could happen to us in a nonconventional war, and the desire to take vengeance and to eradicate our enemies. The personality-disordered individual needs many years of therapy to be able to contain those conflicting feelings and not to be drawn toward the extremes. It is a developmental task incumbent upon us all to move from the childish world of black and white to a world that has shades of gray. We have only to recall the intensity of the panic that seized us when Iraq fired ballistic missiles at us during the Gulf War, which we have already repressed. It is our fear of being destroyed versus our desire to destroy. We can only imagine what our fate would have been had we not restrained ourselves in the Gulf War, had we paid Iraq back in equal measure. A nonconventional war may have broken out, they may have used biological or chemical weapons against us (we have forgotten the anthrax germs they possess). Iraq has already used chemical warfare against Iran. When two states get carried away, when two people are at the brink of a fistfight, it would be good if there were one side that could swallow its honor and make more moderate, integrative statements, to prevent being drawn into war. We were that side in the Gulf War, thanks to the United States, the good parent, that helped us contain our insult and restrain ourselves.

Our conventional ability helps us grow up in a more balanced and less threatened way. Relying mainly on nonconventional arms to defend ourselves would arouse our deepest fears of eradication and would not leave us room to make mistakes, which is psychologically and developmentally intolerable. Even if we assume that a war such as the Yom Kippur War broke out because of mistakes of our own that we could have avoided, we are allowed to make mistakes. Indeed, it is fortunate that we did not use our nonconventional arms, even as a threat, because we could not live with such anxieties.

But even the nonconventional arms, in additional to the conventional ones, played a role throughout the years, first of all because of the existential danger that faced us, and second because of the balance of terror that has existed in this region for a while. Iraq has chemical and biological weapons. Iraq and Iran are close to producing nuclear weapons. Nonconventional weapons, when they exist alongside conventional ones, soothe us to a certain extent. We understand that we can hurt the Arabs, so that if they do destroy us, we can surely take revenge. But our nonconventional arms also give us the power of deterrence, which can keep them from crossing the red lines we set. Both the aspect of deterrence and the aspect of revenge are emotionally soothing. Without our nonconventional weapons, which unconsciously soothe us, we would be much more anxious. If the Arabs had nonconventional arms and we did not, that would surely be an invitation to destroy us. Nonconventional weapons have the same effect that a child's self-confidence has in the growth process. We have to be empathetic toward ourselves and understand how important that existential security is to us.

Israel's policy of ambiguity over the years is an example of the paranoid emotional stance, which limits our thought to "war thinking." It is a trap from which it is very hard to change to "peace thinking" or to healthy and normal growth processes. But first, let us try to understand the logic of the paranoid emotional stance. According to that stance, Israel was wise in hiding its nuclear capability for years as part of its policy of ambiguity. We neither said we had nuclear arms nor that we did not; we just kept silent. We understood that both our weakness if we said we did not have nuclear arms, and our tremendous power if we said we did, could arouse aggression. Our restraint contained a quiet strength that did not provoke war, like a child in the class who everyone knows is strong, but who does not flaunt it, and gets into fewer fights.

In a state of constant confrontation between us and the Arabs, with the Arabs feeling hurt and humiliated by us, we have to be very careful not to arouse unnecessary anger by our own militant statements. We as a state have picked up something true in our unconscious. We understood that when somebody is angry at you—justifiably, from his point of view—it is better to bow your head, be quiet, and not annoy him further. Quiet humility is more soothing than angry explanations. We all know moments when we would do better to stay silent than to add oil to the fire. It is interesting that we have not been able to understand the way in which the Arabs experience the conflict. As a state, we have not been able to see how they are right from their point of view, but on the matter of our nonconventional capabilities we have acted toward the Arabs empathetically. We have understood how hurt they are and have chosen to bow our heads and be silent, rather than increasing their hurt by flaunting our might. There is no doubt that the Arabs have been deeply insulted by us, and when someone else accuses us of aggression and considers himself justified, bowing our head is what we need rather than challenging him, because an escalation of the conflict is at our doorstep. We have avoided as much as possible dragging the region into a nonconventional arms race.

It is interesting to examine the strength of unconscious messages. After all, the Arabs know, as does the whole world, that we have nonconventional arms, but our silence, our restraint, convey a message of restraint to the Arabs too. The ability to take a step back from a provocation, to examine it, and not to be drawn into an immediate reaction is an emotional stance of freedom that conveys power. It is the emotional stance that prevented a serious deterioration in the Gulf War.

In therapy, when the patient is very threatened by his environment, the goal is to show him other options. Fear blocks creative thinking and the ability to see other options. In therapy we often hear statements such as, "there is nobody to talk to," or "if he did such and such to me, or said this or that, how can we talk?" During the clinical discussion it may turn out that these people have not even considered the possibility that they could go over and talk to the person, ask, explain, or inquire. We know that as soon as the patient goes from a paranoid emotional stance to a more depressive tendency his integrative ability will increase, and suddenly more options will open to him. We know that increasing the flexibility of one's thinking is not only a cognitive process but is effected by emotional aspects.

So much for war thinking, the kind of thinking that does not let you see beyond what was described here. Later on, when I describe another kind of thinking, "peace thinking," that comes from a depressive rather than from a paranoid emotional stance, I will criticize the policy of ambiguity. We will see once more that what you say does not matter; it is how you say it that does. In other words, the question is what emotional message you convey to the other side. The emotional message you convey is more important than the contents; we have seen this repeatedly in the previous chapters.

Patients ask therapists again and again, "What should I say?" We know you can say almost anything. The question is how. It is less important whether or not we admit we have the bomb. What is more important is the emotional message that goes with that statement. Will we say, for instance, "If you attack us that will be your end because we have nuclear arms?" or will we say, "We have nuclear arms, but we are interested in mutual disarmament, so that we can all live here in peace. Therefore we are prepared to be under international supervision, on condition that it includes all the states of the Middle East." Such a message, in which you are willing to give up your power, is a corrective experience in our relationship with the Arabs, and does not hurt and insult as does the "ambiguity" message. Ambiguity is surely better than open aggression and threatening the Arabs with nuclear arms, but it is not as good as a message of peace. Because the ambiguous message is actually quite combative, saying, "Watch out; you don't know what I can do." It is a message that is unable to take another important step forward and ask how you can use nonconventional power as a lever for peace. Toward the end of this chapter I will present the alternative to the ambiguity policy.

Usually we repress the existence of the nonconventional threat. When the threat does come up, it puts us, as we have seen, in a paranoid emotional stance, until we repress the threat again and drive it out of consciousness. That is why we go through a startled awakening every time we hear that Iran is close to producing a nuclear bomb, that Syria has chemical missile heads, that Iraq has the capability of spreading anthrax, and who even remembers the first Gulf War, and the second one that nearly happened, and maybe there was a third threat too. I will try to bring our repressions of this matter into consciousness and deal with them with an emphasis on the depressive attitude. The depressive emotional attitude allows us to deal with the nonconventional threat while maintaining our integrity as well as maintaining a correct emotional bond with the Arabs, just as in the development of the individual. On the emotional level it is a matter of going from a paranoid stance to a depressive one. On the cognitive level it is a transition from "war thinking" to "peace thinking."

The repression of this total threat is at the root of human nature. These mechanisms lead people not to think about the hole in the ozone layer, not to have routine cancer tests, not to think about our impending death, and so on. There is a lot of information we choose to repress so as not to feel the pain and anxiety it arouses. Terminal patients too often repress what they know about the state of their health, and continue living their lives until the last moment as if nothing happened. But sometimes a person wakes up and understands he is about to die, considers what he wants to do in the remaining time, and changes his priorities. On his deathbed he will ask what really was important to him of all the things he did, and what mattered less.

We are at a stage where we have to bring all of the repressed material into consciousness, put it on the table and think how we would conduct our relations with the Arabs, considering the fact that we may be attacked by nonconventional arms one day. We may be destroyed. How do we compute this important information into our national priorities? How do we sort out the important from the trivial? And what really matters to us? I think this hypothesis, that we are living under a growing threat of destruction, is a very important hypothesis that we repress.

When the bomb falls, whoever is left will ask themselves where they went wrong. They will surely feel they missed something important. They were busy arguing over another inch of land more or less, busy defending our positions. Out of defensiveness, true; out of anxiety, true; but when the blow hurts so badly, as any child knows, we go into a depressive state and are ready to accept things we would not accept under other circumstances, out of a deep understanding that not everything we want is possible. When the bomb falls, those who remain will ask, "What could I have done differently?" But the question will be asked from a different emotional position, not a paranoid one as we are in today, which says, "I will stand my ground and not give them anything, because I need to be strong, because I am no sucker." Then we will not be strong anymore. The question, "What could I have done?" will be asked from a depressive emotional stance that says there is no choice but to compromise. Even after the bomb falls we will think that we had to insist on our red lines, our minimum. As in the cold war between the United States and the former Soviet Union, nuclear disarmament has to be mutual. Excessive concessions and weakness invite aggression, but that will not be the reason why the bomb is dropped on us. *The bomb will not be dropped because of our weakness; it will be dropped despite our might.* It will be dropped for the most tragic reason imaginable. It will be dropped because we hurt and *insulted* the other side. Insult itself can activate the bomb because we are not actually threatening to attack them, and dropping the bomb is an emotional act. But we hurt them emotionally; because we are hurt and threatened, that is the essence of the tragedy. But these are insights you reach only after a really terrible blow, like the blow the Japanese suffered when the bomb was dropped on their country in the Second World War. At that time not only does the tremendous desire for peace come up with the decision to do everything possible so as never to fight again, but one's entire way of thinking changes (according to the Japanese constitution, maintaining an army and war are forbidden ways of settling conflicts). This is what I am aiming at—changing our way of thinking.

From the emotional stance called "depressive," the world looks different. It is a stance that recognizes our limits and knows that we cannot do everything. That is the whole difference. Then, after the bomb, the emphasis will not be on another piece of land, but on relationships, emotions. The question will be asked, why we could not understand where the other side was emotionally. We talked about agreements and conditions that they did or did not keep. We were right; they did not keep agreements; but being right was of no avail. We were not wise, we were just right, and that is why things turned out as they did.

Life, like relations between people, like relations between nations, is not a court of law where you seek justice; it is an attempt to really understand the other. After the bomb falls we will not care about "Orient House" in East Jerusalem, or about one settlement more or less. Then, when we are sad, we will understand that we should have said that an Arab child is equal to a Jewish child, that we are responsible for every Palestinian child injured by our bullets, no matter what he did and who was right. We are simply responsible because we control the area, we are big and strong, and therefore we are responsible. Had we declared that such a child and his family deserve treatment and compensation, it would promote peace and defer the atomic bomb more than any concession. Or if we tried to help the Palestinians economically in every way, or if we simply respected them at the roadblocks and made sure they did not stand in line for hours before working for hours, that would stop the bomb. What is going to make our enemies drop the bomb is their feelings not their minds, not their wisdom and logic. It is known that the major decisions in life are controlled by emotions, while the minor ones are controlled by the mind, because feelings come from a deeper place in the soul.

Only the correct emotional stance can stop the bomb. But those are post-bomb thoughts, not for now. The Hundred Year War ended with a peace agreement because there was nobody left to fight. After the bomb there will also be peace, but it will be very sad, as in Hiroshima after the war. A terrible blow turns grandiosity and the joy of victory to deep sadness that bring up what was hidden before. I hope we are not inviting precisely the thing we fear most, the sad ending a child sometimes needs in order to take an honest look at himself.

In a state of total threat the hardest thing to do is to move from a paranoid emotional stance to a more depressive emotional stance, which allows a different kind of thinking, such as confidence-building measures. When someone declares war against you, it is not easy to avoid being drawn into their mentality, and to continue thinking in terms of peace. But that is what a good parent does in a confrontation with his children. In that situation, statements and actions that bring the sides closer and build trust can be perceived by the other side as concessions and weaknesses. But if those statements and actions do not really come out of weakness but rather out of a position of power and a commitment to changing the emotional climate, they have tremendous value. We are not sufficiently aware of the psychological aspect of such processes that build trust between both sides. Under the threat of nonconventional weapons the fear is tremendous, and emotions play a central role. *Therefore, gestures of conciliation have a great value.* That is because such gestures soften and modify both sides' fears—King Hussein's gesture when he visited the bereaved families of the slain girls, for instance, or Netanyahu's television appearance when he addressed the families of the victims of an accidental shooting at an army roadblock.

There are far too few examples of such gestures in our region. It only proves how much we need such statements. *If there is one thing that can prevent them from dropping the bomb on us, it is sympathetic words.* We have to be creative in gestures too, not only in wars. When a husband brings his wife flowers, even if he is not doing it wholeheartedly, and even if it seems to him somewhat artificial at a certain moment, he still did go, buy, and send the flowers, and his wife appreciates that action that can create a new dialogue of closeness. In the same way, a good parent seeks to say an honest good word to his child, being aware they have been critical of each other for some time. If we would repeatedly announce that we are prepared to have ties with Iran, for instance, even if we did not get immediate results, there could be benefits in the future. When an adolescent is very angry at his parents, the parents' ability to leave the door open despite the rage directed at them, and the parents' ability not to "go all the way" as their child is doing, will bear fruit one day. Those precious small invitations to a relationship do seep in slowly and remind the child that she has a place to go back to. One day, and it happens all the time, she will come back to us with the gift she was given in the distant past. The child took it with her all those years, and will reach a maturity that allows her to accept our offer. Suddenly she will ask the parent she was so angry at for all those years to baby-sit her children. That is why it is so important to be creative in seeking goodwill gestures, *to change the psychological climate.*

In our current condition we are undoubtedly inclined toward a paranoid stance rather than a depressive one, thereby inviting what every arrogant person invites, which is hurt, humiliation and insult, which will bring us right back to the emotional place we wished to escape. After the bomb we will understand that what really mattered to us was to live, and that is all. After the bomb we will realize that we were misunderstood, and misunderstood ourselves too. It was hard for us to give up the Golan Heights and give the Palestinians a place in east Jerusalem; it was really hard, but now we would give it up with no hesitation at all. If the other side were more patient it would wait with the bomb for us to relax, gain security, and stop being so threatened and defensive. When we feel safer we will be able to give up more. Such is the paranoid personality, that when it receives a lot of empathy it relaxes from the threat. Or conversely, when a paranoid personality takes a terrible blow from its surroundings, only then can it turn inward and experience the depressive emotional stance that was unattainable before. True, the other side will suffer losses too, maybe greater than ours, but it will be no comfort. Our opponents will surely tell themselves the same things, and that will bring peace closer. They will say that instead of caring about the Palestinians and rehabilitating them, we were busy with hatred and revenge for what was taken from us, rightfully or not, but we missed the main point. We sought justice and not life. Then the Arabs will say, What do we care about Jerusalem or more settlements? Why didn't we take care of our children? They will understand how hard it was for us to give to them, and how they failed to understand themselves.

People who are about to die, or people who receive terrible blows, change their whole worldview. Relationships and emotions become more central than any logical considerations. A dying man wants his dear ones near him, first of all. He wants the contact and the touch. Surely he will not continue arguing with his wife or negotiating with her over some small detail of who is right. He will be sad about the many years they failed to reconcile and love. He will not think he is right; he will be sorry for what he did not achieve. When someone close to us dies we are often sorry we did not manage to say warm words to him, and were too busy criticizing. Here too emotions come before logic.

If we embrace the depressive stance now, there is a chance we can prevent them from dropping the bomb on us. We do not need to receive a terrible blow to change our worldview. Some people, unfortunately, do need such disasters. We need to turn to emotions, not to rational arguments about justice. *Every Jew who lives in Israel has to understand that he has displaced an Arab from the house in which he lived, and take responsibility for him.* We must recognize the suffering we caused the Palestinians and internalize our heavy moral obligation to try to help them as much as possible. As long as that Arab is unhappy there will not be peace. As long as the Palestinian state does not thrive as ours does, there will not be real peace. We could tell them that in this familial relationship their good is our good. Giving up our red lines would promote nothing, it would be suicide. We cannot let the refugees back into Israel because we deserve a safe and thriving country. And mainly, we need not feel guilty because we deserve to enjoy life. It is our fate to live with the knowledge that we have badly hurt others without meaning to. That during our birth as a state someone else was hurt. Such a child is not at fault, but does have to help his brother whom he hurt (see the section, "Palestinian Refugees"). That child has a very difficult emotional-developmental task, which is to grow up without guilt feelings, but with a deep understanding and realization that it is his duty to help his suffering Palestinian brother. Only if we adopt a more depressive stance will we suddenly be able to make order out of that difficult emotional complexity. This child can and needs to run forward and flourish, but his fate is to become an expert at understanding sadness, because only when you keep a place for sadness in your heart do you understand another's sorrow.

That is the psychological dynamic of every serious life crisis of mourning and loss. That is when people turn toward their feelings. Their voices become softer. They make do with less. Let us try to understand the different views, the two different states of consciousness that are inaccessible to each other. When you are in one state you cannot understand how you thought and felt in the other. On the one hand, the victorious state of bravado, which is omnipotent, knowing, and right, is familiar to everyone from some point in his life. That is not the attitude that will prevent the bomb from being dropped. On the other hand, the attitude that gives the stage to relationships and feelings rather that to the joy of victory is the one we should adopt. It is a different way of seeing. It is a view that means putting our relationship with the Arabs first. What we give or don't give matters less than how we do it. The how is important; it is what determines the relationship that is built and the feeling that remains. In that depressive emotional position we will not get unduly entangled in details or ask who won or who gained more. The shape will matter more than the contents. The question will not be what the Palestinians did or did not get in Jerusalem, but how the agreement was made, whether it was reached in a good atmosphere or not, and how we live together. Suddenly we will understand that what counts is how the process is being handled right now, and what feelings the sides had during the talks and at their end. The emphasis will be on the process and not on the end point with its balance of gain or loss. True, it will be hard for us to dismantle the settlements, but perhaps in an interim phase, while we try to reach better long-term agreements, the settlements can build factories that provide good jobs for Palestinians. Perhaps giving the Palestinians social benefits and the minimum wage would also be a better start than arguing over another inch of land. The paranoid emotional stance is blocking our thinking; that is clear. If we came in with a positive attitude and really wanted to help them we would not get stuck on the details. There is so much that needs to be done that it does not matter where we start, as long as we get started.

It is a matter of a *more mature way of thinking*. We know it well from therapy, where we take a close look not only at the contents of the patient's life, his problems with others, for instance, but the relationship he builds with us here and now. The form becomes the essence and we teach him out of what happens in the clinic, out of the relationship with the therapist, to look, learn, and understand his difficulties in relationships. If the patient speaks in an insulting or aggressive manner, for instance, or shuts us out because of his hurt feelings, all that says something about how he relates to others. Surely the zealots understood that after the Second Temple was destroyed and they were on their way into exile. The Germans understood that when they awakened from their grandiosity at the end of World War II. We all understand that when we come out of our grandiosity and regret what we failed to see.

Legislating social laws to protect Palestinian workers, for instance, guarding their rights and their honor and reducing the use of closures and curfews to allow Palestinian children to go to school, will prevent the bomb from being dropped much better than more army divisions. Treating the Palestinians with respect is no less important than our nuclear capability in preventing such a war. As I have already said, the bomb will fall despite our might, because of their insult. The same is true for terrorism. Treating the Palestinians in such a manner is no less effective than a good Shin Bet. It is time to determine emphatically that torture, which may have a short-term benefit of drawing more information out of the person, in the long run incites hatred and vengeance. Such emotional scars do not allow dialogue for years, just as conciliation is almost impossible between a parent and the child he has sexually abused. The person who was tortured, his family, and his people will not forget and will not forgive what happened for years. Therefore, beyond the humanitarian aspect, which is important to us as a people, torture does not pay off. The psychological dynamics of nuclear warfare are the same dynamics as the ones that apply to a suicide bomber, but on a national scale. The same emotional rules of rage and terrible insult motivate both the suicide bomber and the leader who decides to use nonconventional arms.

Therefore, instead of making statements about "Jerusalem under Israeli sovereignty forever," it is time to say, "There is room for everyone in Jerusalem," or "Jerusalem is a symbol of conciliation between the different religions." And that is without saying anything about what is actually done, because the spirit in which the message is conveyed comes first. A child can accept a parent's "no" and recognize the parent's boundaries as long as they are conveyed empathetically. That emotional attitude, which puts emotions and relationships at the center rather than possession and victory, is what will allow a deep conciliation between us and the Arab world in the future and prevent a disaster from happening.

We have noted the need to call for a historic conciliation between Judaism and Islam. Even though today it looks more like a dream than a reality, calling for such conciliation and understanding is vital for peace in our region and would promote calm, because articulating something is half the solution. Silence reinforces the assumption that there is no one to talk to on the other side. We know from therapy that even the deepest fears look different when they are articulated. The ability to translate one's deepest anxieties into words is an important part of a child's emotional development. It is the part that teaches him how to soothe himself. The Gulf War, with all of its anxieties, taught us the power of hatred and how feelings guide it. If there were only a different atmosphere between us and the Palestinians, perhaps Iraq would never have fired missiles at us.

We live under a serious nuclear, biological, and chemical threat, and we repress it. Raising this into our consciousness and realizing that we are living under the shadow of devastation would lead us to a different way of thinking. In that thinking emotion plays a central role. The thinking is that we are all in the same boat and should strive to reach a safe shore. Even if our partner in the boat is beating us, we should, for the benefit of both of us, continue to paddle and hope he calms down. We will either both be saved or both drown. We should help the other party be saved because we will have the same fate. That common fate invites us to think about our emotional bond and put it at the center, rather than one detail or another. We should do all of our thinking together. We should think what would suit us, and listen well to what it means for the other side. The bomb will fall, as I said, not because of our weakness, but despite our might, and it will be activated by insult and hurt. If we treat the peace process like a psychotherapeutic process and put our emotional bond with the Arabs at the center, we will be able to prevent the bomb from falling and reach real peace.

The closest we have ever been to nonconventional warfare was during the Gulf War. Saddam Hussein's rationale for the fighting was his concern for the Palestinians. But it is only thanks to our repression mechanisms that we fail to see the connection between Israel's bombing of the Iraqi nuclear power plant under Begin, with the insult this caused Iraq, and their firing of missiles at us. It was easier for Hussein to explain his firing of the missiles by his concern for the Palestinians than by the deep insult he felt (although those are not mutually exclusive options), while we, out of our paranoid attitude, are unable to make the connections and understand the other. We know well how threats hurt our ability to think and prevent us from seeing other options. We chose to be victims rather than people who have some responsibility for what is happening and the ability to change it, and the world supported that view. It is possible that as part of the peace talks with the Palestinians and the atmosphere of the peace process, which did not exist in Shamir's time, Hussein would not have fired missiles at us. He also declared that he would accept any agreement we reached with the Palestinians. He is not crazy, as I have noted, and the fact that we see him as such in order to distance him from our comprehension is to our detriment and requires examination.

A nuclear war can break out because of such a misunderstanding. The other side will be seen as insane or manipulative rather than as someone who has to be listened to, who is speaking from his heart. We have to understand what Hussein said, because the situation at the time was on the brink of nonconventional war, and unfortunately Hussein remained in our consciousness as a madman. The same is true for the Palestinians who danced on the roofs (therapists know it is not that hard to understand madmen). Understanding the dynamics of such a war is very important, because it is the prelude to a nuclear war if and when it happens. There will be a Moslem leader who identifies with suffering, let us say of the Palestinians, which we cannot understand, and we will be unable to say anything soothing, not to speak of doing anything. Hussein identifies deeply with the discrimination the Palestinians feel, and he wants to help them.

During the first Gulf War and during similar dangers afterward, Israel took a waiting approach, which was not easy at such times. It was a restrained approach that contained our anxiety and enabled us not to use our power unnecessarily in a way that would have escalated the situation. That approach proved itself as correct in the face of domestic protests to the effect that we could restrain ourselves no longer and had to respond. We were not drawn into the split Hussein invited us to fall into; we did not move from the emotional stance of victims to aggressors. We could contain our feelings, thanks to our good and soothing parent, the United States. Still, our thinking continued to be war-type thinking rather than a kind of thinking that could promote peace. We restrained ourselves but failed to understand what Hussein was saying. We were unable to be empathetic and to see the world through his eyes. It is very possible that in conditions of a peace process like the one we are in today, Hussein would not have fired missiles at us. It is also possible that a ceremonious invitation to Hussein to come talk to us about various subjects, including the Palestinian issue and Jerusalem, would change the whole picture, if only thanks to the declaration and the openness. But when we feel threatened it is so hard for us to see beyond the threat and send a message of peace.

Had we not destroyed their nuclear reactor, it is reasonable to suppose that nothing would have changed. They would not use nuclear arms against us, just as they did not use chemical or biological weapons against us, even though they have been able to do so for years. So that bombing the reactor was unnecessary. Besides the emotional blow we dealt them, we gained nothing. The bombing may have delayed their nuclear arms program for a few years, but nothing more. At the same time, they developed biological and chemical arms. We cannot stop them from continuing to arm themselves unless we introduce a new way of thinking, peace thinking.

In our minds it is clear. The Western world, which Hussein hates so much, is good and just, while the Arab world and Hussein in particular, are the bad guys. I am not even trying to say that this is not true and that the United States should not have attacked Iraq. I only think, as someone who lives in the Middle East, that it is important not to turn someone into a madman, and to try to understand the deep insult Iran and Iraq feel from the Western world in general and from Israel and the United States in particular. There is no doubt that the impulsive and backward world feels humiliated in the face of the developed world it experiences as arrogant, cold, and distant. A religious country like Iran feels as if the Americans "have no god." We say a person "has no god" when we want to say he has no limits. That is how the Iranians view the freedom the Americans allow themselves. The choice to embrace religion is taken by people who are afraid of freedom and seek order in their impulsive, primary, and turbulent world. Therefore, we can understand their fear and hatred of those who have no god and look as if they have no moral restraints. If that state is also as strong as the United States or another Western state, then the fear of what it represents is increased by the fear of its strength, and assumes demonic proportions. We have already discussed those qualities when we tried to understand how our political right feels toward the left, how the religious feel toward the secular, and how the Arabs feel toward us. In order to be empathetic to that religious Moslem world we have to understand that the Arabs are afraid first of all of Western culture, and only then, as a reaction to their fear, they hate it. In clinical work you always find insult and injury in the person before he develops aggression and hatred. That understanding enables us to be empathetic toward the aggressor. We can also understand that it is no accident that the former Soviet Union had closer ties than the United States with religious, undemocratic states. Religious regimes and totalitarian regimes are fundamentally similar. Both use tremendous force to contain tremendous drives.

The Iranians and the Iraqis merge their hatred of the West and the insult they believe the Jews inflicted on the Arabs in general and the Palestinians in particular. To them, our behavior toward the Palestinians is yet more proof of the profound injustice the Western world deals to the Arab world. We and the Americans are experienced as one entity. For our own good, we would be well-advised to listen to what that child is saying when he cries all the time that he is being mistreated. We cannot allow ourselves the American luxury of being apathetic and not emotionally understanding the Iraqi and Iranian experience. Iraq says that it is asked to submit to nuclear supervision while Israel is not. They feel the United States automatically supports Israel. The Palestinians are deprived and nobody in the Western world gives them a hand. Are we really unable to understand what they are talking about? If we cannot understand what they are saying, if we cannot do that simple exercise in empathy, to stop for a minute and look at the world through their eyes, we are in bad shape. *It is a more devastating disability than military weakness.*

In the Gulf War, even the Arab world rallied against Hussein and his take-over of Kuwait, but the Palestinians danced on the rooftops and hoped Hussein would win. That is how deeply we offended the Palestinians. Surely it is true that the United States supports us more than it does the Palestinians. They feel closer to our pain than to theirs; it gives us, not them, generous aid. Similarly, the United States is closer to us and identifies with us more than it does with the Arab world. We are the ones who will ultimately have to live with the Arabs and understand them more than will the Americans. The United States is like a parent who pampers one child but deprives the other. The pampered child will ultimately pay a price. The American position of automatically supporting us may be blocking us, as an overprotective parent does to his child, and might be making it hard for us to understand the world in general and the Arabs in particular. We cannot hide behind the American apron forever without coming into contact with the Middle Eastern world we live in. The Arabs ask why the Western world attacks Iraq but not Israel. We too conquered land. True, there is a big difference, but you can't argue with feelings. In feelings there is no right and wrong.

Therefore, it is incumbent upon us to understand Iraq, Iran, and other countries of that type. I seriously question the assumption that "there is no one to talk to" there, because we live with them, and we will be the first to pay the price of the nuclear bomb that falls. Then we will not be able to say we are right because it won't matter anymore. And if someone asks what we should do then, as a patient will often ask the therapist, I will tell them that from a different emotional position, from understanding the other, from a depressive rather than a paranoid position, from peace thinking rather than war thinking, every-thing is different. When two people are fighting one can say to the other, "you are wrong," but he can also say, instead, "I understand your pain." The person who chooses the second reaction will be less focused on what he is or is not giving up. The person who chooses the first reaction will be overly focused on what he is or is not giving up.

We must lead a process of conciliation and peace even with the most extreme Islamic regimes. Our fate has decreed that we have to be world experts in peacemaking. We have to be the ones who export peace to the world. We have to specialize in how to be empathetic to the other. We, who are so torn from within and without, if we want to live, have to practice the ability to set the world's trickiest question aside for a minute: who is right.

All the aforementioned can be achieved by a dramatic appeal for religious conciliation between Judaism and Islam, as I have said: we could issue a ceremonious invitation to states such as Iraq and Iran to participate in the responsibility for arrangements at Islamic holy sites and in the discussion of Jerusalem. We can do so with empathetic statements that we can sustain even if the Americans don't like them, with a dramatic call for mutual disarmament of nonconventional arms, with an invitation to take part in the peace process, with a recognition of the importance of their long-standing support of the Palestinians over the years, and so on. We must, for instance, oppose many of Hussein's actions. We also have to take part in world sanctions against Iraq. *Just as in the case of the Palestinians, only by offering an alternative to war in the form of a warm and dramatic peace message, coming from a real understanding of the other and of what he needs in order to grow, out of an ability to identify with him, can we make uncompromising demands.* We have to make a dramatic appeal to Iraq to make peace with us. In our consciousness as it stands today, that would be fawning. In our current view, that would be giving up everything we believe in. That is not the case. In fact, the opposite is true. We need a lot of emotional strength and maturity to make such an appeal. Those are abilities we sorely lack today. It would be a great achievement in our paranoid state to be able to raise our heads above the water and see that over there, in Iraq, there is not a monster, there is a person, even if his name is Saddam Hussein. And if he has paranoid tendencies, like many of us, then an empathetic emotional approach is even more likely to change the picture. That is how a self-confident parent should respond to a child who is having difficulties. In the family of nations, both Iraq and Iran are children who are having difficulties.

It is possible that we owe Iraq an apology for bombing their nuclear reactor (the apologies they owe us notwithstanding). In general, we should learn to apologize more (e.g., as Barak did toward the Mizrahi Jews). We should understand that apologizing does not demean us but is an invitation for a relationship. When we apologize, we are respecting the other's pain even if we are absolutely right. An apology is not measured by the standards of a court of law; it is merely an emotional expression of recognizing the other's pain, which we had a part in causing. We had good reasons to bomb the Iraqi reactor considering Iraq's threats against us. Yet, it never did use its nonconventional arms against us even though it possessed them. It only used words, but we raised our hands first. But what does it matter who is right ? Many children, as I have noted, have never heard their parents say they were sorry they were wrong, even once in their entire childhoods. But if the parent does say it even once, the child will not forget it for his whole life. The apology is so important, bowing our heads, understanding that we hurt someone. If such conciliatory statements came today from a party seen as a great and strong monster such as Israel, it would have an unforgettable magical effect (I already discussed the need for us to apologize to the Palestinians). Surely Hussein deserves a good word for saying he will accept any agreement we sign with the Palestinians. He surely deserves a good word for his deep identification with Palestinian suffering (it is even hard for me to write this; after all, I am in the same trap). If we paint those countries in black we will get war. Maybe even an unconventional war.

Nonconventional arms introduce a new dimension into human evolution that has to do with the war of survival. Until such weapons were developed, each side traditionally tried to strengthen itself, and its survival depended on its might. In a nonconventional war you lose the ability to win, that is, to destroy the enemy and stay alive. Therefore, it is an invitation to more depressive feelings. The paranoid emotional attitude, or war thinking, can exist in this situation only by repressing the nonconventional threat, as we do. The United States and the former Soviet Union have already gone through that change from a paranoid to a depressive state. They went from a cold war and mutual threatening with nuclear arms to mutual disarmament. The transition to a depressive emotional state that recognizes the other and is willing to disarm has to be mutual, or else it is suicidal. In simple words, the life of one side depends on the other. The evolutionary stage in which "if we are *strong* we will survive" is over. A new stage has begun, in which "if we are *communicative* we will survive." A few more nuclear bombs won't make a difference anymore, but an emotional bond with the enemy will help. This position, that a relationship is more important than force for survival, is new in the history of conflicts and war. Man is the only living creature who can destroy himself, but man is also the only living creature who can reduce his strength by choice. Mutual surrender to each other's strength, the internal relinquishing of the desire to win, brings up sadder tunes. Paradoxically, the era of nonconventional arms and the depressive approach it entails take us directly to thinking about human rights, equality, and democracy, the need to help the weak, the poor, and the deprived, not only because each of them has the future potential of causing a nuclear conflagration, but mainly because only through depressive glasses can we recognize the other.

But such an emotional stance, which puts the ability to communicate in the center, is not at all new in the human evolution of individual development. In the family, traditionally, whoever communicated survived. That is why babies are programmed from birth to smile at the world and communicate with it in order to invite their care. That is how boys solve their first oedipal war: instead of fighting their fathers, they identify with them out of love. That is how the child goes from the paranoid stage to the depressive stage in his development process, and recognizes the parent as a person with separate needs and wishes from his own. Mutual dependence requires identification and love. If we can adjust ourselves to the other, understand him, help him, and mainly—and this is the absurd—love him, we will survive. It can, of course, raise unpleasant associations, for a raped woman to love her rapist, for instance. How can we identify with the enemy and love him? It is reasonable to assume that is how a child feels at various stages of his development, when he sometimes has to identify with a parent he experiences as hostile, to justify him and finally to love him (I intentionally am not using the analogy of spouses, who can separate. A parental relationship is for life. Nor can we divorce the Arabs.)

But it is not new for countries to go from a state of war to a state of warm peace. The United States helped the Russian economy at the end of the cold war. Countries in today's world help each other. The United States helps us and others. The international community helps our peace process and is emotionally invested in it. There is an understanding that countries depend on each other. Our future depends on our ability to have a dialogue with Iraq and Iran. We have to be the world's experts on peace; experts on seeing both sides of a story, who understand what we must not give up and what we must give up. We should be experts on humane relationships between countries, and export our expertise to the world. The nuclear era turns the world into a global village, into one family: Whoever bonds survives. Whoever soothes himself and others survives.

It is a serious omission for us to rarely ever discuss the nonconventional threat on the national level. This massive repression has far-reaching implications for our whole worldview. First of all, we are not reading reality correctly, which is grave militarily. We panic every time the nonconventional threat is mentioned. Then, for instance, we discover that we do not have enough gas masks. It turns out that the wish to spare the public from panic, and not letting the public in on the existing threat at the appropriate time, creates greater panic. The desire to repress our anxiety will not work for long, and it will come back again every time we are reminded of reality in some way or another. But that is not the main thing. The educational value of an open discussion of the nonconventional threat would be tremendous. I have already stated that awareness of the nonconventional threat could serve as a powerful curb to omnipotent and paranoid thinking. That is because it raises the need for an emotional bond. Nonconventional weapons necessarily invite us to recognize the other, their wishes and their needs, and in that way encourage a more depressive way of thinking. It is a fundamentally antireligious stance. Our god is no longer omnipotent, and others have the ability to destroy us. A quiet, sad, and restrained discussion of the nuclear threat is what we are missing in the political discourse in Israel, a depressive stance that recognizes the limits of our power and that suits the reality surrounding us.

Nuclear arms bring us back to the question of how we live together, not how we die. It makes us aware of the details of life, not the details of victory. Suddenly the hungry Palestinian child and the hungry Israeli child from Ofakim are important. The inability to be victorious in war, and the possibility of being annihilated, raise questions of emotional bonds and make us look inward. An open discussion of the nonconventional threat would promote a mood appropriate to the reality in which we are living. Then we will understand that we are like a terminal patient who wants to be with his family until he dies. The only difference is that if we act correctly our fate as a nation and as a world will not be that of a terminal patient. But we can no longer deny that we live under the shadow of the threat of annihilation. More countries will acquire nuclear arms over the years, and the solution has to be through emotional communication and dialogue, not through force.

The change we have to go through in our awareness and emotional experience is from a paranoid emotional stance to a depressive one. The ability to respect the details of life, which we lack today, is like a good mother who is sensitive to the details of her child's feelings and sensibilities. As of today, we are like an onlooker who is unable to identify those sensibilities. I am talking about respecting the other and recognizing his feelings, a respectful and equal treatment of Israeli Arabs, for instance. We will need to separate church and state, and not allow a certain group to impose its lifestyle on another group. Surrender would actually increase the confrontation and the danger, as happens in the case of surrendering to drives to which one should stand up. Separating church and state is necessary for many states in order to stop religious grandiosity, to give space to more depressive thinking at the expense of omnipotent thinking. Many countries, including Israel, are like a powerful grown child who has yet to acquire the skills to restrain his power and to use it constructively. A deep understanding of the pain of Palestinian refugees and our moral obligation to help them will have to coexist with our feeling that we are not to blame and that we too deserve a state and prosperity and so on. Only then will there be a real recognition of the many differences that exist among us. An open discussion of the nonconventional threat and a release of our repressions will force us, as has happened around the world, to be less militant. The era of force is coming to an end. If that is not a first-rate educational discussion, what is?

What is the personality profile of *the leader who uses nonconventional weapons first?* The use of nonconventional weapons is in fact both murder and suicide. We know a lot about murder and the hatred and revenge that motivate it. All murders come from aggressive and destructive drives. We know too a lot about suicide. It is aggression directed at the self, which is expressed, in its mild form, in depression (e.g., the depressed person attacks himself and feels worthless). When depression is deep and the ability and desire to carry it through exist, the result is suicide. Suicidal people feel deep yearnings to merge with "mother earth," to regress to a quiet and protected place. Those are feelings of warmth and intimacy the suicidal person lacked in childhood because of a pathological relationship with his parents. The suicidal person also tends to imagine how his family will mourn him, see that he was right, understand how much he suffered, regret what they did to him, and so on. In many cases he also imagines his life continuing in another time and place (Palestinian suicide bombers are promised a place in the afterlife).

Therefore, strong tendencies toward aggression and depression have to exist in the personality of the leader who drops the bomb. That leader is likely to have thoughts about what will happen after the bomb. He will envision those who remain mourning, and be gratified. He may think that then, finally, everyone will see how much he suffered, and be sorry for what they did to him (or to his people). He might envision everyone talking about him and how important he was, which was not the case before (as with the Palestinian martyrs). His satisfaction might come from knowing that nobody will be happier than he; everyone will share the same fate. And he might have fantasies of starting a new life in another time and place.

Using nonconventional weapons is, as I noted, both murder and suicide together. Whoever drops the bomb first will realize that he is annihilating the other and himself at the same time. That is because the other side will pay him back in kind. Let us examine cases of murder-suicide, and try to understand the psychological dynamics that guide them. Samson committed suicide, according to Jewish tradition, and killed the Philistines. "Let me die with the Philistines," he proclaimed. It happened after he was tortured and had his eyes gouged out, and he was burning with vengeance. He felt he had nothing to lose. The Palestinian suicide bombers also come from a background of considerable deprivation, and sometimes feel they have nothing to lose. We will use the nuclear bomb for revenge, when we are sure we are being annihilated. The other side's role is to make sure we do not feel our lives are worthless, because then we might do anything. Therefore, a leader who has his back against the wall, who feels he has nothing to lose, might use nonconventional arms. Our role is to see to it that both the leader and his people do have something to lose; in other words, to see that that leader does not face an existential threat (e.g., Saddam Hussein). Similarly, if such a dangerous leader's nation suffers severe deprivation to the point that the people have nothing to lose, that would be an invitation to conventional and nonconventional terrorism. That is why the boycott on Iraq has to be carried out very carefully, out of humane thinking that respects the population.

Now for the personality profile of the leader who uses nonconventional arms. Palestinian suicide bombers experience deep insult that ignites rage and hatred. They feel insult over their deprived state and what was taken from them. They are bursting from within, this time not just as a metaphor, but as a matter of fact. Their aggression is directed not only at others out of a wish to hurt them, but also at themselves in their choice to commit suicide. They do not choose to plant a bomb and run away, or to open fire on passersby in a crowd. They choose, and this is the interesting point, to die with the people they hate and whom they want to hurt. The desire to die with the enemy contains a yearning for enmeshment with the enemy and an inability or will to separate from him. Now they are equal to the enemy, sharing one fate. That happens in unrequited love, when one partner murders the other and commits suicide. In the collective memories of others, the two were together and stayed together. Such acts carry the hidden message that if we die together, we will actually continue being together. It is a way to avoid the separation the murderer wants to avoid. In other people's collective memory they were together and stayed together.

It is the same in the case of a parent who kills her children and then commits suicide so that the children won't stay alone, so as not to part from them. There is a great personality difference between someone who murders someone else, someone who chooses to commit suicide, and someone who chooses to do both. In the first two cases there is separateness, and each person has a different fate. That is not the case in a murder-suicide. *A nonconventional war is possible only for someone with the kind of personality that does not allow him to separate from the other whom he hates.* Hatred usually represents a strong separateness and is translated into an attempt to hurt the enemy in every way, while caring for oneself. But such a leader will have a lot of hatred along with a great difficulty in separating from the object of his hatred. It is a very particular pathology. In the case of a suicide bomber or a leader who drops the bomb, his goal is that in collective memory everyone will share one grave. The terrorist can imagine his body mixing with the bodies of the people he hates without any separateness or difference. Maybe they will lie together in hospital, one bed next to the other. Every time the Israelis remember their casualties, they will also remember the suicide bomber, whose identity will probably be known. Sometimes you see a small child get so frustrated that he runs up to his father or to a big child and tries to beat him up, against all odds. The main thing is to hurt him. The parent within us knows how desperately that child needs a hug. A soldier who is in distress and storms the enemy out of despair also wants to kill the enemy and himself together. In the last two examples the child and the soldier put themselves at the same level as those who are stronger than they are. They do not mind hurting themselves, as long as there is no difference between them and the other. In other words, they have a deep yearning to be with the other.

There are patients who never say a good word to the therapist about their treatment. They might even make themselves fail so that we, the therapists, fail with them. They know their success is our success; yet they would rather we both fail than that we both succeed. They will try to drag us into their pathology and prove to us in every possible way that we are both wretched. They will hug us with a "death hug" and refuse to let go. Such patients are actually saying,

"I am willing to suffer, as long as we can be together." That is because "if I make progress in therapy, we will be together less and we will each have a separate fate" (the therapy will end or the therapist will succeed as a therapist and the patient will succeed in what he is doing). The suicide bomber and the leader who drops the bomb choose the only course that combines their fate with the fate of the other one. Any other course, whether conventional war or even peace, gives each side a *different* fate. We know the kind of children who will do everything to hurt themselves and their parents at the same time. They will deliberately fail to prove to the parents that they are bad parents, so that they are both sorry together. The goal is to feel intimacy. The *paradox* is that the leader who will use nonconventional weapons is seeking intimacy and bonding. But it will be very difficult to see that, because he will induce and create situations of confrontation.

In the world of clinical psychology it is hard to make predictions. That is partly because some of the variables are hidden. It is possible that that leader's difficulty in formulating a separate identity will express itself in constant conflicts and provocations against a neighboring country or countries. He will unconsciously ask for emotional involvement with those countries and draw them into getting involved with him. He will not show a clear will to win the war, because he will sometimes take actions that are sure to fail. He does not want to win because he does not want to be separate. For the same reason, he does not want to lose either. He will do everything to make both the other side and his suffer. But all of these emotional materials might be repressed and might not come out until the last moment. It would be interesting to examine the psychological profile of the Palestinian suicide bombers to see whether they fit this description.

In summary, the personality of the leader who might use nonconventional weapons tends to be both depressive and aggressive. His emotional experience will have both insult and rage. The leader's past will show traces of both characteristics. On the cognitive level his thinking about what will happen after dropping the bomb will have magical or religious traits. On the emotional level, the most salient trait in that leader is the deep yearning for a bond. One of the most obvious indications of this trait is a strong feeling of "stickiness" this leader will arouse in people. He will be the kind of person who draws you into constant confrontation and commingling and does not leave you alone.

Let us look again at the policy of "ambiguity" and its alternatives. On the practical level, the policy of ambiguity did not stop the Arabs from knowing that we have nuclear arms and treating us like a nuclear superpower. The policy of ambiguity did not prevent the process of the region arming itself with weapons of mass destruction (Iraq and Syria have nonconventional weapons and Iran is very close). Nor has the policy of ambiguity deterred Arab countries from attacking us in various ways, despite our nuclear arms. Such was the case in the Yom Kippur War, the Lebanon War, the Intifada, and the Gulf War. We have to understand that the ambiguity policy, that silent restraint, that militant defiance, is very insulting to the Arabs. We are like a giant casting its shadow on the whole region. Egypt confronts us about this and demands that we agree to mutual disarmament, because it sees our might as an insult. The deep insult, of us being stronger than the Arabs and having nonconventional weapons, in addition to the deep insult they have received from us for years, have induced them to attack us even though they knew we had nuclear arms. That is the power of insult, that it is illogical and can go to the edge or to the end. The policy of ambiguity actually encouraged a nonconventional arms race rather than preventing it as we expected, but this could have been predicted by anyone with an understanding of psychology. That is because ambiguity is a very militant message that provokes attack. It is a message of war rather than a message of peace. The message says, "Look out for me; you don't know what I can do."

As of today, there is a balance of terror and a cold war between us and Syria and Iraq. That is not how the media portrays things, and it is a shame it does not. It serves repression. It might be late, but better late than never. We should issue a dramatic statement that we are prepared for a mutual nonconventional disarmament in the Middle East. Such a message in the dramatic language of the Middle East would significantly promote peace on the conscious level and especially on the unconscious level. That is because such a threat touches upon the deepest existential threats of the nations of the region. A statement that we are prepared to give up our force is the deepest test of our willingness for peace. Such an agreement should include a curb on conventional armament, so that the nations of the region can invest their meager resources in economic and social development instead of war, and the mutual threat will come to an end. We have to understand that our ambiguity is more provocative than calming. It has long ago become an insult to Arab intelligence. Even the Egyptians are not demanding our unilateral disarmament from nonconventional arms, but they are demanding, justifiably, that we use our nuclear capability as leverage toward peace. That could be done by openly stating that we have it and expressing our desire to rid our region of nonconventional arms. If we declare today that we have the bomb, it will be a sign of honesty, openness, an invitation to disarmament, and a catalyst for peace. In that way we would be the leaders of the process of reconciliation rather than being led by it.

Such a statement of our willingness to mutually disarm can be accompanied by a dramatic call for religious conciliation. Those two components, the nuclear and the religious, should work together toward conciliation in the Middle East. The feelings nuclear arms arouse are fundamentally similar to religious feelings. They have many traits in common: existential anxieties, total control, swinging between feelings of impotence and omnipotence, extreme narcissism, and so on, because the feelings aroused by nuclear arms, like the feelings aroused by religion, come from the same unconscious, archaic places in the soul. Therefore it is natural to combine them into one dramatic statement.

The other option is to continue treating the Arabs like fools and flaunting our ambiguity.

The real question we should ask ourselves is whether we are really emotionally prepared to go into a peace process where there is supervision and where we can no longer destroy the Arabs. As of today, we are afraid of letting go of our ability to destroy them. The question is whether what we really want is security or the ability to annihilate them. There is no doubt that if instead of ambiguity we declared that we have nonconventional arms and we are willing to give them up as part of a comprehensive peace, it would promote peace more than our ambiguity. While UN inspectors searched for nonconventional weapons in Iraq, the Iraqis raised a demand for mutuality. They demanded that we be inspected too. We definitely had an opportunity to agree to that, on condition that other states in the region join in. We might have been able thereby to advance the inspection in Iraq, which was cut short by the Iraqis, as well as promote broader processes of conciliation between us and the Arab world in general. In such circumstances we would have been leading a peace process rather than being led. A declaration of our willingness for mutual nuclear disarmament in the region would slow down dangerous processes of nuclear armament rather than speeding them up, as our policy of ambiguity has done. We must understand that when one side does not say what it has, it is actually threatening. After all, fear of the unknown is the biggest fear. But when the strong party says it is prepared to give up its strength, what greater message of peace could there be?

It is hard for anyone to give up his strength. This is especially true of the paranoid personality. We understand that the nuclear arms we had deeply soothed us and not always consciously. It might have been necessary to help the Arabs come to terms with our existence. But this does not necessarily imply a policy of ambiguity, which in an historic perspective has surely failed to prevent a nuclear arms race. An alternative result can be to use the fact that they cannot destroy us as an impetus toward peace. In my opinion the policy of ambiguity was not necessary and was actually harmful from the very beginning. It is good that we have nuclear arms and cannot be destroyed, but the simple question is why we use our power to insult and threaten instead of using it to promote peace. How could we make such a mistake for so long? The answer is very simple; we know how strong the effect of emotions is on our way of thinking and reasoning. We were and still are in a paranoid position and are unable to think about peace. Today, when we no longer have a nonconventional advantage over the Arabs and they too can destroy us, and besides we are in a peace process, is it not time for that major threat to the region to turn into a symbol of peace? Such a message, that we should have issued long ago, could change the Middle East altogether, because it is a message of trust and growth rather than of threat. Rabin explained at one of the peace ceremonies why people shake hands. It is to prove that you are not holding a weapon. In our policy of ambiguity we are refusing to shake hands, so that the others don't see what we are holding. That is our mistake, our distorted sense of reality, which caused the Intifada, the Yom Kippur War, the Rabin assassination, the belief that we could defeat terrorism by force, the Lebanon War, and more. It reflects our difficulty in getting out of the mind-set of threat and war and thinking in terms of peace. We thought that the threat was from without rather than within. Our traditional emotional attitude shows our paranoid tendencies. It should have been obvious that a message of threat would cause the other side to arm itself more than a message of peace. Even if someone wants to destroy you, a message saying, "I am strong and you cannot destroy me, but I am willing to have real peace and stop threatening you," is wiser and more mature message than the threatening restraint that is expressed by ambiguity. The combination of our strength and our willingness for real peace is the right way. What did we have to hide all those years? But we could not conceive of an emotional stance of willingness to disarm. That was a thought that was not possible for us. For us to weaken ourselves at a time when we are trying to fortify ourselves as much as possible? True, for years we said we would not be the first to attack with nuclear arms, but we did not lead an emotional message of peace but rather a provocative message of war. A child who grows for years in an atmosphere of threat will have a hard time letting go of his power when he first acquires it as an adolescent. Iran is not developing nuclear weapons in order to disarm quickly. Now it will be harder to ask it for a mutual disarmament. They will ask us, "Where have you been? Why haven't you issued that message years ago?" Better late than never. Such a declaration by us would promote the peace process.

Postscript

I have to admit that there were basic things I could not see or even did not want to see. Again my unconscious surprises me. Since the breaking out of the second Intifada in October 2000 many Israelis have had to admit that there were things they did not want to hear or see. They wanted to hope that the other side would give up the "right to return" (the Palestinians' desire to return to their lands and homes inside Israel). They wanted to believe that peace is within reach but they woke up to a different reality—the Palestinians have not yet recognized the legitimate existence of Israel. They have said many times that they are not going to compromise about the "right to return" but we did not want to hear that because it is painful for us. It is not the first time we have heard something unpleasant that we don't want to hear. The Holocaust is another example. I believe every nation, as every person, has its unconscious and if we are aware of it the chances to be surprised are lessened.

In these days we can, of course, think about September 11, as a monumental and horrible surprise that the United States had not wanted to see. It was pleasant to repress and forget the hatred of some parts of the Islamic world toward the West. Hatred that is still, even today, incomprehensible to many Americans, so that they ask themselves, Why? These Americans are unable to switch position and to be for a minute a person from a Third World country looking at the United States.

And what a panic ensues when these repressions, emerge, breaking through our defenses. Suddenly, we are so afraid of anthrax, nuclear weapons, or other forms of unconventional warfare that we repress our fears again because they are so hard to deal with. This is the nature of the human being who does not want to be examined for a malignant disease, does not want to know, only to discover it, too late.

I'll try to explain what is going on today between Israel and the Palestinian Authority according to one of the most profound principles of growth and development. Developed by Margaret Mahler, it is called "separation individuation." When a child is born it separates itself from its mother physically. Mahler described in detail the steps of separation individuation in the first three years of a child's life. How he pushes the mother away when he is held on her chest and how he tries to distance himself from her. Later he goes away from the mother and comes back to her to check if everything is OK (to fuel himself). At the age of three years (generally) he succeeds in internalizing the image of the parent. Anna Freud said that at this age the child is mature enough to go to kindergarten and be separated from his parents because he has now internalized the image of his parents.

The truth is that all our lives we are dealing with this question of separation—in the domain of our thoughts—what is mine and what is not mine. Where do I end and someone else begins is not only a question of territories but also emotions. Many of us project our feelings onto the other and make wrong attributions, so it is not clear to us what emotions and thoughts are ours and what are not. For example, if I think that the one from the other side of the border is a monster and in this way I project onto him all my aggression so that I feel very pure (paranoid stance), I have not established separateness. And if I imagine that he loves me because of my internal need to be loved and it is not the reality, again I am dependent on him and not separated from him (depressive position). You see, the question of separation is built into the human experience. Human beings as nations (peoples) might have problems in establishing this autonomy. Many nations build their individuation as a child through rebellion and fighting. The child two years old has to say, "No" in order to feel he is different from his mother and has his own opinions; so does the rebellious adolescent.

Let's start with Israel, a nation that most of its life has crossed borders in the exile and has not had clear borders of its own. More than that, the passage from religion to state is a passage of the Jewish people from the kingdom of imagery to reality. It is a growth process in which one needs to find his own borders (physically as well as emotionally). We don't have to be surprised that some of the Jews still think about the Promised Land up to the Jordan River and cannot recognize the Palestinians' rights. The reality is very painful for them and they are in the middle of a mourning process that will enable them at its end to realize that not everything is possible. The Israeli settlements in the West Bank and Gaza, a few Jews in the middle of an Arab sea, is another example of the Israeli difficulty over the years, to know where do I end and someone else begins. Israel has invested so much blood, money, and especially emotional energy into the settlements instead of directing its libido to the right place—inside, for growth—to the immense poverty inside Israel, for example.

Israel, therefore, does not direct its emotional energy to fulfilling itself but rather to mixing with the other—this is a problem of separation.

The Palestinians have the same difficulty that we have, of being separated, although we are very different one from the other as, for example, the West is different from the East. The Palestinians who are coming from hierarchical and oppressing families and governments feel many times in their lives that they have only two possibilities: to rebel or to surrender. If you are afraid of someone, a parent or a leader, you are not separated from him because you are involved with him, at least in your thoughts, all the time. In this way Israel, although being the occupier, gets more aggression than it deserves because of an internal rage of the Palestinians against other authoritative figures in their lives. To kill yourself together with the enemy, as the Palestinian suicide bombers do, represents concretely the problem of separation. Those terrorists imagine themselves getting mixed with the enemy, their body parts and blood buried together, and remaining in the collective memory of the people as one. They really, in the deepest levels of their unconscious, don't want to be separated. Does it not remind us of the "right to return" and the wishful thinking to mix with Israel instead of building their own state on the side of Israel? It means, of course, destroying both sides.

It is not an accident that the Palestinians today don't speak about their independence. They are not aimed at this target—although today everyone (the whole world and, in Israel, even Sharon) agrees that they could declare their independence. It is very hard for them to be separated, to take the responsibility of being independent and to invest in themselves. They don't try to build anything like schools, hospitals, and economic infrastructure. In this way their libido or their emotional energy is not directed to the right place—for growth—but instead, to fight Israel. (We can think of an adolescent who fights with his parents instead of trying to fulfill himself.)

What Israel has to do is unilaterally withdraw from the occupied territories, in this way establishing its own borders. Then, decrease gradually, and through agreement the supply of working places, water, electricity, and so forth, to the Palestinians in order to encourage them to take responsibility for their own lives. It is amazing that at a time of such a war, we still supply them with all their needs. It does not come from our philanthropic position but from our dependency and inability to separate. That is also the reason why we do not succeed in blocking the borders more effectively against terrorists. Our unconscious does not want us to do so. In psychotherapy we encourage the patient to speak about it and to understand it. That is what Israel needs today—to understand deeply how it is a prisoner to its unconscious and to the past. After two thousand years of dependency on other countries it is not so easy to grow toward independence.

Some of the Palestinians' anger toward us is not only because of the occupation but also because they are dependent on us. We, unconsciously, enjoy this feeling of superiority. But we know that only very dependent people want others to be dependent on them. These people create circles of dependencies around them—and so does Israel. That is why I say that in this respect, Israel and the Palestinians are similar.

Our unilateral withdrawal will help the Palestinians rebel against the other two occupations in their lives: their corrupted regime and their authoritative families. They simply cannot fight on all fronts at the same time. True, it will be a "sad peace" and not a happy one because the dream of the "right to return" will not be solved to their satisfaction, and to give up a dream, as the Jews know, is not so easy. Terror will continue, but to a lesser extent—as in Lebanon. But less is a lot for us. That is why I suggest this new term, "a sad peace."

Index

Abraham, 15, 17, 88

Acting out, 54, 81, 126

Adolescence: emotional growth in, 31; omnipotence in, 24; rebellion in, 109

Aggression: avoidance of dealing with, 111; curbing, 4, 44; denial of, 44–48, 107; emotions leading to, 125; of extreme right, 44; fear and, 48, 51; identification with, 39, 49, 50, 69, 70, 132–138; past injury and, 39; peace process and, 44; as reaction to hurt, 46; recognition of, 67, 115; reluctance to renounce, 44; repression of, 50, 111; sympathetic attitude with, 149; toward Palestinians, 91; unconscious, 46; verbal, 144; weakness behind, 39

Agranat Commission, 52

Ahimeir, Ya'acov, 49

Akiva (Rabbi), 89

Anger, 10, 160; dissipation of, 25; identification with aggressor and, 135; recognition and, 25

Anthem, national, 63–66, 73; change needed, 64; egocentricity of, 63; fear and, 64; of paranoid nation, 64; as spirit of nation, 65

Anxiety, 1, 23, 24, 30, 73, 104; covering up, 7; existential, 33, 52, 179; lack of belief in power and, 40; obsessive rituals and, 31; repression of, 55; revealing, 39

Arab peoples: acceptance of existence of Israel by, 27; agreements with, 21, 22, 26, 28, 69, 70, 77, 135, 140; alleviation of tension with, 103; boycotts against Israel, 144; common fate with Jewish peoples, 168; contempt toward, 12; credibility of, 139; defensive lying by, 140, 141; defensiveness of, 11; desire to eliminate Israel, 53; development of limits for, 22–23, 129; difficulty in separation and, 141–142; ego forces and, 136, 143–146; emotional attitude of, 136; emotional bond with, 99, 100; emotional conciliation with Israel, 128; expectations of Jewish peoples, 150–151; family structure, 134, 148, 149; fantasies of destruction of Israel by, 27; fear of domination by, 11; feelings of injustice toward West, 171; feelings of shame and, 145, 146; feelings of Western favoritism to Israel, 171; image of mothers in, 148; inclination to bargain, 141–142; inequality in encounters with, 151–152; insults and, 122–130, 134, 138, 139, 143, 149, 152, 170, 179; international support for, 42, 43; Israeli, 29, 32, 48, 63, 101, 143; Israeli attitude toward, 131; Jewish peoples and, 122–156; knowledge of Israel's nonconventional weaponry, 161, 178; lack of consistency in, 145; lack of fear of Israel, 40; language of, 134, 146–156; legitimate desires of, 25; need for apologies to, 172, 173; recognition of feelings of, 59; similarity of government to family structure, 148; speaking to, 146–156; suffering of, 21; thoughts of, 130–146; viewed by Jews, 11; warmth in relationships by, 146, 147, 148, 149

Arafat, Suha, 144